The Day of Atonement

A Guide to the history, liturgy and nature
of the Jewish festival of Yom Kippur

A Companion volume to
"A Myrtle Among Reeds"

DAVID PRASHKER

THE ARGAMAN PRESS

The Argaman Press

ISBN: 0615982638
ISBN-13: 978-0615982632

To my friends, colleagues and students on Project SULAM,
who taught me far more than I could ever have hoped to teach them,
during my two years as a teacher-mentor.

CONTENTS

"Wooing, wedding, and repenting is as a Scotch jig, a measure, and a cinque-pace: the first suit is hot and hasty like a Scotch jig--and full as fantastical; the wedding, mannerly modest, as a measure, full of state and ancientry; and then comes repentance and with his bad legs falls into the cinque-pace faster and faster, till he sink into his grave."

William Shakespeare, Much Ado About Nothing

"And here, shipmates, is true and faithful repentance; not clamorous for pardon, but grateful for punishment."

Herman Melville, Moby-Dick; or, The Whale

"No evil dooms us hopelessly except the evil we love, and desire to continue in, and make no effort to escape from. "

George Eliot, Daniel Deronda

"Chronic remorse, as all the moralists are agreed, is a most undesirable sentiment. If you have behaved badly, repent, make what amends you can and address yourself to the task of behaving better next time. On no account brood over your wrongdoing. Rolling in the muck is not the best way of getting clean."

Aldous Huxley, Brave New World

Chapter One: Forgive Us Our Trespasses

In Judaism there are no beginnings – perhaps not even the *"Bereyshit"* itself, the beginning of all beginnings.

To speak of the Day of Atonement is to isolate a point in flux, and to pretend that it stands alone. But it doesn't stand alone, and it refuses to be isolated. It's the culmination of the Ten Days of Awe which do indeed mark a beginning, that of the New Year, but it's also the inception of the new spiritual year. It's annually repeated, identical in every way – yet always different, because every human act is always different. A *Yom Kippur* that falls on a *Shabbat* cannot be the same as any other *Yom Kippur*; nor can that which falls on a certain anniversary, or in the light of a specific personal or political circumstance. If in this book I treat *Yom Kippur* in isolation, as though it were identical and constant, it's only for the pragmatism of the book, and not for the limitation of the atonement.

The date in question is the 10th of *Tishrey*, falling in the autumn, the seventh month of the Jewish calendar, though the 1st of *Tishrey* is now regarded as *Rosh ha-Shana*, the calendrical New Year. In Leviticus 16:29:

"And this shall be a statute for ever unto you, that in the seventh month, on the tenth day of the month, you shall afflict your souls, and do no work at all, whether it be one of your own country, or a stranger sojourning among you."

The eternality of repetition of the single moment. The dedication of an extra *Sabbath*. The rendering universal. Three colossal divine and human actions in a single verse.

"For on that day," the passage of Leviticus adds the explicit to the intrinsic, "He will forgive you, to cleanse you, that you may be clean from all your sins before the Lord."

But who is "he"? The phrasing is ambiguous, and Hebrew doesn't supply, as English does, a capital to denote the deity. From the preceding it might imply that "he" is your countryman and/or the stranger sojourning among you; from the succeeding, God Himself. And what of your forgiving him, or Him, so he/He too may be cleansed? That too is implicit, for you are his/His countryman, you are the stranger within his/His gates.

"It shall be a day of rest unto you, and you shall afflict your souls, by this statute, for ever."

You shall afflict your souls. From the evening of the 9th to the evening of the 10th, twenty-five hours in total. But what precisely do you have to do, that your soul may be properly and fully afflicted; that atonement may become at-one-ment?

We shall see.

1

✡

In *Yoma* (8:1), a tractate of *Talmud*, and in *Yad, Shevitat Asor* (1:4, 3:9) five forms of affliction are defined, namely prohibitions against eating and drinking, washing oneself (for pleasure), anointing the body, wearing shoes (of leather), and sexual intercourse. But the Rabbis will always build fences around the *Torah*, to protect it. Today, we don't even clean our teeth, lest the swallowing of water or saliva count against us as drinking; we don't wash at all, because a definition of pleasure is implausible, and what greater joy can there be than dousing off the grime and sweat in the luxury of a centrally-heated bath? And we wear no shoes of any kind, nor anything of leather. So we intensify affliction, and in so doing deepen our atonement. It's unnecessary, but commendable.

As King David sings, in Psalm 35:13: "I humbled my soul with fasting. And as for my prayer, may it return to my own breast."

Children are exempted, though they too should go barefoot. In *Tosepha Kippurim* (4:1-2), and in *Sefer ha-Yeshar*, one of the Responsa of Rav Tam, a 12th century grandson of Rashi, it's regarded as a parent's duty to feed his children with his own hands, even while abstaining on *Yom Kippur*: an act of Nazaritic masochism in the view of many. The Kara'ites, for example, who openly disagreed with this; for them, the children too should bear the burden of affliction, not just at the age of *B'nei Mitzvah*, but as soon as they're young enough to understand.

"Wherefore have we fasted, they ask, and You see it not? Wherefore have we afflicted our soul, and You take no knowledge? Behold, in the day of Your fast You find Your purpose, and exact all Your labours."
Thus Isaiah (58:3), emphasising the intrinsic over the extrinsic. We fast, not to make atonement to God, but within ourselves. But wanting God to see, and to approve our doing so, for we're always in a child-parent relation with our God, and what child can bear to act without parental audience? By fasting, we validate God, as well as ourselves. Isaiah makes metaphor out of the act of fasting, reflecting in it both the material and the spiritual drought; he rebukes Israel, not for fasting inappropriately, but for failing to make the act of fasting antithetical. The act of fasting must lead back to the taking-in of food, in the same way that it was itself a lapse from eating.
"Behold, you fast for strife and debate, and to smite with the fist of wickedness; surely you do not fast so that your voice can be heard on high? Is it such a fast that I have chosen? A day for a man to afflict his soul? Is it to bow down his head like a bulrush, to spread sackcloth and ashes under himself? Will you call such a fast day acceptable to the Lord? Is not this,

2

rather, the fast that I have chosen? To loosen the chains of wickedness, to undo the bands of the yoke, to let the oppressed go free, to break each and every yoke..."

Yom Kippur, not as a day of mourning, of lugube and lamentation, but as a fast for freedom, an abstention that liberates the body with the soul. Even through the soul. But there's a contradiction here. Isaiah's purpose in the fast stands in complete disagreement with the Rabbi's purpose in the *Talmud*. Which is correct? Which are we to follow? According to the *Pirkei Avot* - the "Ethics of the Fathers" - authority had passed from the Prophets to the Rabbis, and so we should follow the *Talmud*; but this transition is only on the say-so of the Rabbis, and self-evidently they're biased in their judgement. Then who should we follow? Fasting for our own sake, or for God's? Fasting to forgive, or to be forgiven? Fasting as a metaphorical or a literal act? I'm inclined to think that, even despite the seeming contradiction, it isn't impossible to choose both.

So central was this theme of liberation in Biblical times, in the Jubilee year the *shofar* was sounded on *Yom Kippur* to testify the setting-free of slaves, the restoration of land to its ancestral owners (Leviticus 25:9-10).

But presumably, today, that tradition dare not be revitalised, lest the stranger who is within our gate be so far increased by the return of the dispossessed brothers, sisters, uncles and cousins of the stranger who is within our gate, that Israel becomes swamped by strangers, and the Jew finds himself voted into exile by a Palestinian majority!

"Is it not to share your bread with the hungry," Isaiah continues, "that you bring the poor and the outcast into your house? When you see the naked, so you will cover him; and do not hide from the nakedness of your own flesh..."

The individual atonement nourishing the communal.

"Then shall your light break forth as morning, and your health shall spring forth speedily; and your righteousness shall go before you; the glory of the Lord shall be your reward. Then you will call, and the Lord will answer; you will cry, and He will say 'Here I am'..."

Atonement as purgation, a making clean, of the soul as well as of the slate. But Isaiah's concepts aren't those of the Rabbis who supplanted him and his fellow Prophets. What Isaiah hints in these lines is the fulfilment of the "*Shemoneh Esreh*", the "Eighteen Blessings" (light, health, righteousness, reward, etc); but in his form of atonement, the entire process is personal and internal. One can achieve atonement *even without God*. The Rabbis wouldn't accept that.

"If you take away from the midst of you the yoke, the putting forth of the finger, the speaking of iniquity; and if you bring forth that which you have

3

prepared for yourself and give it to the hungry, and if you nourish the afflicted soul, then shall your light rise in obscurity, and your darkness will be as at noon; and the Lord will guide you continually, and satisfy your soul in drought, and make fat your bones; so you will be like a watered garden, like a spring of waters whose waters fail not..." (Isaiah 58:9)

The mere act of charity is sufficient. Give to the poor and you become a God to the poor, delivering the afflicted soul from its affliction. But like the 5th commandment, charity goes against the grain of human nature and requires a reward. An ironical reward too: give to charity and you will become rich.

Within these acts of giving lies something deeper too. The concept of "Justice, Not Vengeance", as the Nazi-hunter Simon Wiesenthal called his autobiography. Atonement funded by confession, not accusation; by forgiveness, not extenuation. Abstention as an aspect of eating, another of the intrinsic processes. And finally, the wholeness of self which is at-one-ment, endorses the wholeness of God's Universe.

"So they shall rebuild the old waste places, so they shall raise up the foundations of many generations, and you will be called the repairer of the breach, the restorer of the dwelling-places."

In short, Messiah.

But the inversion of the Christian Messiah. There, Jesus is the *Azazel*, who takes the sins of all the world upon his back and is sacrificed to shed them; here, each man is his own *Azazel*, confessing his individual sins, making his individual sacrifice in their name, receiving clemency in the first person singular. And as to the Jesuitic motto, that Man cannot live by bread alone. Fast, so that you may eat. Fast totally, so that the whole world may be nourished. Fast, so God may reward you. Fast, so that you will appreciate the true value of bread. The alternative to earthly bread is not spiritual bread, but abstinence.

Fast, says Isaiah, in order to bring the covenant to fruition.

✡

A tradition which is tantamount to a superstition: the date on which Moses descended Sinai with the second set of tablets, the restored law, was the day of *Yom Kippur*. And not just the day of, but the very first *Yom Kippur*.

Then why do we not mark the fact?

Perhaps because it's only one of several similar traditions, and because we've grown sceptical about the number of historic dates that get associated with festivals simply because some Rabbi in a sermon somewhere found it convenient to draw an analogy. *Yom Kippur* is also regarded in the *Aggadah* (the section of the Talmud which contains homiletic and non-legal texts) as the day on which Abraham circumcised himself; and of course it's regarded as the true date of the *Akeda*, the "sacrifice" of Isaac on Mount Moriah – which would have been a logical date, had Abraham gone ahead and sacrificed Isaac, rendering him, like Jesus later, the *Azazel*; but God stayed Abraham's hand, and it was the paschal lamb of Passover that was sacrificed, not the billy-goat of *Yom Kippur*. *Leviticus Rabbah* (21:4) declares that this is the one day in the year when Satan has no power to accuse the children of Israel. One has to remain sceptical, especially in this latter regard.

✡

Should married women participate, according to the orthodox *halachah*? In Numbers 30:14, endorsed by *Yoma* 74b, "Every vow, and every binding oath to afflict the soul, her husband may establish it, or her husband may declare it void."

In the days of chattel-marriage, it was her husband's decision. But today? Is it not the case that, in the opening pages, in *Kol Nidre* itself, all vows, all binding oaths, are nullified, which must even include those of marriage? Then women too are free to fast.

✡

The ancientness of the fast-day is attested in Leviticus 23:24-32:

"And the Lord spoke to Moses saying, 'Speak thus to the children of Israel. In the seventh month, on the first day of the month, you shall have a day of rest[1], a memorial with blowing of horns, a holy convocation…and on the tenth day of this seventh month there shall be a day of atonement; it shall be a day of holy convocation, and you shall afflict your souls, and offer an offering made by fire to the Lord."

How much harder then than now. Not simply to fast, but to participate in the ceremonies of the cooking of the meat sacrifice even while you fast. Perhaps we should say our prayers today, not in the synagogue, but in the kitchen.

"And you shall do no work on that day, for it is a day of atonement, to make an atonement for you before the Lord. And any soul that does any work that day, he will be destroyed from among his people; and any soul

---

[1] I have left the translation as "have", but I would prefer "make". To have a day of rest implies laxity, a doing nothing, a mere cessation of activity. To make a day of rest requires actions, and as such the day is positive, not passive. There are those who would translate the line as "take" a day of rest, which is even less again.

that does not afflict himself, he shall be cut off from among his people. You shall do no manner of work; this is a statute for ever, for all generations and in all dwelling-places. It shall be to you a day of rest, and you shall afflict your souls, in the ninth day at evening, from evening until evening, shall you celebrate this *Sabbath* of *Sabbaths*."

Harsh punishment indeed for those who disincline. Destruction and extirpation – not simply excommunication, but a complete rooting out, so that there can be no future generations. To cut off a man is only half his punishment however. In Judaism, full punishment necessitates cutting off his seed as well. Such is the status of *Yom Kippur*.

And as to the *Sabbath* of *Sabbaths*. The *Sabbath* is one of the five covenants between Man and God (the others are the Noachic Rainbow, the act of circumcision, the *Torah* and the Messiah). If the *Sabbath* is supremely holy, how much more so a fast that's called the *Sabbath* of *Sabbaths*?

How ancient though is the festival, given the questions that surround the text? Modern scholars of the *d'vei* of Bible Criticism will argue that Leviticus isn't Mosaic at all, but reflects the practises of the Second Temple period. Then *Yom Kippur* is only two and a half thousand years old, and not the full three and a half! For this too, very sorry.

No one disputes the Mosaicity of Numbers however, and Numbers 29:7-11 reiterates the ediction of the fast day:
"And you shall have, on the tenth day of this seventh month, a holy convocation, and you shall afflict your souls, and you shall not do any work that day. And you shall offer a burnt offering to the Lord for a sweet savour; one young bullock, one ram, and seven first-year lambs, all these creatures completely without blemish. Their meat offering shall be of flour mingled with oil, three tenths for each bullock, two tenths for each ram, several tenths for each of the seven lambs. One of the kid goats for a sin offering, beside the sin offering of the atonement, and the continual burnt offering, and the meat offering, and the drink offering."
This isn't affliction, this is torment. Hard enough to make the twenty-five hour fast; but here, in Temple times, the bruise was pressed upon, like a heel on bone. Meat offerings, the sweet savour of roasting lamb, beef, goat, grilled in batter on the holy altar, its tantalising odours permeating prayer. And because it's *kurban* – the full burned offering – not even the compensating certainty of an eventual banquet. This is salivation induced without reward – salivation without salvation. Worse. We're not even permitted to taste the salivations.

✡

The Book of Jubilees (5:17-18), a pseudepigraphic volume from the Second Temple period which influenced both the midrashic authors and the sect of the Essenes, claimed that the date of *Yom Kippur* was a commemoration of the date that Jacob heard of Joseph's death and mourned for him; the sacrifice of the male goat, the *Azazel*, according to Jubilees, was a reminder of the goat his brothers slaughtered in order to have blood to stain Joseph's coat of many colours and thereby convince Jacob of the tragic fate that had befallen him. The Kara'ites have always followed this version of events, regarding the fast day as a day of mourning, and it may be a residue of this fate that led mediaeval communities to institute the practise of lighting twin memorial candles, one for the living and the other for the dead.

It seems to me an oddity, however; so odd as to be implausible. Jacob, after all, was in the throes of a deception; his mourning was false, because Joseph was very much alive. Are we really founding our repentance on a charlatan sacrifice and a deceived father? Are we to understand that our prayers only have the same measure of validity that Jacob's *Kaddish* had, which is to say precisely none, for we would be repenting into a void?

Philo, writing in the 1st century CE in Alexandria, takes the opposite view from Jubilees. Jubilees makes it a day of mourning, and therefore sadness; Philo regards it as pure joy, because we are purified, washed clean and purged. Born again, like new-born babes, unsullied by our lives' experiences. Of course, Philo had the advantage of being ascetically-inclined on all the other three hundred and sixty-four days of the year: he didn't regard venal indulgence as the real source of human joy, as let's be honest the majority of us do. Food, drink, dance and sex reflected mankind's lowest desires and lusts, not his highest hedonistic satisfactions. Abstinence for Philo was a genuine pleasure, where for most of us abstinence is precisely the affliction described in Scripture.

But the Sages do take Philo's side in this. *Genesis Rabbah* (2:3) calls *Yom Kippur* "The Great Day", Ta'an (4:8) has "The Great Fast", as do Sifra, Acharey Mos and Tosef Hul (5:9). God gave the day to Israel with love, and so we should enjoy it. I say this, not because I know that many Jews endure it, but don't enjoy it. I say it, rather, because I intend throughout this book to follow Philo and the Sages' guidance, and to enjoy not just the festival, but also the research into the festival, and the writing about it. Do not expect the mourning of the Book of Jubilees or the solemnity of the afflicted. Expect the writings of a man who sings the hymnal of his self-atonement in full throat and with deep enjoyment of the inner sounds.

Judah ha-Levi, the greatest of the Sephardi poets of the Middle Ages, declared *Yom Kippur* (*Kuzari*, 3:5) to be that on which the human soul, freed from the chains of the body, could attain the peak of its perfection in the service of God. My hope is that this book will say amen to that.

✡

Nothing begins where it begins. A fast, like a banquet, requires preparation.

In *Orach Chayim* (604:1), and clarified in *Mishnah Berurah*, we are enjoined to fast on the eve of *Yom Kippur* with the same intensity that we'll fast on *Yom Kippur* itself. The two are forms of the same act, and no Jewish ritual, ceremony or mere get-together is imaginable without food, whether indulging in it or abstaining from it, and in either case taken to the most extreme degree.

At noon, so custom and *Masey Ephrayim* (605:18) dictates, a festive lunch. Then, after visiting the *mikveh* and *davening Minchah* – taking a ritual bath and praying the afternoon service – the *Se'udah ha-Maphseket*. No wine, no alcohol, but the *challah* is dipped in honey as it is on *Rosh ha-Shana*. No fish, no spicy foods, nothing that's hot or made of milk or eggs or garlic – the purpose it to ready the stomach, not to ruin it. Chicken rather than beef – it's lighter. It's also considered virtuous to share this meal with the needy, and to recite Psalm 126 before consuming it:
"*Hodu l'adonay ki tov, ki le'olam chasdo*…Give thanks to the Lord, for He is good; His mercy endures for ever."

✡

Kapparot

But before any of this, the strangest of all rituals – *kapparot*, performable at any time between *Rosh ha-Shana* and *Yom Kippur*, but deemed best of all (most efficacious, in the way of white magic) at just after dawn on the eve of *Yom Kippur* itself.

There's nothing in the Bible, nor in the *Talmud*, to suggest *kapparot*. It was an invention of the *ga'onim*, the Babylonian sages of the 9th century, though even they were in disagreement as to what should happen. Rashi, in *Shabos* 81b, describes a ritual entirely at odds with the one described, for example, in *Rosh*, in *Yoma* 8:23, in *Tur Orach Chayim* 605; and unusually it's the Rashi which is out of use.

At *Rosh ha-Shana* the Book of Life is opened, in which our deeds for the past year have been recorded, and where, come *Yom Kippur*, they will be judged in order to determine our karma for the coming year. Through the Ten Days of Awe, through the five prayer services of *Yom Kippur* especially, we have the chance to make amends, through penitence, and convince God to write our names in the Book of Life for a happy, healthy, prosperous and joyful next twelve months. But nothing that pertains to God's creation can be taken from the world. So where, if we are forgiven, do our sins go? For they must go somewhere. In Temple times, they went into the body of the *Azazel*; but now, now that there is no Temple? *Sifra, Acharey Mos* 8:1, tells us that the Day itself is now sufficient, and supplants the *Azazel*; but clearly the orthodox don't accept this ruling. For now they go – into the body of a rooster. Or a hen, if a woman is performing the expiation. And why a rooster? Because the Hebrew word *"gever"* can mean both a man and a rooster.

The ritual, then, is one of symbolic transference, spiritual as well as etymological. By a process akin to self-exorcism, a person's sins depart him and enter the fowl instead; deceived, apparently, by linguistics. Or simply too giddy, too punch-drunk, to spot the chicanery. The chicken is taken in the right hand (some recite the phrase *"Nephesh tachat nephesh* – a life for a life"* while doing so), lifted above the head, and then swung around three times, a process not unlike consuming three consecutive pina coladas in a smoke-filled discotheque. However, before swinging, the *"Beney Adam"* is recited, a construction of Psalmic out-takes (107:10, 107:14, 107:17-21), with two verses of Job (33:23-24). Only the opening phrase is original to the prayer.

"Children of Man, who sat in darkness…I have found atonement."

Then the formula for transference, varied according to who is performing the ritual, in what company, on whose behalf.

"This is my substitute, my vicarious offering, my atonement. This rooster shall go to its death, but I will have a long and pleasant and a peaceful life."

Originally, and preferably still today, the hen and rooster should be as white as purity, but as the relentless pursuit of the white dove, the bird of Asherah, was a pagan virtue, Jews were encouraged not to be too choosy. Like the penny in the old man's Christmas hat, if you haven't got a white hen, a speckled one will do; and if even that's beyond your means…in 9th century Babylonia it was customary to use baby rams (in recollection of Abraham's substitution at the *Akeda*), or even simple vegetables such as peas or beans. As sacrifice became forbidden with the destruction of the

Temple, so no animal fit for sacrifice could be subjected to *kapparot*, lest the act be misunderstood. It's also acceptable, since the *kapparah* is destined for charity, to use money. The rooster will be slaughtered and given to the needy for a meal – though fortunately we Jews are not an animistic people; there is no suggestion that he who eats the rooster will absorb the sins.

The act of transference itself transfers. The sins to the fowl, the fowl to the hungry. And the entrails of the fowl, given by the hungry to the needy birds and beasts. Nothing may be wasted.

How should a pregnant woman perform *kapparot*? (These are the sorts of question that have sustained an industry of Jewish scholarship for two millennia.) For herself, a white hen. But she must also atone for her unborn child. With the same hen, or with a second one? And if a second one, since she cannot know the sex of the unborn child, should she use a rooster or a hen, or one of each, to be on the safe side? And maybe they're twins.

What do you mean, it doesn't matter? Of course it matters. To save a single human soul, the Rabbis teach, is equivalent to saving the whole world. Believe me, it matters.

✡

Not all the world approves of the ritual of *kapparot*, and it isn't hard to see why. Vegetarians and animal rights campaigners have their own reasons, and they're probably valid. But in Jewish tradition other reasons apply. In the Responsa *"Darchei Emon"*, Rabbi Solomon ben Abraham Adret, the *Rashba*, opposed *kapparot* precisely because it transferred the rite of sacrifice from Temple to courtyard, from *Azazel* to rooster. Post-modernists would take pleasure from such symmetry, but to Adret it was contradictory; the Temple practice was God's Law, the *kapparot* mere heathen superstition, and the one could not be allowed to stand substitute for the other. Adret's teacher Nachmanides – his "other" teacher; the *Rashba* always regarded Jonah ben Abraham Gerondi as *"my* teacher" – shared his pupil's view, as did Joseph Caro who, in the *Orach Chayim* (the book being clarified in the *Mishnah Berurah*), derogates it as "a stupid custom". (*Orach Chayim* 605)

It was the cabbalists who really gave it credence, and thereby a tradition; and this may explain why it's particularly prominent amongst Hassidic Jews today. What more mystical act than this symbolic transiration, this ghostly passage from body to body as though a sin was no different from a wart or a louse or a virus? Isaac Luria and Isaiah Horowitz both advocated it, and Moses Isserles not only decreed it compulsory, but ordained for it all manner of ceremonies that attached it unequivocally to the cult of sacrifice – the laying of hands upon the animal, for example, the slaughter in the immediate aftermath of the rite, the accompanying *Vidu'i* or confession.

One final thought on *kapparot*. In Yiddish, the term is used for any futile effort, any waste that might have been avoided, any loss of goods or cash or time. Is there, in this, a measure of criticism to be deduced?

✡

The *Kittel*

Much of the ritual and ceremony of *Yom Kippur* derives from the *Pirkei d'*Rabbi Eliezer ben Hyrcanus, one of Yochanan ben Zakkai's pupils at Yavneh (the Rabbinical academy in Palestine which the Romans allowed to survive after the destruction of the Temple in 70 CE), and Rabban Gamliel's companion on his "mission" to Rome in 95/96. His teacher once famously said of him (it's quoted in *Avot* 2:8) that "if all the sages of Israel were balanced against Eliezer, he would still outweigh them". In chapter 46 of his *Pirkim*, he compares Israel on *Yom Kippur* to the angels, concluding that our state of repentance makes us free from sin, and thus on a par with the heavenly host. For this reason we may adopt their special practices, but only for today. So we recite aloud the *"Baruch shem kavod"* in the *Shema*. So we prostrate ourselves during the *Aleynu*. So also do we wear the *kittel*, a simple white tunic whose source is Daniel 10:5:
"Then I lifted up my eyes, and looked, and behold a certain man clothed in linen, whose loins were girdled with fine gold of Uphaz." This is understood to have been an angel, because "I, Daniel, alone saw this vision, for the men that were with me saw it not" (v7), and it is the only physical description of an angel which the *Tanach* ever affords us. There are two problems however.
The first is that *"badim"* (which has several uses, and several meanings, including "lies", "falsehoods" and "separations") only refers to the thread or yarn from which linen is made, and is white only through the human process of retting.
The second is that we now know Daniel to have been a work of fiction, composed to serve an allegorical purpose during the Greek occupation of *Erets Yisrael* after Alexander of Macedon; and it isn't customary in Judaism to educe laws out of known fictions.

The source is Daniel 10:5 but the ruling is from the *Orach Chayim* (610:4), and in fact states that we should dress in white for a quite different reason: because white is the colour of the Jewish shroud and will thus inspire repentance in us by evoking death. It's precisely this which lies at the heart of that great modern payyatan Leonard Cohen's "Who by Fire", sourced in the *Yom Kippur* liturgy but chorused at his own invention: "Who shall I say is calling?" The inference is Death, the One Who Judges Souls, and Moses Isserles, co-author of the *Shulchan Aruch*, would not dissent.

The *kittel* itself, the ankle-length white robe that makes a man look like Wee Willie Winkie without his candle, was in fact an invention of the North Italian and Provençal communities in the era of Immanuel of Rome, the man who taught Dante the sonnet and *terza rima*. A second, entirely unconnected custom also owes its origins to this time and place, though it may have been brought in by German Jews escaping from the Rhineland: that of lighting candles in the home, to preclude cohabitation which is forbidden on *Yom Kippur* (no, I'm not clear how it would be effective; perhaps with an absence of curtains the neighbours would be less likely to notice); this has now become a memorial candle, but with a surreal difference; it's lit specifically in memory of the living, alongside a second candle for the dead. (*Machzor Vitry* also informs us that, in Germany, on *Yom Kippur*, in mediaeval times, charitable donations on behalf of the dead were offered, and the litany of donors and the size of their offerings read out, after the reading of the Law, during *Shacharit*. I wonder if there's any mileage in this notion for the United Joint Israel Appeal's annual campaign?)

At what time should we don the *kittel*? Custom decrees "before the *Kol Nidre* service", but this is unspecific. Immediately before? Upon arrival in synagogue? Before leaving home? Unusually for Judaism, the decision on this is left to the wearer.

Mishnah Berurah advocates that women too should dress in white, but not a *kittel* – God forbid the intrusion upon male hegemony! – because the dead, both male and female, are shrouded in the *kittel*, and *Yom Kippur* as Judgement Day requires symbolic reminders of death and judgement. This elucidation bewilders and disturbs me: the explanation wants to imply that we *should* all, male and female, wear a *kittel*. In truth, the exclusion of the female from so doing was never a matter of religious law but only of social status, an emphasising of the patriarchal authority.

✡

Prayers before prayers

Minchah, the regular afternoon service, eternal substitute for the "*tamid*", the afternoon sacrifices in the Temple in Jerusalem. *Berachot* 26b tells us the sacrifice could not be brought until at least a half-hour after mid-day, but that anything up to three and a half hours was regularly waited. Late afternoon is best of all, because it was in late afternoon that Elijah (1 Kings 18:36) called on God at Carmel to light his pyre and confound the priests of Baal, and it was in the late afternoon that Isaac (Genesis 24:63) went out to pray. But this is the eve of *Yom Kippur*, and it's no ordinary *Minchah*. Its *chazan* should be someone fit to lead the prayers of *Yom Kippur* itself, and he should wear his *tallit* (Rashi in *ha-Pardes* is the source of the ruling on this: we should don the *tallit* for the evening service because this way we can say the blessing for the donning of the *tallit* before *Yom Kippur* commences). Collection plates should be left in synagogue, so merit may be acquired through the *mitzvah* of charity. And the prayers should be *davened* early in the afternoon, to leave time for the preparations for *Yom Kippur*.

Begin with *Ashrey*, as is customary, then half-*Kaddish* (I do not propose to explain again those daily customs that I have already explained in "A Myrtle Among Reeds"; my reader, if interested, is invited to consult that book). The centrepiece of *Minchah* is the *Shemoneh Esreh, the* Eighteen Benedictions of the *Amidah*, augmented during these Days of Awe by specific supplementals, and in most communities chanted to a very different, a slower, more rhapsodic, more lugubrious melody, mournful yet uplifting.

✡

There are several additional phrases in this *Minchah Amidah*:

"Zachreynu le-chayim, melech chaphets ba-chayim, ve-chatveynu be-sepher ha-chayim, le-ma'ancha elohim chayim – remember us for life, O King who desires life, and inscribe us in the Book of Life, for Your sake, O Living God."

A simple enough request. God the Abstract, God the Metaphor, is personified, anthropomorphised, in all the *Rosh ha-Shana* and *Yom Kippur* liturgy, mostly as a King – the King of the Universe – but also as a King-Judge who is His own Clerk and Court Recorder. It's an infantile atavism, and one that I continue to regard as allegory not literality, elsewise God would be little more than the red-gowned, white-bearded Santa Claus invented in the 1930s by Coca-Cola to sell their tooth-dissolving beverage; and the duty of penitence would be reduced to farce. Nonetheless, this is the conceit: that God on *Rosh ha-Shana* opens the Book of Life, to judge us and to decree our fate for the coming year. The Book will not be closed until the last instant of *Yom Kippur*, and the fervour and sincerity of our penitence is meant to curry favour. Prayer is equivalent to petition. Clemency may be obtained by grovelling or piety. Like flies to wanton boys are we to God! Like flies – unhuman, our humanity stripped. What is required – mechanically, robotically – is our obedience. I imagine this God much as Solzhenitsyn imagined Stalin in that extraordinary chapter of "The First Circle", or as Mandelstam did, with his "cockroach moustaches", in the epigram that got him inscribed in the Book of State Enemies and exiled to the *She'ol* of Siberia.

"Mi kamocha av ha-rachamim, zocher yetsurav le-chayim be-rachamim – who is like You, merciful father, who recalls His creatures mercifully for life?"

Most translations bestow an exclamation mark, where grammar implies the question mark that I have used. This is a paean, not a rhetorical device. But surely *"le-chayim"* means "to life" and not "for life" – and as such it carries inferences of resurrection or reincarnation. Is the mistranslation a modern sidestepping of what anciently was quite acceptable? Can we read into a simple preposition an entire recasting of the principles of faith?

"U-chetuv le-chayim tovim kol beney vritecha – and inscribe all the children of Your covenant for a good life."

The first two additions came early in the *Amidah*, in the middle of *Avot* and before the closing phrase of *Gevurot*. This third addition - which requires no commentary - follows the *Modim*, and almost immediately after it comes the fourth.

"Be-sepher chayim berachah ve-shalom, u-pharnasah tovah, nizaker ve-nikatev lephaneycha, anachnu ve-chol amcha beyt Yisra'el, le-chayim tovim u-le-shalom – in the Book of Life, Blessing and Peace, and of Prosperity, may we be remembered and inscribed before You, we and Your entire people, the family of Israel, for a good life and for peace."

Placing the four appendices together like this unbalances the main emphasis of the *Amidah*, which is otherwise unaltered from any other recitation. The appendices render it specific to *Yom Kippur*, but they do not modify it.

✡

Vidu'i

There is, however, a significant modification to the end of the *Amidah*, for at *Minchah* of *Yom Kippur* we add for the first time the long *Vidu'i* or "Confession" that will be repeated at every phase of *Yom Kippur*.

Why do we confess and what are the sources for *Vidu'i*? The answers are

14

manifold. But first the sources:

i) Genesis 4:13 - Cain complains about his punishment and is given protection against any who would try to take his life. The Rabbis insist that there's an inference here of confession, arguing that God wouldn't grant clemency without an act of confession. But nothing in the text overtly renders this; and anyway it isn't clemency that Cain receives, nor really protection, but only a curse against the perpetrator of his death.

ii) 2 Samuel 12:5-17 - After the killing of Ur-Yah the Hittite, plotted by King David in order to obtain his wife Bathsheba, the prophet Nathan castigates the king. David doesn't overtly confess his sin, but presented with an allegory he condemns the perpetrator as worthy of death. He is punished, and fasts in penance, after which redemption is once more possible. This, not Cain, is the first true example of atonement; and the second is also David's, after the disastrous attempt to bring the Ark up to Jerusalem, for which an entire national ceremony of confession and self-affliction was prescribed.

iii) Psalm 32:1-5 – "Blessed is he whose transgression (*pesha*) is forgiven, whose sin (*chata'ah*) is covered. Blessed is the man to whom the Lord does not impute iniquity (*avon*), and in whose spirit there is no guile...I acknowledged my sin to You, and my iniquity I have not hidden. I said, I will confess my transgression unto the Lord, and You forgive the iniquity of my sin..."

The triple concept of *pesha*, *chata'ah* and *avon* is crucial to the process of atonement; three entirely different types of sin, each with its own consequences. Biblical usage suggests that a *pesha* is stronger than a *chet*, where *avon* is full-scale iniquity, the deepest level of sin. A *chet* will incur a forfeit or a fine, but is expiable and may only be an error. A *pesha* has the sense of wilfulness, even of protest or rebellion against the Law and against God; it requires a sacrificial offering at the Temple. This is why the words for pardon are also varied - a *selichah* for the *chet*, a *mechilah* for the *pesha*. *Selichah* is forgiveness, *mechilah* the full pardon, relative strength to relative strength. Only on *Yom Kippur* itself do we ask for and receive the highest level, beyond *selichah*, beyond *mechilah*, the full *kappara* which gives the day its name, the complete obliteration of our sins from the record books, the nulling and voiding of the entire page, so that we may start again afresh, at-one.

iv) Psalm 51 (the Bathsheba Psalm; but as my parentheses indicate, it's used in several other important contexts besides this one):

"Have mercy upon me, O God, according to Your lovingkindness; according to the multitude of Your tender mercies blot out my transgressions.

Wash me thoroughly from my iniquity, and cleanse me from my sin. For I acknowledge my transgressions, and my sin is ever before me.

Against You, against Your self, have I sinned, and done this evil in Your sight; so You are justified when You speak, and clear when You judge.

Behold, I was shaped in iniquity, in sin did my mother conceive me.

Behold, You desire truth in the innermost parts; and in the hidden part You shall make me know wisdom.

Purge me with hyssop, and I shall be clean; wash me, and I shall be whiter than snow.

Make me hear joy and gladness; let the bones which You have broken rejoice.

Hide Your face from my sins, and blot out all my iniquities.

Create in me a clean heart, O God; and renew a right spirit within me."

v) *Al tashlicheyni*:

"Cast me not away from Your presence; do not take Your holy spirit from me.

Restore to me the joy of Your salvation, and uphold me with Your free spirit.

Then I will teach transgressors Your ways, and sinners shall be converted into worshippers.

Deliver me from blood-guilt, O God, God of my salvation, and my tongue shall sing aloud Your righteousness."

vi) Opening of the *Amidah*:

"O Lord, open my lips, and my mouth will recount Your praises.

For You do not desire sacrifice; if You did I would give it; but You take no delight from burnt offerings.

The sacrifices of God are a broken spirit; a broken and a contrite heart, O God, surely You will not despise?"

vii) *Ayn Kamocha*:

"Do good, in the goodness of Your pleasure unto Zion; build the walls of Jerusalem.

Then You will be sanctified with the sacrifices of righteousness, with burnt offerings and every other kind of offering; then they will offer bullocks on the altar."

viii) Psalm 69:6-14:

"O God, You know my foolishness, my sins are not hidden from You…
When I wept, and chastened my soul with fasting, that was to my reproach. I made sackcloth my garment…
But as for me, my prayer is unto You, O Lord, in an acceptable time."

ix) Psalm 41:5:

"I said, Lord, be merciful unto me, heal my soul for I have sinned against You."

All of which seems to make mockery of the Temple practices. If God didn't desire sacrifice, why did this continue to be the central function of the Temple, the central rite of the cult? If God took no delight in burnt offerings, why did he give Moses such detailed regulations for its practice, why did the Prophets so frequently call back the Children of Israel to this as the predominant form of worship?

And there are still more sources. In Genesis 38:26 Judah acknowledges, not the unintentional sin, but the talismans that prove it. Achan, in Joshua 7:19-21, is the first to be explicit: "Indeed I have sinned against the Lord God of Israel, and thus and thus I have done" – arrogant in the admission, almost to the point of nonchalance, disdain; his sin was the personalising of significant amounts of booty; his punishment stoning. Confession in his case didn't lead to redemption; but God was angry with all Israel, Achan was the scapegoat, and "the Lord turned from the fierceness of His anger'. Communal redemption at the price of the individual.

Booty was also the issue in 1 Samuel 15:24-25: "And Saul said to Samuel, 'I have sinned, for I have transgressed the commandment of the Lord, and your words; because I feared the people and obeyed their voice. Now, therefore, I pray, pardon my sin and turn again with me, that I may worship the Lord." Clutching the Prophet's gown as he turns away, the gown tears, and Samuel makes of this an allegory for Saul's punishment, declaring that "The Lord has rent the kingdom of Israel from you this day.' Saul repents this too, and joins Samuel in worshipping God contritely, though it's evident he fears Samuel's wrath more than the Almighty's. In fact Saul isn't redeemed, because he fails to perform properly the act of contrition, but the anecdote functions as a Rabbinic precedent nonetheless; it's the precept, not the exemplar, which provides.

There are paradigms too. In Exodus 32:31 Moses leads the children of Israel in communal contrition after the idolatry of the Golden Calf. In

Leviticus 16, the High Priest performs the aboriginal *Yom Kippur* rituals; in Ezra 9 and Nehemiah 1 and 9 we can read the founding ceremonies of the Second Temple period. Talmudically the sources for these *Vidu'im* are *Yah*, *Ma'aseh ha-Korban* 3:6 and 3:14-15, and *Yoma* 3:8.

Maimonides declares (*Teshuvah* 1:1) that "it is a positive precept…to confess the sin when desirous of repenting.'
The key phrase of confession – "Truly we have sinned" – is found in *Yoma* 87b.

Other than *Yom Kippur* the most important occasion for confession – a residue of atavism in Judaism, implying a belief in the afterlife – is on the death-bed. *Shabat* 32a urges a seriously ill person to make confession, but to do so before witnesses, who should first issue the reminder: "Fear not. Many who have confessed nonetheless recovered from their illness, whilst many others who did not confess still died." I like this anti-fatalism, balancing as it does the atavism. The act of confession is ancillary to the act of dying. God doesn't regard it as knocking on the gates of Heaven, nor as an Open Sesame.

"I acknowledge before You, O Lord my God and God of my ancestors, that my cure and my death are in Your hands. May it be Your will to send me a perfect healing. But if my death is fully determined by You, I will, in love, accept it at Your hand. May my death be an atonement for all the sins, iniquities and transgressions which I have committed before you. Grant me the great happiness that is stored up for the righteous. Make known to me the path of life; in Your presence is fullness of joy; at Your right hand bliss for evermore."

Was ibn Gvirol[2] thinking of these lines when he wrote his extraordinary poem, a human cry in the wilderness of all this liturgy: "His Illness"?

> Forgive me, my God, and overlook my sins,
> Although one cannot fathom their number or their depth.
> Remember, for my sake, your kindness, Lord,
> Pay no heed to the sins of dust and earth.
> Even if the decree has gone out against my life,
> Annul it, my God, make it of no effect.
> Consider my illness as my redemption,

---

[2] Solomon ben Yehuda ibn Gvirol, known in Arabic as Abu Ayyūb Suleiman ibn Yahya ibn Jabirūl and in Latin as Avicebron, regarded as one of the greatest poets of Spain in the 11th century

And let my pain ransom me from death.

Two forms of confession, the first of faith, the second of error. And what a splendid retort to Death, to transform it into the very act of contrition which redeems a soul for Paradise. No, not Death – but rather the act of dying. All that physical and metaphysical anguish, transmuted into eternal life!

But dying should be unselfish.

"O father of the fatherless and defender of the widow, protect my dear family, with whose soul my own soul is bound. Into Your hand I commend my spirit; You will redeem me, O Lord, God of Truth. *Amen* and *amen*."

Suicide is precluded then. But all of this requires considerable lucidity, perhaps more than can realistically be expected of the terminally ill, let alone the unexpectedly cut down. The latter prayers are mere phrases, familiar to the regular worshipper, each one repeated several times. Even a man in final agony can mouth a single sound.

"*Adonay melech, adonay malach, adonay yimloch le'olam va'ed.*"

Recited three times.

"The Lord is King, the Lord was King, the Lord will be King for evermore."

"*Baruch shem kavod malchuto le'olam va'ed* - blessed be His holy name; His kingdom shall endure for ever."

Also recited three times. And seven times, this:

"*Adonay hu ha-Elohim* - the Lord, He is God."

Finally, at the very instant of death, the central tenet of the Jewish faith:

"*Shema Yisra'el, adonay eloheynu, adonay echad* - Hear O Israel, the Lord our God, the Lord is One."

What greater expression of optimism, and of faith, than to expire praising God? (And of course it's the same for the mourner, who is never allowed to mention the deceased in his prayers, but prays only the *Kaddish* , the justification of the judgement, the praise of God who has taken away the father, mother, sister, brother, daughter, son.)

The criminal facing execution is likewise urged to make confession. I regard this as one of the great moral paradoxes of Judaism, but also one of its virtues. A criminal has broken laws whose source are God; the men who judge him and condemn him are bound by those same laws, and act as God's arbiters on Earth, ruling in His name. If they've demanded death, it's because God requires it; if they've declined clemency, it's because God denies it. And yet, at the instant of execution, the criminal may confess, and still take his place in Paradise; which is to say that God, acting as the Supreme Court of Appeal, may overrule His judges, and Himself. How can this be? Does it not diminish Law itself? Does it not imply that confession may reprieve sin, and thereby condone it? The answer to this conundrum lies in *Sanhedrin* 6:2, probably ibn Gvirol's source: "May my death be an expiation for all my sins", from which the death-bed *Vidu'i* is drawn. To ask for expiation is not automatically to receive it. The criminal is urged to give his soul the chance of Paradise. Nowhere (except in the mouth of Heinrich Heine, who doesn't count[3]) nowhere is it suggested that God will always concur.

Two other traditions regarding the *Vidu'i*. It's said that, in ancient times, the dying would recite the long *Yom Kippur Vidu'i*, translating it into the first person singular. Even if certain sins didn't apply, a text of such sanctity may not be expurgated, and so the dying man (or woman) would confess even those sins not committed; and in that way every dying woman (or man) became the *Azazel*, the universal scapegoat, and each dying person had the propensity, in theory, to redeem the whole world. Each of us, then, is potentially the Messiah.

The second tradition is still practised. On the eve of his wedding, at the *Minchah* prayers, the bridegroom should recite the *Yom Kippur* confession, in its plural form, on his own behalf, and on behalf of his bride-to-be. A wedding is a coming to judgement. To sign a marriage contract is to take possession of the Book of Life.

✡

There is a form of the *Vidu'i* which prologues *Tachanun* on each day of the year; but it's brief, and not just a prologue but the prologue to an addendum. From this margin it moves to the very centre at *Yom Kippur*, repeated at every service, sometimes twice – once silently, once congregationally. And long. Even Stalin, even the black-clad Inquisitors of

---

[3] Heinrich Heine (1797–1856), German-Jewish poet and journalist who converted to Christianity to get around anti-Semitic professional restrictions. When a priest came to his death-bed to offer him confession as a last chance of forgiveness, Heine replied, "Of course God will forgive me; that's His job."

St Dominic, never extracted a confession so intense, so explicit, so pious, so passionate.

Eloheynu:

The first phrase is from Psalm 88:3, the second from 55:2, the remainder a variation and elaboration of 106:6. It's a confession of the intention to confess, a confession that there are sins that need to be confessed, but it isn't yet *Vidu'i*. It's a strange arrogance too. It demands an audience of God, demands clemency from the audience, and does so on the grounds that "we are not so brazen" as to deny sin; *au contraire*, we are differently brazen, we expect to be excused for unnamed crimes simply because we admit the error. This exalts the act of confession to a posture of extenuating circumstance.

Ashamnu:

The litany of confession then begins, each phrase nailed, stamped, affirmed, by striking the left side of the chest with the right hand – the side closest to the heart, struck with the stronger hand: a left-handed person should reverse the process. Today we strike lightly, but I suspect that once, like the Flagellants of Islam, the self-infliction of pain was fundamental to the ritual, though not, this being Judaism, to the point of drawing blood. What kind of confession is it, after all, that's rendered voluntarily, rather than elicited by torture, even self-torture?

Ashamnu – we are guilty. No specific crime is named, but "*shemanah*" is regarded as spiritual desolation, consequent upon rebellion against God. The inference is deliberate, conscious, intentional breaches of God's laws.

Bagadnu – we have betrayed. Ingratitude and disloyalty, breaches of the laws of trust without which family, tribe, society, humanity cannot hold. To betray Man is to betray God. And vice versa.

Gazalnu – two very different meanings, two very different sins, contained in the single term. First the obtaining of goods by theft, by force, or by wrongdoing, meaning burglary or rape or brown envelopes. Micah (3:2) uses the term for flaying skin (presumably an ancient exemplar of the anti-animal-skins lobby); 2 Samuel 23:21 has one of David's bodyguard taking by force the spear of his Egyptian adversary; 1 Chronicles 11:23 and Job 24:9 have an orphan "plucked from its mother's breast", while Genesis

31:31 has Jacob fearing that Laban would take back his daughters by force.

But the Rabbis impute to *"gazalnu"* a spiritual and moral meaning in addition – the concept of fulfilling personal responsibilities, or of failing to, in the case of this confession. How do they derive this? By linking theft of or from others to theft of or from God. Since we were appointed custodians of Creation on the 6th day of Creation, our responsibilities are apparent. As with *"bagadnu"*, so with *"gazalnu"* – to sin against Man is to sin against God. In this way does each of us inhabit, simultaneously, a personal and the universal sphere.

Dibarnu dophi – we have spoken slander. Like *"ashamnu"*, *"dophi"* exists in the Hebrew but appears here in its Aramaic usage, from the age of the Rabbis, not the Priests. Biblically it occurs only once, in Psalm 50:20, where its meaning is close to the Arabic *"daphah* - ruin"*, or "destruction". As far as the confession is concerned, any act of tale-telling, any pejorative inflection, even any instance of hypocrisy may be regarded as *"dophi"*, though the latter is tendentious, being founded on a tenuous linguistic pun: *"du-phi"* being obscurely interpretable as "two mouths", one speaking to, the other behind, another person's face or back.

These four phrases combine to make the opening avowal. Like all the *Vidu'i* they construe an alphabetical acrostic. Like all the verses, it's customary to chant a melody without words between these and the ensuing.

✡

But why do we recite the *Vidu'i* at *Minchah*, before *Yom Kippur* has even started? The *Rambam*, Moses Maimonides, who codified the *Vidu'i*, says we cannot go to Heavenly Judgement if our conscience isn't clean; so we must repent in order to be able to repent; an act of fastidiousness that is worthy, though surely tautologous? Maimonides also makes it a matter of pragmatism and expediency – lest we fall ill and cannot repent. Rashi insists not just on *Minchah*, but before the last *se'udah* (meal) as well; in case a person overeat, and die choking, unconfessed. Surely it would be better after the *se'udah* – to counteract the sin of gluttony?

He'evinu – I dislike all the translations available for this term: "we have caused perversion, wickedness, corruption" being the most common. The root is *"avon"*, which is closely linked to *"ayin"*; both imply a state of nothingness, of emptiness, of void, a vanity, even a futility, but several Psalms (e.g. 55:4 and 90:10) use it to mean calamity or misfortune or adverse circumstances, which is somewhat less than zero. It's recurrent in Job (22:15, 31:3, 36:21 et al), which perhaps isn't that astonishing. Here the form is *"hiphil"* or causative – we have engendered a nothingness, we are responsible for a personal calamity: upon our heads the zero. There's no obvious English equivalent however; at least, not in language; in action English is just as capable of corrupting good people, overturning sound value systems, turning idealists into cynics, making the pure wicked, the selfless greedy, and transforming the straight and narrow into a labyrinth; we simply lack a word for it.

Ve-hirshanu – a slight cheating of the acrostic here, the use of the prefix *"vav"*, in the Biblical form of the *"vav* consecutive" but without the inverted future tense; the phrase should read, to be grammatically correct, *"ve-narshe"*, but this would spoil both the rhythm and the rhyme. The admission here is that we've sinned by causing others to sin, whether by influence or coercion. The *"rasha"* is a sin of deed, not of thought; planned, not spontaneous.

Zadnu – we have been proud, or haughty; in its many Biblical uses anyway. The Rabbis treat it as wilful sin, those that we not only commit but seek to justify, validating them with complex philosophical rationales, mitigating them intellectually (so the ideology of Reform Judaism could be construed as *zeydim* to the Orthodox – seeking *Toraic* or *Talmudic* legitimacy for driving to *shul* on *shabbat*, say, or seating men and women side by side; so the Orthodox use of a *shobbas goy* could be construed in the same way by Reform Judaism). *Zeydim* are greater sins than *resha'im*, because anyone who can justify his misdeeds intellectually is almost certain to repeat them; and besides, and still worse, if you can justify your misdeeds intellectually, then you are also claiming a level of knowledge and intelligence which suggests you should know better.

Chamasnu – again the Rabbis have interfered with the meaning, in this case softening it. Art Scroll gives "we have extorted", but this is minimalist. *"Chamas"* means to oppress or to use violence, and it's frequently instanced in the *Tanach* (Genesis 6:11, Psalm 140:2, Judges 9:24 to name but three). No doubt extortion involves or threatens violence, but the term in its modern sense - the Arabic equivalent is well known as the eponym of a terrorist movement – resounds with gun-fire and bomb-blast. The Rabbis defend their construction with the legal precept *"pachot mi-shavah perutah"*, which is to say "less sin than wrong-doing", less heinous than trivial, but still a breach of ethical purity: the act of taking advantage of those weaker than yourself.

Strangely, I can find no link anywhere in the Rabbinic sources to one anomalous use of *"chamas"* in the *Torah*. In Exodus 23:1, part of the original Book of the Covenant: "You shall not make a false report. Do not put your hand with the wicked to be an unrighteous witness." Unrighteous witness is rendered as "*ed chamas*".

Taphalnu sheker – we have made up lies. The prettiest of etymologies this. "*Tophal*" is really a *Talmudic* figuration, though it does appear twice in the *Tanach*, once in the Babylonian Job (13:4, 14:17), and once in the late Second Temple period Deuteronomy (1:1). The root of the figuration is a single *Tanachic* reference, Psalm 119:69, where the Psalterer states "*taplu alay sheker zeydim*" – the sin lying in the "*zeydim*", not the "*taplu*". "They have woven a patchwork of lies about me, to accuse me of them." From this the Rabbis drew a new interpretation, and frequently in the *Talmud*, as in this use in the confession, "*tapal*" no longer means "to patch" or "to sew", but explicitly "to make up lies".

These six constitute the second stanza of the *Vidu'i*, joined as before by an unworded melody. When the *Vidu'i* is chanted by the congregation in the repetition of the *Amidah*, the cantor sings each word or phrase alone, and the congregation then repeats it; but the melody is sung by all at once.

Ya'atsnu ra – we have knowingly given bad advice. It could be translated as "we have counselled evil" or "we have counselled evilly", which are not at all the same. "*Ra*" and "*resha*" in Hebrew are strongly connected, sometimes deliberately juxtaposed (in the 11th line of *Yigdal*, for example – "*noten le-rasha ra ke-rishato* – He will mete out punishment to the wicked and to the evil, each according to his wickedness"); "*ra*" is the milder of the two expressions, being generally more a matter of external appearance and superficial manner, whereas "*resha*" reflects the inner heart and soul and mind. To Martin Buber, the German-Jewish philosopher of religious existentialism, "*ya'atsnu ra*" lay at the heart of his philosophy of "I and Thou". Every human being bears the responsibility to attend carefully to other people's needs and fears. To give bad advice knowingly is to abuse trust, to put at risk. It's a sin of humanity, not divinity; of the social not the heavenly realm; but no less wrong for being that.

Kizavnu – we have been deceitful. We have told lies. We have made statements that we knew to be false. We have made promises with no intention of keeping them. Hebrew doesn't distinguish white lies from other colours, nor little white lies from other sizes. Falsehood is falsehood. Confess. Confess honestly.

Latsnu – we have mocked. But should this not be "*latsatsnu*"? At what point did Hebrew drop the second *tsade*? This isn't the place to discuss the matter; I merely point out the anomaly. The 19th century German philologist Gesenius[4] defines mockery as a "frivolous contempt for what is good and what is upright". But the two together are an oxymoron. Harnessed, they become cynicism.

Maradnu – we have rebelled. Contumacy and sedition. Defiance of God's will. Refusal to obey a law of *Torah* or *Talmud*, because it doesn't fit into our personal concept of justice or morality. This is the sin of Sisyphus, of Camus' "*L'Homme Revolté*". This is my sin – and I confess it, but I shall go on committing it, again and again, because it's also the assertion of my humanity and my individuality. So I acknowledge that the Rabbis are right to say, "this is the worst form of sin, for it cannot be blamed on error, passion, or fear..." But not the second part of that sentence "...but is performed to demonstrate that the perpetrator does not believe in God." Because I do believe in God – in God the beating pulse, God the blood-jet of the cosmos. I simply don't accept that certain of His laws, written for a slave-group asylumed in the desert, remain appropriate to city-man, in the 3rd millennium CE. Nor do I accept that God wants my obedience at the price of my humanity (the evidence is in the tale of Abraham bartering at Sodom and Gomorrah), which is defined precisely by my capacity to decide for myself what is justice and what morality. In precisely the same way, one can be a passionately committed Zionist, and still abhor the policies of Ariel Sharon, and still abhor the colonisation of Palestine by Jewish fundamentalists.

There is a huge irony surrounding "*maradnu*". Like "quisling" and "boycott" in English, the root of the name, rather than the root of the sin, is an historic individual who committed it. 1 Chronicles 4, listing the family of Judah, notes Mered, the second son of Ezra, whose rebellion lay in marrying outside the tribe (the technical term is exogamy); worse even, he took a daughter of Pharaoh named Bit-Yah. The same root leads to "*Merodach*" (Tolkien may have been aware of this), which in Jeremiah 50:2 et al is a Hebrew variation on Marduk, the Babylonian god of war whose place in the constellation of the heavens was the planet Mars, and whose name is regarded by Latinists as the source of "*mord*" and "*mort*", meaning "death". *Maradnu*, then, is also rebellion against God through the worshipping of idols. Why is this ironic? Because Marduk becomes Mordechai in the *Purim megillah*, the Hebrew adaptation of the Persian epic of the Spring, the story of Queen Astarte-Esther and Haman the ikon of the sun-god, and it was precisely Mordechai's refusal to bow down to idols

---

[4] Heinrich Friedrich Wilhelm Gesenius (1786–1842) was a German orientalist and Biblical critic; his lexicon of Hebrew and Chaldean provides the most thorough etymological study of the Hebrew language, the tracing back of words to their original roots.

that caused such trouble to the Jewish people.

"*Ashamnu*", I discover elsewhere in my reading, is also known as the "*Vidu'i Katan*", or "small confession", by contrast with "*al chet*" which is called the "*Vidu'i Gadol*" or "great confession". Both were formulated in *ga'onic* times.

Both prayers are recited as "*Selichot*" in the weeks before *Yom Kippur*. In many non-Ashkenazi synagogues, "*Ashamnu*" is included whenever the *Torah* is read on weekdays; in Hassidic synagogues, daily.

All these phrases are given in the first person plural, not singular. We are making communal confession. All of us have done these things, even those of us who haven't committed the sins ourselves. The sin is societal, not individual, even when the individual, standing within the congregation, prays in silence and alone. But it's always "*ashamnu*" not "*ashamti*", "*bagadnu*" not "*bagadeti*". I prays for we. The individual confesses for the whole community; the forgiving of the whole community redeems the individual.

Moses Isserles, in the *Orach Chayim* (607:2) allows a worshipper to confess even those sins he's certain he hasn't committed, precisely because the communal takes precedence over the individual.

The third stanza begins:

Ni'atsnu – we have angered and provoked God. Again a softening by the Rabbis – do they think it so hard to confess even our lightest sins that they're reluctant to press us to admit our heaviest? The verb "*na'ats*" contains more than mere angering and provocation. Derision. Contemptuous rejection. Despising. In Deuteronomy 32:19 it leads to God's complete abhorrence of His people, and in Isaiah 52:5 to His rejection of them.

Sararnu – we have been stubborn. From Hosea 4:16: "*Ki kepharah sorerah sarar Yisra'el* – for Israel slides back like a back-sliding heifer"; the allegory links the Prophet's son who refused to submit to his parents with the relationship between Israel and God. Stubbornness becomes an exemplar, a pretext for a sermon. We have become indifferent to God's laws, and so fail to keep them. Comfort and prosperity have become an indulgence, when they ought to be an opportunity. Animals backslide by throwing off the yoke and harness. Israel does the same to God.

Avinu – the simple, active form that previously gave "*he'evinu*". As we have made others do, so we have done ourselves, reducing to zero when we should have been building to eternity; not adding to the human sum, but subtracting from it. *Avinu* doesn't require translation, nor explanation. *Avinu* embraces all the sins, implies them, includes them, encompasses them. The *Vidu'i* is an inventory of human failings so commonplace there can be no excuse for silence. *Avinu* is the epicentre of that maelstrom.

Pashanu – we have transgressed. In the scale of sins, a *pesha* is amongst the least severe, little more than a fault or flaw, the probable original of Jesus' "forgive us our trespasses". It's stronger, however, than a *chet*, and merited a sacrificial offering as penitence in Temple times (Micah 6:7). The Rabbis regard any breach of a single, specific commandment as a *pesha*.

Tsararnu – we have caused distress to others. In the poetry of sin, as in its scales of measure, terms connect with terms. *Latsnu* with *ni'atsnu*, *pesha* with *resha*, *avinu* with *he'evinu*, *sararnu* with *tsararnu*. It may or may not be coincidental – with poetry it's usually better not to enquire. *Tserira* as persecution is itself a metaphor – originally the word meant "to bind in cloth", which is how (Exodus 12:34) the children of Israel gathered up the unleavened dough by night, and fled from Egypt.

Kishinu oreph – we have been obstinate. "Stiff-necked" is the Vulgate's splendid term – St Jerome's late 4th-century Latin translation of the Bible; "*Ve-arpechem lo takshu od*" it says, in Deuteronomy 10:16: "Be no more a stiff-necked people." Still, we kept the other half of that verse: "*U-maltem et arlat levavechem* – circumcise therefore the foreskin of your heart." What an extraordinary phrase!

So ends the third stanza of avowals; and the fourth begins:

Rashanu – we have been wicked. As *avinu* to *he'evinu*, so *rashanu* to *hirshanu*. We have induced others to these sins, but we have also committed them ourselves. Which is worse? The Rabbis don't say. They distinguish levels of sin, but they don't personalise. This is one of the key differences between the Semitic and the Hellenic outlooks, and it's reflected in the grammar. In Hebrew, as in Arabic, one states the action, then sufficates the pronoun (*rashanu*); in the Latin languages it's the obverse, pronoun before action (*we have been wicked*). The fact that the deed has been performed at all is more significant than he or she who has performed it, good or bad. So there's sin, confession, penitence, forgiveness; but there's no individual personality.

Shichatnu – we have corrupted. Or we have ruined. Or we have committed crimes. Words in every language are multivalent, so need a thesaurus as well as a dictionary to translate them fully. *Shechitah* is the ritual slaughter of animals; why does this aspect need confessing? Because to take life, even humanely, even according to the strict rules of *kashrut*, is nonetheless to take life, and even if it's done to sustain life by providing food for nourishment, still it's right to acknowledge what process is involved and the fact that blood is spilled. I like this. I like the fact that we confess not just our bad deeds but also the unhappy implications of our good ones. It describes a better balance in the universe. It dualises fault. It allows intention to provide extenuating circumstance.

But that's only the easiest meaning of *shichatnu*. Throughout the *Tanach* (Genesis 9:11, 19:13, Joshua 22:23, 2 Samuel 24:16 et al) a picture is painted of annihilation, by flood, by war, by the pulling down of walls, by murder. So far is *shachat* identified with devastation, it came eventually to mean a pit, and finally the "The Pit" itself, the dark hole of *She'ol* which is Judaism's Hades, this latter possibly by confusion with "*shu'ach* - a snare". So Psalm 7:16, 9:16, 35:7 and 94:13 use it as a trap for wild beasts, some kind of dug hole camouflaged with leaves and branches. By the time of Job 33:24, echoed in Psalm 55:24, it has come to stand for "going down into the grave"; and logic says that *shachat* would have been the word used by Joseph of Arimathea when he offered his family sepulchre as a burial place for Jesus. Then "*shichatnu*" must imply murder, or destruction of some other, equal kind. Why then do I read, in Art Scroll:

"*Shichatnu*…we have committed sins that corrupt our character…sins that are *tantamount* [my italics] to idolatry, such as arrogance, extreme anger, and apathy towards charitable causes…sins that are related to sexual immorality, such as vulgarity and eroticism." Yes, all this needs confessing too – but as "*shichatnu*"?

The final letter of the alphabet is given three sins – a matter of poesy, not piety, I suspect. Flaubert would have enjoyed the precedent.

Ti'avnu – we have performed abominations. Or "we have become abominable". *Ti'avnu*, like *kizavnu*, *ni'atsnu* and *shichatnu*, is rendered in the passive, as though by some curious act of destiny these sins have befallen us, rather than us perpetrating them. It offers an unlikely alibi, seems almost plaintiff – as though we're asking for, and the Rabbis are supporting us, extenuation. But what kind of action makes us abominable? Something that degrades us, shames us, even in our own eyes. Masturbation is regarded as such an abhorrence, as are homosexuality and bestiality. But Deuteronomy 7:26 states that it's simply the setting-up and worshipping of idols in our homes.

Ta'inu – we have gone astray. Self-evident. No need for explanation.

28

Titanu – you have let us go astray. The *hitpa'el* or reflexive form of *ta'inu*. But how extraordinary, to inculpate God, to include Him in the communal confession, to make Him part of We! It's all, apparently, God's fault. We sinned, we failed to obey His laws – but at the last it's His fault. He should have stopped us. He should have created us more perfect. He should have withheld free will. He should have written us better in the Book of Life last year. He should have chosen another species for His custodian.

No, this is the worst abomination of them all, the most heinous sin there is, this palliation of confession, this passing of the human buck! No, remove this *titanu* from the *Vidu'i* . Either we confess or we conceal. But to evade responsibility in this way – no, it's enough to make a man resume the whole *Vidu'i* from the beginning.

✡

After the alphabetical acrostic, three verses of address. This is a familiar form in Jewish liturgy, the supplicant courtier gabbling sycophancies at the heavenly king, speaking not for the words but against the embarrassment of silence.

Sarnu – two phrases, one from Job 33:27 ("He will sing to men and say, 'I have sinned and perverted what is right, and it is not proper for me.'"), the second from Nehemiah 9:33 ("However, You are just in all that has come upon us, for You have dealt faithfully, but we have acted wickedly."). The first acknowledges the generality of our sins, and their futility; the second acknowledges the righteousness of God, and anticipates forgiveness. Heine's God.

Mah nomar – "What can we say before You, who dwells on high, and what can we tell You, who inhabits the highest heavens; for is not everything that is hidden revealed to You, and You know it?"

The line could be interpreted as self-defeating, a theological tautology: why make confession to God, after all, when God knows everything anyway? To which the answer is quite magical: it's really to ourselves that we need to make confession; to ourselves, who are capable of concealing our own sins even from ourselves, who don't always know what we know. Confession as an element of education.

But also a psychological necessity. The Greek *katharsis*, self-achieved. A *Talmudic* anticipation of the work of Sigmund Freud.

Atah yodeyah – an elaboration of Proverbs 20:27, augmented by Jeremiah 11:20. The remainder is Rabbinic. Because God knows everything, even that which is hidden, "forgive us all our sins"; which is to say, those sins we also know, and have confessed, but also those sins we don't even know we've committed, but which God knows, and which also therefore need to be atoned.

The phrase defines again the three kinds of sin: *avonot*, *pesha'im* and *chatotot*. It's the *chatotot* which form the substance of the immense mantra *"al chet"* that ensues. A *chet* is an error committed unintentionally or through carelessness, where an *avon* was a deliberate sin, and a *pesha* was not only deliberate but contumacious.

✡

Al chet

The second great confession of *Yom Kippur* is, like the first, an alphabetical acrostic; doubly so, in fact, each letter given two lines, so that the whole poem becomes forty-four lines, with three repetitions of the refrain, after the tenth letter (*yud*), the sixteenth (*ayin*) and the twenty-second (*tav*). Each line commences with the same formula, *"al chet she-chatanu lephanecha* – for the sin that we have sinned before you", until it becomes a mantra, the body rocks with the soul, and confession is rendered cathartic as well as purgative.

"Be-ones u-ve-ratson – by compulsion or of our own free will."
"Be-imuts ha-lev – through the hardening of our hearts." (c.f. Deuteronomy 2:30, 15:7)
"Bi'vli da'at – in ignorance."
"Be-vitu'i sephatayim – through our rash and ill-considered mutterings." (c.f. Leviticus 5:4, Psalm 106:33)
"Be-galu'i u-va-sater – tacitly or covertly."
"Be-gilu'i arayot – wantonly."

The Joyceian subtlety here is almost untranslatable. From *"galu'i"* to *"gilu'i"* is a mere vowel, and in Hebrew the vowels aren't even written down, so only their precise meanings prevent them from being interchangeable. *"Gilu'i"* and *"arayot"* both imply nakedness, but the tautology is poetic, not grammatical: "in the nakedness of our nakedness".

"Be-dibbur peh – through the words of our mouths."
"Be-da'at u-ve-mirmah – premeditated or deceitfully."
"Be-har'hor ha-lev – in our innermost thoughts."
"Be-hona'at rey'a – in hurting our friends."

A wonderful missed opportunity for poetry here. *"Hona'at"* is a complex

30

grammatical construction, the *hophal*, a passive form of the causative conjugation, here rooted in *"avon* - to do wrong". *"Rey'a"* can be a neighbour, a companion, a friend, even a lover, but there's also the noun *"ra'ah"*, indistinguishable by its consonants from *"rey'a"*, which means "bad" or "evil". Why not, then, *"be-hora'at rey'a"*? It would balance *"har'hor"* better, like *"galu'i-gilu'i"* and *"Vidu'i -ve'iydat"* below.

"Be-vidu'i peh – through insincere confession."
"Be-v'iydat zenut – through our acts of vice."

Too complex to translate. A *"va'adah"* is a conference or congress or committee in its modern usage, from the Biblical root *"ed"* meaning a witness or an act of testifying; in this the link with *vidu'i*, confession. But there's also homophonic word-play once again, because *"va'ed"* means eternal. The second word *"zenut"* informs the problem, but fails to resolve it. *"Zonah"* is generally regarded as "a whore", whence *"zenut"* means fornication; but *"zenut"* is used specifically to mean the worshipping of forbidden gods and goddesses (perhaps because ritual prostitution and public congress were associated with their rites) – as in the story of Judah and Tamar in Genesis 38. So *"zonah"* is really a hierodule, not a whore. So *"ve'iydat zenut"* should be the generality of "eternal idolatry" and not the insinuation of prostitution. I've settled on "acts of vice", but it represents a preference for inadequacy over emptiness.

"Ve-zadon u-vi-shegagah – deliberately or inadvertently."
"Be-zilzul horim u-morim – in disdain of our parents and teachers."
"Be-chozek yad – by abuse of power."
"Be-chilul ha-shem – by blasphemy."
"Be-tipshut peh – by the stupidities of our mouth."
"Be-tumat sephatayim – by the profanities of our lips."
"Be-yetser ha-ra – through our Evil Inclination."
"Be-yodim u-ve-lo yodim – consciously or unconsciously." (oh yes, long before Rabbi Freud or Pastor Jung)

And then the first instance of the refrain.

Before I give it, though it may seem like pedantry, let me note that this process of enunciating sin, of splitting its atoms down to their protozoic particles, is fundamental to the building of a moral code. Sin isn't simply sin, a generic abstract. Sin may be a thought, an action, an intention, a failure, an accident, and each must carry its own level of responsibility and punishment; and perhaps our problem with the word today is only that it's been so far associated, in Catholicism especially, with sexual practice, that we can no longer take the term "sin" seriously; perhaps it would be better to substitute the term "breaches of the moral code". I cannot imagine any but the most hardened sinner having difficulty accepting that all of us breach the moral code from time to time, and that confession and repentance are a better panacea than jail. To build a legal system, we must first define right and wrong. To participate as an ethical individual, each of us must have the capacity to differentiate, not simply the vast sea of rights and wrongs, but tides as well.

"Ve-al kulam eloha selichot, selach lanu, mechal lanu, kaper lanu."

This, then, the refrain, sung not chanted, twice on each occasion. As we've differentiated sin, so here we differentiate forgiveness, at three levels of depth. The first, the most superficial, *selichah*, is forgiveness itself – an alternative to punishment. The next, *mechilah*, is pardon – the overturning of judgement, the quashing of punishment. Deepest of all, *kapparah* – the word which gives the festival its eponym and is the goal of *Yom Kippur* – implies complete atonement, the sin forgiven, the punishment for the sin acquitted, and then, still more, the very record of the sin removed from the files and pulped.

"For the sin that we have sinned before you…

"Be-chaphat shochad – by offering bribes."
"Be-chachash u-ve-chazav – by false promises and false testimonies."
"Be-lashon ha-ra – by gossiping and rumour-mongering."
"Be-latson – by mockery."
"Be-masa u-ve-matan – in the way we conduct business."
"Be-ma'achal u-ve-mishteh – in what we eat and what we drink."
"Be-neshech u-ve-marbeet – through interest and profit."
"Be-netiyat garon – through arrogance."

"Netiyat garon" is a figure of speech whose source is Isaiah 3:16, "Because the daughters of Zion are arrogant, they walk about with their necks stretched (*"netuyot garon"*) and their eyes wanton, walking and mincing as they go, making a tinkling with their feet."

"Be-sikur ayin" – No!

Alphabetically this should now be *samech* (ס), yet the traditional text gives *"sikur"* with a *seen* (שׂ), the variant form of the penultimate letter of the alphabet. Correctly *"be-sikur ayin"* is spelt with a *seen*, as indeed it's so spelled in every text I've examined, and the sense of the phrase connects perfectly

32

to the previous verse, the rude-peering eyes here paralleling the wantonness of the *"netiyat garon"*. But would not *"be-sikur ayin"*, spelled with a *samech* and meaning "painted eyes" serve just as well?

However, for it to work, the echo line would need to match. And as to the echo-line...

"Be-siyach siphtoteynu" – if this too is accepted as a *seen*, then it could mean any of the products of our lips, from idle chatter to open quarrelling. This is the form given in the prayer books. But if we reinstate the *samech*, we have the root *"su'ach"* which means "to triumph" or "to conquer"; and this too would work in parallel with *"be-sikur ayin"*; indeed, work even better, because it would balance the look of arrogance in our eyes with the haughty sounds we utter with our lips; two kinds of arrogance.

I am therefore proposing formally a correction to the text, reinstating the *samech* to its correct alphabetical position, while maintaining the meaning of the phrases. Over to you, Elders of the *Beth Din*, for inevitable rejection.

"Be-sikur ayin – through the arrogance in our eyes."
"Be-siyach siphtoteynu – through the haughtiness on our lips."
"Be-aynayim ramot – through over-ambition."
"Be-azut metsach – through brazenness."

The figures of speech in the last pair confirm my correction of the text. Once again the body-parts (eyes, lips, now forehead, are used metaphorically. I've rendered *"aynayim ramot"* – literally "great eyes" though it could also mean "the springs of water in the mountain-shrines" – as "over-ambition". *"Azut metsach"* could also be "the fortifications of the town of Gaza"!

After *"azut metsach"* the refrain again. Then:-

'*Be-pherikat ol* –
'*Be-phelilut* –

There's a treatise to be written on this couplet. But in brief. The accepted translations are "in throwing off your yoke" and "in judgement"; but I believe it's the manner in which we approach God that's intended here, and not the ways in which we reject Him. *"Ol"* as yoke is a rare form; it occurs in Numbers 19:2 and Deuteronomy 21:3 as a literal yoke, the one laid on a beast of burden; and figuratively in 1 Samuel 6:7, 1 Kings 12:11 and Isaiah 9:3 for servitude of man to Man; it's nowhere used to signify human servitude to God, because Judaism doesn't regard *"avodah"* as servitude, despite the double-meaning of *"avodah"* as "worship" and "service". But if "*ol*" were rendered with a second-letter *vav*, which is the normal variant, we would register "*avel*", meaning "wickedness", as the verbal root.

A similar reading is valid for "*phelilut*", where the root-verb "*palal*" is only rarely used to mean judgement (*Mishnah* explains this as deriving from its *pi'el* form, where it has the sense of "cutting"; but even this is an accident of the Chaldean language used by the Babylonian *amorim*, where "*peylī*" means "to decide"). In its common usage "*palal*" is prayer or supplication, with the reflexive form the standard still today, and the derived participle "*tephillah*" used for the act of prayer itself.

I beg the Rabbis' forgiveness, ask their pardon, and yearn for atonement, in making this second correction of their errors in as many lines; but still, I prefer to render the couplet:

"*Be-pherikat ol* – in turning aside from sin."
"*Be-phelilut* – in approaching You in supplication."

"*Be-tsediyat reya* – in destroying evil."
"*Be-tsarut ayin* – in the wells of sorrow."

Let me say immediately that I reject these last two translations, which are in fact my own and not the Rabbis'. They are, nonetheless, etymologically plausible, and demonstrate what we've already seen, the Nabokovian love of word-play. "*Reya*" and "*ayin*" have both occurred previously in this text, so I shan't rehearse the explanations. "*Tsada*" can mean "to destroy" in the sense of mowing or scything, but it's also used (c.f. 1 Samuel 24:12) for "fixing the eye", which is to say focusing the mind – note the link to "*ayin*" here. "*Tsarah*" has two derivations, of which "*tsarah*" with a final *hey* (צרה) means "sorrow" and "*tsarar*" with a final *reysh* (צרר) can be any kind of rival, but particularly the so-called "female adversary", the consort of *ha-Satan*.

The Rabbinic explanation of the couplet is:

"*Be-tsediyat reya* – through entrapping a neighbour."
"*Be-tsarut ayin* – through a begrudging eye."

And I'm loath to disagree for a third time. However, it does appear that a theme runs through these couplets. Where previously the levels of sin were denoted through our own actions, here there appears to be a survey of our attempts to overthrow sin, but which enterprise is itself of necessity sinful – this was the main thrust of my novel "The Flaming Sword" nearly twenty years ago. To kill Hitler would still be murder – and still therefore a breach of the commandments, requiring *Vidu'i*. And to ask God's forgiveness without perfect obeisance, to stutter in prayer; even these may be sins.

"*Be-kalut rosh* – through lack of seriousness."

"Be-kash'yut oreph – through obstinacy."

Like *"tsarut ayin"*, *"kash'yut oreph"* repeats the *"ashamnu"*.

"Be-ritsat raglayim le-ha-ra – in our enthusiasm for wrong-doing."
"Be-rechilut – through profiteering."

In modern usage, *"rechilut"* has come to mean ""slander or "gossip-mongering", but in the Bible a *"rochel"* was a wandering merchant, of the sort to whom his brothers sold Joseph.

"Be-shevu'at shav – through false oaths."
"Be-sinat chinam – through gratuitous hatred."

Why another *seen* (ש), if not to prove my point about the missing *samech*? Or was there no *sheen* to offer? Note the letter-play in *"shevu'at shav"*!

"Bi-tesumet yad – in failing to look after what we have agreed to look after."
"Be-timhon levav – in breaking the commandments."

These, again, are my alternative translations, offered because I'm too completely astonished (I use the word advisedly) by what's given in the texts even to reprint them. The common translation of these two lines manifests a quite extraordinary absence of scholarship amongst the Rabbis. The first, *"bi-tesumet yad"* is simply rendered literally, as "the extending of the hand", which at least implies "lending a hand" even if the sin lies in failing so to do. "Confusion of the heart", or "astonishment of the heart", which are the literal translations available for *"be-timhon levav"* don't even have that virtue of proximity. The fact is the two phrases relate to two specific legal precepts, and if the Rabbinic translators were to look, they would find both in the *Torah* – but perhaps they're so focused on the *Talmud* that they forget to look elsewhere.

"Tesumet yad" is found in Leviticus 5:21, "If a soul sin, and commit a trespass against the Lord, and lie to his neighbour about something he agreed to look after on his neighbour's behalf…he shall restore that which was delivered to him for safe-keeping…and the priest shall make an atonement for him before the Lord, and he shall be forgiven his trespass in this matter."
This is hugely significant. In the closing couplet we move from the generality of sin to its specifics, and learn that this act of atonement in which we're participating is a legal process and not just a moral or a spiritual

one; that it's happening in the actual, not the virtual; in the concrete, not the abstract.

"*Timhon levav*" broadens this to the truly universal. The phrase belongs to that extraordinary catalogue of curses and punishments which are heralded in Deuteronomy 28:15 by the statement, "It shall come to pass, if you will not heed the voice of the Lord your God, to observe all His commandments and laws and statutes, that all these curses will come upon you..."

"*Tesumet yad*" refers to forgiveness after contrition, "*timhon levav*" declares the fate of the uncontrite, a journey into a Hell of Dantesque proportions, one that is rather more than mere "confusion of the heart" (Deuteronomy 28:28).

Follows the third rendition of the refrain, and then, just in case any doubts linger over my commentary on "*tesumet yad*", a listing of those sins for which precise retribution in the form of sacrificial atonements is stipulated – I imagine that, in the original ceremonies, in Temple times, these lines were chorus to the actual bringing of the sacrificial offerings, or at the very least mimetic.

The opening mantra is "*Ve-al chata'im she-anu chayavim aleyhem*...For the sins for which the obligatory retribution is..."

Olah – an elevation offering.
Chatat – a sin offering.
Karban oleh ve-yored – a variable offering.
Asham vaday ve-talu'i – a guilt offering for a definite or a possible sin.
Markat mardut – a rebel's quotient of lashes.
Malkut arba'im – forty lashes.
Mitah bi-yedey shamayim – the death penalty at the hands of the Heavenly Court.
Karet ve-ariri – excommunication and childlessness.
Arba mitot beyt din; sekilah, serephah, hereg, ve-chenek – the four death penalties available to the *Beth Din*, namely stoning, burning, beheading and strangling.

But none of this will happen. "*Tesumet yad*" precedes "*timhon levav*", but it also precludes it. Instead of the four methods of death, there are also the three levels of forgiveness. Even the order of the *Vidu'i* confirms that, moving from forgiveness through pardon to atonement. In asking for these things, and in this way, we are taking for granted, as Heine did, that they will be given.

✡

"Ve'al chata'im" requires a further paragraph, to delineate the verdicts that pre-sentence the named offerings. The list is provisional – which is to say, I'm using the Art Scroll commentary, about which I have very grave reservations (its explanation of *"al chet"* is almost entirely fanciful, but then there are modern agendas which prorogue the ancient agendas). It makes, nonetheless, a useful starting-point, a place to argue from.

Olah – for sinful thoughts; for failure to perform positive commandments.

Chatat – Maimonides (*Hil Shegagot* 1:4) lists forty-three pre-sentences; the punishment is for careless, unintended errors.

Karban oleh ve-yored – six pre-sentences here, and the value of the offering means-tested; the punishment is for false swearing.

Asham vaday ve-talu'i – five pre-sentences (but again the Art Scroll fails to enumerate them); false swearing is again the cause of punishment; but this sentence also applies where there is doubt over a *chatat*.

Makat mardut – not an offering at all, but lashes, "for the positive violation of a Rabbinic prohibition; to coerce a recalcitrant to perform scripturally ordained positive commandments; and whenever the court deems it necessary to prevent widespread abuse of Scriptural or Rabbinic law." I've quoted the Art Scroll commentary verbatim, simply because no one will believe me otherwise. Yes – lashes. Yes – the Rabbis are claiming equal status with God in decreeing punishments. Yes – coerce. O God of Justice, you had better take your whip out, for I, for one, intend *"mardut"* against this sentence.

And against several more that follow.

Malkut arba'im – in fact only thirty-nine though *"arba'im"* means forty, as if that makes it better. The punishment for breaking a negative commandment by perpetrating the forbidden act, and in the knowledge that it's forbidden. Proof requires two witnesses. Acts include eating cheese hamburgers and playing golf on *Yom Kippur*. Maimonides has the full list in *Hil Sanhedrin* 19.

Mitah bi-yedey shamayim – the death penalty (though not by crucifixion, which was a Roman, not a Jewish device).

And no, it wasn't for murder, nor for rape; they're merely human offences. For eating the *"terumah"* – the offering laid on the altar – if you were not a Cohen or were ritually impure; indeed for performing any part of the Temple Service whilst *"tumah"*. Oh, and for writing such paragraphs as these – which is to say, for speaking in a critical or disparaging tone.

Karet va-ariri – thirty-six transgressions (*Kereisos* 2a lists them) for which excommunication and childlessness are the punishment; though it isn't explained how the latter is to be enforced (I don't imagine they were barbaric enough to go in for obligatory vasectomies and hysterectomies). Because Art Scroll only lists a small few, I can't comment further, but there does seem to be a weighting towards cultic practice rather than general ethics and morality – here are included tabu relations, working on *Shabbat* and *Yom Kippur*, eating *chamets* on Passover and, most oddly, "failure to circumcise oneself".

The number thirty-six is also worth a mention, since thirty-six is also the number of "*tzaddikim*" or "just men" believed to exist in the world at any time; thus making here a perfect symmetry of righteousness and transgression.

Arba mitot beyt din – *Sanhedrin* 7 gives the details. Stoning, burning, beheading and strangulation are the four options; any one of them, I guess, preferable to crucifixion.

✡

Al mitsvat aseh

Technically, "*al mitzvat aseh*" is the completion of "*ve-al chata'im*", though it has the feel and construction of a separate paragraph. We are still in confession mode, and now add:

the 248 positive commandments
the 365 negative commandments
those that can be remedied by a positive act
those that cannot be remedied by a positive act
those that were instructed through revelation (or: those that we are aware of)
those that were not instructed through revelation (or: those we are not aware of).

The latter couplet is then further qualified:

those that were instructed through revelation but which we have already confessed in open declaration [in the previous section of the *Vidu'i*]

those that have still not been instructed, nor revealed, but which nevertheless are known to you [I think this is one of the great moral-philosophic moments, the request for forgiveness for those sins we don't even know are sins, that we don't even realise we have committed – a man, after all, may sneeze, and the virus kill another man a thousand miles away. How far are we responsible for our actions? The Rabbis would say: entirely. But confession yields forgiveness, then pardon, finally atonement.]

The text itself elaborates this:

"The hidden sins belong to God, but the revealed sins are ours, and our children's, forever."

This is one of the keys to understanding Job. In Judaism, the sins of the father may be visited even on the great-grandchildren; so if you suffer or are rewarded undeservedly, it may be a consequence of your ancestors, not yourself.

"For You are the forgiver of Israel and the pardoner of the tribes of *Yeshurun*..."

Yeshurun needs some explanation. In the *Tanach* the term *Bene Yisrael* is used to denote all of Jacob's descendants and the land, but the Prophets after the division of the kingdom refer to the northern part as Ephrayim, after a leader of that name rather than the tribe. Later it became Jeroboam's kingdom, with Shomron as its capital city. Poetically, Ephraim was known as *Yeshurun*, and it's one of the favoured references of the school of Bible Criticism in dating Deuteronomy as Second Temple, because *Yeshurun* is the favoured term of that book (Deuteronomy 32:15, 33:5, 33:26). It also occurs in Isaiah 44:2. The significance of this name isn't easy to deduce, especially as it only makes these four appearances. The first three letters of *Yeshurun* and *Yisrael* are identical in appearance, though one is in fact a *sheen* and the other a *seen*. The root is "*Yashar* - to be straight" or "upright", and "*Yesharah*" is used in 1 Kings 3:6 to mean "integrity". It thus serves as a perfect epithet for Israel - the righteous people of God being in Hebrew *Yishar-El*. It may even be that *Yisrael* was an alteration or an error for *Yishar-El*, though it's much more probably a word-play of the later poets.

"...in every generation, and beside You we have no king who pardons and forgives."

The quoted phrase, "the hidden sins..." is from Deuteronomy 29:28. The phrase "and beside you" is a variation on a phrase in *Nishmat*, recited in *Pesukei d'Zimrah* on a *Shabbat* morning and one of the most potent images of God as *poetikos*, the continuing act of creativity - Hinduism makes the same distinction, between Brahma as Creator and Vishnu as Sustainer.

✡

Elohay ad she-lo

Another of those prayers in which Judaism becomes Islam, which is to say surrender and submission, but then goes further, because the ancient rites of grovelling propitiation reduce a man to servile servitude, the undignified status of a worm – and not just any worm, but specifically the one evicted on its belly out of Eden. I hate this face of my religion, and spit on it. Those who accept it don't, of course, regard it as servitude. They would say it's an acknowledgement of God's vastness and majesty, a recognition that "we are so small against the stars". But we're also "so large against the sky"[5], and don't need to stoop and truckle.

The second phrase, "I am dust...", takes its cue from Genesis 3:19, and in doing so confirms my reference to the worm.

What's interesting about the prayer is its total contradiction, inferring rejection, of the notion of an after-life. "I am dust in my life and will surely be so in my death." This is plain and unambiguous. When we die, we're buried and decompose. Ah, the mystics would say, but the spark of life, the individual soul, it must go somewhere; it isn't a light that's simply switched off.

Genesis 3:19 would disagree.

"*Elohay netsor*" is the familiar paragraph that always closes the *Amidah*. See "A Myrtle Among Reeds" for details. The same is true for "*yehi ratson*".

The individual's repetition of the *Amidah* ends here. The *chazan*'s repetition is identical.

✡

Minchah however isn't yet over. Like all prayer services, it ends with *Kaddish* and the *Aleynu*.

Kaddish for *Minchah Yom Kippur* is sung to a different tune from the customary: much slower, more mournful and lugubrious in the opening phrases, but positively joyful, table-thumping by the time you get to "*titkabal*". The only other variation between this and other recitations of the Full *Kaddish* (*Shalem*) is the doubling of the "*le-eloh*", to emphasise just how very exceedingly great is God. Some add a definite article before "*shalom*" in the closing verse – the first "*shalom*", not the second.

---

[5] From Leonard Cohen's "Stories of the Street"

Aleynu is as normal, sung or chanted, including the omitted parenthetical "*she-hem mishtachavim*" in the first paragraph and the optional "*al tira*" that follows. *Kaddish yatom* (known, incorrectly, as the "Mourners' *Kaddish*") comes next – again the "*le-eloh*" doubled, as it will be through the whole of *Yom Kippur*.

✡

Minchah for *Yom Kippur* is now complete, but the preparations for the evening begin at once. I've given most of the details earlier in this chapter, but there's one last feature yet to mention.

As with *Shabbat*, so with *Yom Kippur*: the *Eruv* has to be established.

First the *Eruvei Chatseirot*, the Merging of Courtyards; then the *Eruvei Techumin*, the Merging of Boundaries. These are *Talmudic* inventions, designed to secure the sanctity of the Holy Day while simultaneously simplifying it for practitioners – within the *Eruv* is akin to being within the home, where many of the Holy Day prohibitions don't apply. By merging courtyards, adjacent houses may be deemed a single dwelling-place; so food may be carried between them, prams pushed etc. Individual boundaries for *Shabbat* are reckoned as two thousand cubits from a person's normal dwelling place, and one may not walk beyond that limit, not even to attend synagogue. But by placing food in another person's dwelling, that place may count as the boundary epicentre, and if the two courtyards are then merged, a scope of four thousand cubits is achieved. In Golders Green a vast *eruv* has been established that effectively courtyards the whole Borough of Barnet, and in my view makes a complete nonsense of the *melachot*, the *Shabbat* prohibitions. (However, since I don't observe most of them anyway, who am I to comment?)

Eruvei Chatseirot involves a simple blessing ("…and commanded us concerning the *mitzvah* of *eruv*") and a voiced statement of legalistic inclination known as "*ba-hadeyn*":

"Through this *eruv* we may be permitted to carry out or carry in from the houses to the courtyard, and from the courtyard to the houses, from house to house, from courtyard to courtyard, and from roof to roof" – in Biblical times the flat roof served as a living room – "all that we require, for ourselves and for all Jews who live in this area." This is self-validatory, not a stamp of God nor even of the Rabbis. Some translations present it in the form of a question ("may we be permitted…"), which at least allows the pretence of divine approval; though even without an affirmative sign the *eruv* is inaugurated, so perhaps even the asking is rhetorical, a mere formality.

The same blessing is used for *Eruvei Techumin*, but the validatory statement is much briefer:

"Through this *eruv* we may be [or "may we be"] permitted to walk two thousand cubits in every direction from this place during *Shabbat* and *Yom Kippur*."

Appended to the statement for *Eruvei Chatseirot* is an interesting parenthesis, whose recitation is optional. Having inaugurated the *eruv* for today, it also pre-establishes it for those who will come in the future – "and to all who move into this area – *u-le-chol mi she yitoseph boh*". Why in parenthesis? Because Jewish history inspires no optimism in the future? Or is it truly optimistic, anticipating expulsion, prophesying return?

✡

The Blessing of the Children

One of the most ancient rites informs one that will always remain modern. *Yom Kippur* is an ordeal, and no parent would send their child off to such an ordeal without fears and reservations, and consequently without a blessing. Go, and go well. I will be with you. But also: I will not be with you; which is to say, each of us will cross this desert alone, even though we form a company. Because every man is ultimately alone who makes the inner journey.

André Brink, describing Estienne Barbier's *vortrekker* voyage into the hottentot heartland of southern Africa in 1738, wrote that: "In a way, one might say, each one of us on that expedition had joined for reasons of his own. We were all in it together; we all wanted to obtain cattle and sheep; the farms were in need of stock. But deep in his heart each man had set out on a private quest…"
So is *Yom Kippur* for each of us.

The *Yom Kippur* blessing is rooted in Jacob, but Jacob wasn't the first. Cain and Abel brought their offerings to God-the-father for His blessing long before, and there too (it's a constant theme in Judaism – Jacob and Esau, Ephraim and Menasheh, Perets and Zerach: tales of twins with hints at ultimogeniture) the younger is given priority over the elder. The obvious model for the blessing ought to be Jacob's "*Hikavtsu*", the death-bed will-and-testament blessing of his sons in Genesis 49 – but frankly the Rabbis have always been too frightened of the obscure riddles that comprise that text. Drummond, in "Oedipus Judaicus" (1811), demonstrated the calendrals of the text, its horoscopy, equating the tribes with the

42

constellations, the map of Israel, like the map of the pyramids, with that of the heavens; this was Robert Graves' source in "King Jesus" and elsewhere. Far too dangerous for the Rabbis however, who are quite content to wish a hearty "*mazal tov*", but don't really wish the idolatrous superstition to be translated – it means "may the stars align in your favour".

Ephraim and Menasheh then, the two sons of Joseph, born to him in Egypt when he was serving Pharaoh not God, dressed as an Egyptian, eating their food, inevitably – how could he not? – participating in their rites and ceremonies (all men, even grand viziers, addressed Pharaoh prostrate and exited backwards). Sons, too, of an Egyptian woman, Asnat, the daughter of the High Priest of the Temple at On – something akin to Disraeli marrying the daughter of the Archbishop of Canterbury: and no suggestion anywhere of an orthodox conversion, a Jewish marriage, not even a Naomic iteration. These were the sons who later acquired tribal territory in the heartland of Israel, in place of their illustrious father who was given none. Extraordinary that such should be a model of the child who merits blessing!

But there's a logic to it too. Who less integral but more integrated than Ephraim and Menasheh? The dispossessed acquiring a place at the centre, with full and equal rights. Yes, this is the ideal model – a Judaism which not only welcomes, but blesses, but places at its centre with full and equal rights, even the children of non-Jewish parents. In the case of Ephraim and Menasheh, one set of Jewish grand-parents is enough.

If only it were true of Judaism today!

"May God make you like Ephraim and Menasheh."
Taken from Genesis 48:20. And then, not just any blessing, but the "*Yevarechecha*" itself, the Priestly Blessing. Do the orthodox Rabbis who reject one-Jewish-parent Jews realise the irony of their making this blessing in the place of God over their own sons?

For daughters the models are the matriarchs, Sarah, Rebecca, Leah and Rachel and Leah (the order is always reversed for the latter pair: as Laban reminded Jacob, it should be Leah first, then Rachel; the elder, then the younger: or is this another case of ultimogeniture?).

A blessing made with both hands on the child's head, though in fact in all the Biblical instances the blessing was one-handed (in the case of Ephraim and Menasheh the hands were crossed).

The largest part of the blessing lies in "*Viyehi Ratson*", the source of Bob Dylan's wonderful "Forever Young". An index of virtues, a tabulation of qualities, that surely every parent wishes for his child, with or without the

Jewish *schmaltz*; but which also defines the Jewish code. It's worth citing in full:

> May it be the will of our father in Heaven
> that He instil love and respect in your heart;
> may you live all your days without sin and with reverence for the Almighty;
> may your desires be for *Torah* and for keeping the commandments;
> may your eyes always see what is there before you (Proverbs 4:25);
> may your mouth always speak wisdom (Psalm 49:4);
> may your heart always meditate in awe (Isaiah 33:18);
> may your hands always be busy in the keeping of the laws;
> may your feet always be swift to do the will of our father in Heaven;
> may He give you sons and daughters who are upright,
>   who busy themselves with *Torah*,
>   and who keep the commandments all their lives;
> may the source of your prosperity be blessed (Proverbs 5:18);
> may He provide you with an honourable livelihood
>   one that brings you sufficiency and satisfaction
>   one that is given through the openness of His hands
>   and not in recompense for offerings of flesh and blood
> a livelihood that will free you to serve the Lord;
> and may you be inscribed and sealed in the Book off Life
>   for a good life and a long life
>   amidst the upright men and women of the tribe of Israel
> *Amen*

✡

Chapter Two: Praying With Sinners

Hadlakot ha-Nerot - The Kindling of the Lights

The preliminaries at last are done. Now the twenty-five hour ordeal – no, that isn't the correct attitude; we enter this voluntarily, like pioneers, like explorers – now the twenty-five hour inward journey may begin.

Always on *Shabbat* and festivals two white candles, each in its own candlestick. But at the onset of *Yom Kippur* two extra candles, both of which should be wax enough, and slow enough, to burn until the fast is done. The *Ner ha-Bari*, the Candle of Health, is lit not by but for every married man in the household; a widow may also light one for herself. The *Ner Neshama*, the Candle of the Soul, the *Yizkor* or Memorial Light, lit for each deceased parent, to atone for their sins. The *Ner ha-Bari* should always be larger than the *Ner Neshama*, so that life may be superior to death, and a healthy soul to an afflicted one: a superstition this, rather than a requirement. There are no specific blessings for the extra candles; they are lit with the regular pair, and the blessing conferred is also transferred.

If *Yom Kippur* falls on *Shabbat*, the blessing reflects the doubling.

"Blessed are You, O Lord our God, King of the Universe, who has sanctified us with His commandments, and has instructed us to kindle the lights of (*Shabbat* and) *Yom Kippur.*"

And the traditional, much-cho-chorused blessing of every festival:

"*Baruch atah adonay eloheynu melech ha-olam, she-hecheyanu, ve-kiyamanu, ve-higiyanu la-zman ha-zeh* - Blessed are You, O Lord our God, King of the Universe, who has kept us alive, sustained us, and brought us to this moment."

It is, of course, the women who traditionally kindle the lights, though there's no reason why men should not do so. Where, however, is disputed. *Shabbat* candles must be lit in the home, but why light *Yom Kippur* candles where we won't see them, and a stray draft might make them dangerous in our absence? So communities vary in this custom – some in the home, some at *shul*, some one at each. The *Yizkor* candle may be lit by men.

The source of the custom of kindling *Shabbat* lights is Isaiah 58:15. The authority of women in this custom comes from Maimonides, who allowed widowers, husbands of sick wives, or men living alone to kindle. The lights must be lit – that's the first priority. Only at the secondary level is priority bestowed on women. The source of this ruling is "*Magen Avraham*". The reasoning is that women are exempt from many time-bound commandments; Maimonides the justicer sought means to compensate.

The blessing employs the singular *Ner*, not the plural *Nerot*, inferring just a single candle. This permits the poor to light just one. More importantly it places the emphasis upon the light that emanates, and not the wick that burns.

Tractate *Shabbas* (23b) states that: "One who is scrupulous in the kindling of lights will be blessed with children who are *Torah* scholars", a statement which is both self-evident and idiotic. From it is derived the "*Yehi Ratson*" which is recited after kindling the *Yom Kippur* lights:

"May it be Your will, O Lord my God and God of my forefathers, that You show favour to me and all my near ones; that You grant us and all Israel a long life and a good life; that You remember us and bless us beneficently; that You consider us for salvation compassionately; that You bless us with great blessings; that You create harmony in our homes; that You cause Your presence to dwell among us. Grant me the privilege of raising children and grandchildren who are wise and understanding, who love the Lord and fear God, people of truth, holy offspring, who cleave to God, who illuminate the world with *Torah* and good deeds, and by working in the service of the Creator. Please hear my supplication at this time, in the merit of Sarah, Rebecca, Rachel and Leah our mothers, and set our light shining so that it may never be extinguished, and let your countenance shine so that we are saved. *Amen.*"

A most beautiful prayer with which to begin any festival, especially that last fleck of sunlight, merging into candlelight, and the light of human darkness, just at the moment when we're about to cross the Hinnom Valley.

✡

Atiphat Tallit - Donning the Prayer Shawl

We enter the realm of whiteness, which is purity, which is innocence, in the sense not of naiveté nor of guiltlessness, but of atonement. Once all wore white throughout *Shabbat*, to denote its sanctity; today the number of occasions has lapsed almost to zero – the bride and groom on their wedding-day; the prayer-leader at the *Musaph* service for *Shemini Atseret*, when the prayers for rain are introduced; the dead in their coffins; and *Yom*

Kippur, though not until the *Kol Nidre*, and not until sunset for the donning of the *tallit*.

The ceremony of donning the *tallit* is identical in every respect to that of *Shacharit* (c.f. "A Myrtle Among Reeds"). But for many, and particularly for the prayer-leader, the *tallit* itself is altered. In place of the normal prayer-shawl a long, white gown, known as a *"kittel"* or as a *"sargenes"* in Yiddish (from the German *"sarg"* or coffin). When we approach God, we wrap ourselves in robes of purity, mantles and garments of the angels. So our body may inspire our soul. So our exaltation may induce atonement in the fullest sense, the mutual sense of Portia's apologia for mercy in "The Merchant of Venice": "It is twice blessed; it blesseth him that gives and him that takes."

✡

The Meditations of Abraham of Danzig

Known as *"Tephillah Zakkah"* or – English lacks an easy idiom to translate this – "a cleansing prayer", it was added only recently to the liturgy (less than two hundred years ago; ancient times if you are American or Australian; far too new for its inclusion yet to be certain if you are Jewish). Avraham ben Yechi'el Michal of Danzig (Gdansk), author of *"Chayey Adam* – Man's Life" and *"Chochmat Adam* – Man's Wisdom", was a student of Prague and a Dayan – a religious judge - of Vilna, whose heyday coincided precisely with the Napoleonic era. A conservative and a pedagogue, he sought to make Jewish law more accessible, by codifying more simply what had already been codified in the *"Shulchan Aruch"*. *"Chevrot Chayey Adam"*, teaching groups which studied the law through Abraham Danziger's books, formed all over Lithuania, and in parts of Germany. *"Tephillah Zakkah"* should be recited, according to its author, before nightfall of *Yom Kippur*, and "praiseworthy is he who recites it on *Yom Kippur* morning too". However the order of recitation isn't Danziger's. *"Ve-liheyot"* was originally the penultimate paragraph; now it's placed after the opening; the reason given is that it contains statements of forgiveness towards others. Since many people won't finish reciting the whole meditation, they might not reach these core statements. I like this: the acknowledgement of differences in our degree of Hebrew literacy. The emphasis on forgiving others before we begin the ceremonies of self-purgation. However – what of those, the vast majority I guess, who don't attempt to read the meditation at all?

Danziger comes from the "free will" rather than the "predetermination" school of Judaism, which makes me initially sympathetic; only his is that form of "surrendered free will" which defines all individual choices morally,

47

and is therefore a tacit and voluntary subordination to predeterminism. God gives Man freedom of choice; God defines what is Good and what Evil; God ordains punishment for sin; Man therefore chooses God, employing his freedom of choice willingly to surrender his freedom of choice, preferring to let God rule him. This isn't free will at all; merely a complex form of slavery, of social conditioning. This is a man buying a train ticket for Oswiecim, rather than being dragged unwillingly by rifle-toting guards into a cattle-truck.

But it's still preferable to full "predeterminism", because that view takes away from Man any measure of responsibility for his actions, and reduces us to mere automatons, robotically performing the defined acts and saying our blessings as we do so (amen). Like God Himself, the predeterminist can say "I am that I am" and feel vindicated; but it's the vindication of a lap-dog. There's no need for justice, mercy or forgiveness in a world founded on predeterminism (and this is true of the genetic predeterminists as much as it is of the divine ones and the astral ones). The paedophile, the parasite and the peddler of hallucinogenic powders are all exonerated – I am that I am. This is my destiny, the fate that I was given. Predeterminism is the nemesis of atonement.

This, however, isn't the message of Danziger's meditation; only its inference. "*Tephillah Zakkah*" is, rather, an exercise in verbal self-flagellation, an extended *Vidu'i* of positively Manichean proportions. Danziger hates his own body, because it's a source of sin. "Woe to me that I have followed my eyes," he moans, "and contaminated them by staring lustfully at women." His ears are chastised for listening to gossip, his sexual organ for "improper arousal and seminal emissions" – indeed "I have examined all my organs and found them defective, from the sole of my foot to my head, there is nothing worthwhile in me."

What a terribly sad, sad man, who thinks God wants nothing from us but the contemplation of the *Torah*, and gave us a body only that we should find it disgusting. Blessed are you, I reply, who gave me eyes to enjoy…but not Danziger, who blesses God for creating him with "a mouth, tongue, teeth, palate and throat…to articulate the sounds of the *aleph-bet*, and Your Holy *Torah*."

With such a view of life, God may, but will Life itself ever forgive him?

✡

After five long pages of this, follows the Confession of *Rabbeinu* Nissim, about whose origins I can say precisely nothing. I have hunted, Lord, but I have not found. Neither in the Everyman Judaica nor the twenty-volume complete, neither in the Maimonidean lists nor the search pages of the world wide web. Only that the text is generally ascribed to Rabbeinu Nissim

Ga'on of Gerona in northern Spain, "who, with Rabbeinu Chananel, led North African Jewry in the 11th century"[6]. Others in fact ascribe the text to Sa'adiah Ga'on, or to Rabbi Nissi, who lived in Persia in the 10th century. Myself, eventually, I don't care who wrote it, nor do I think it matters. Prayer transcends biography, or fails to. This is the confession of the Datsmay.

✡

And so we come, at last, to the great service of *Kol Nidre*, begun with *"Or zaru'a la-tsadik, u-le-yishrey lev simchah* – light is sown for the righteous, and gladness for the upright of heart."

But first the Ark is opened, and all its *Torah* scrolls are taken out, carried on the breast and shoulder round the synagogue so that everyone may kiss its fringes as in ancient times they would have kissed the hems of kings. Once the circuit of the scrolls is finished, all but two are put away, and these two frame the *chazan* while he recites the *"Or Zaru'a"* seven times – seven the holiest of all numbers, the number of Creation, the number of Noah's universal laws, of the *"hakafot"* of Jericho…

Why three at the *amud*, the reading desk? Because Moses was flanked by Aaron and Chur when he prayed for Israel during the assault by the Amelekites (Exodus 17). Because the *Kol Nidre* will transform the synagogue into a *Beit Din*, a Court of Law, which requires three magistrates. This is the same reason why the phrases are repeated thrice.

Kol Nidre is generally mispronounced with the last syllable so foreshortened that all its poetry is expunged, like taking the colour out of the sunset. *Kol Nidrey* please. The prayer is neither part of *Minchah* nor of *Ma'ariv*, but a special service of its own, brief but beautiful, and as essential to the process of atonement as a lodeline to a ship's buoyancy. Indeed it isn't really a prayer service at all, but a legal process, a stripping away of hypocrisy as the essential preparation for confession and forgiveness; for how can we make our new vows with sincerity, when our old vows remain unfulfilled; and how can we ask forgiveness, when our enmity towards others is still on our heads?

So we transform the House of Prayer into a Court of Law, aware that this was the original dual purpose of the Mosaic Tent of Meeting; and with the

---

[6] Not to be confused with the 14th century scholar Rabbeinu Nissim, known as Ran, who was primarily responsible for establishing the practise of reading the last and first chapters of the Torah on Simchat Torah.

Ark open, the congregation standing, and the *chazan* pillared as if by Bo'az and Yachin – the two pillars at the gateway of the Temple – by two held scrolls of the Law, we say, and not once but three times:

"With the approval of the Omnipresent, and with the approval of the congregation; in the convocation of the Court above, and in the convocation of the Court below, we sanction prayer with sinners."

We, the elders of the congregation. But we too are sinners. So we may pray with you. But also, you may pray with us.

But "*avaryanim*" means more than just "sinners". It includes even those who, for whatever reason, have been excluded from the society of their fellow Jews. On *Yom Kippur*, because everyone has the right and needs the opportunity to atone, even the excommunicate are readmitted.

In some communities, before the process begins, a lengthy passage of Rabbinic mystification is read aloud, esoterica relating to the *Shechinah* – the Divine Presence in Judaism, the Holy Ghost in Christianity – from the mouth of Rabbi Shimon bar Yochai, he to whom is falsely attributed the writing of the *Zohar* (Moses de Léon, writing it eleven hundred years "after" Shimon, presumably wanted to bestow on his work the weight of gravitas that came with Shimon's name, for he was a pupil of Akiva and one of the principal proponents of the *Mishnah*). Shimon argues the nature of an oath so utterly abstrusely that its omission by most communities is entirely sensible, and it may well have been one of the passages that Maimonides had in mind when he named his great clarification and simplification of the laws "A Guide for the Perplexed". Nonetheless the passage does contain two important moments. The first includes God and the angels in the process of confession-forgiveness-atonement, which is truly Abrahamic. The second extols God specifically to annul any vows He may have made to prevent the redemption of His people (but surely, after the Noachic Flood, He promised never to do such a thing again?)

There exists, in some though by no means all communities, the abhorrent practise of auctioning off the privilege of holding the *Kol Nidre* scrolls, and in particular the first scroll, which is called for the purpose the *Kol Nidre Torah*. Being called to any duty in the synagogue is a source of special merit, but Judaism isn't usually so vulgar as to designate merit by a man's capacity to give large sums of money, however philanthropically. That form of designation belongs to the United Joint Israel Appeal, and should be left there, where it belongs, under the distinguished auspices of Lord Levy of Stardust.

Three times, each one louder than before, building a great spiritual crescendo out of lines that are intrinsically devoid of crescendo, or even spirituality, lines which in themselves are bland, prosaic, stilted, the formal jargon of judicial process. It requires huge inward intensity – like those dreadful trivial dialogues in Mozart's operettas that somehow contrive to become arias of sublime exaltedness. As one who led prayer services daily for more than a decade, this is one of the moments in the annual calendar that I most look forward to – though sadly it's very brief.

Nor can an English translation give more than the material meaning of the words. A transliteration will at least allow the reader not familiar with Aramaic a Braille version of the hidden vision:

"Kol nidrey, ve-esarey, u-shevu'ey, va-charamey, ve-kunamey, ve-kinusey, ve-chinuyey, de'indarna, u-de-ishtabana, u-de'acharimna, u-de-asarna al-naphshatana."

Entirely single words, separated by commas, until the closing triverbial:

"Mi-Yom Kippurim zeh ad Yom Kippurim ha-ba aleynu le-tovah."

Note that we call it here *"Yom Kippurim"* in the plural, and not *"Yom Kippur"* in the singular. This is the proper and correct form.

"Be-chul'hon icharatna ve-hon. Kul-hon yehon sharan, shevikin, shevitin, betelin u-mevutalin, lo sheririn ve-lo kayamin. Nidrana lo nidrey, ve-esaranah lo esarey, u-shevu'atanah lo shevu'ot."

Everything resides in sounds of words, in juxtapositions of sounds, in echoes and variations within phrases, in rhythms implicit within words – impossible, for example, not to speed up and insert a singable pop-melody with accompaniment of hand-clapping or *bimah*-tapping, when the long adagio of *"al-naphshatana"* breaks into the tripping *"mi-Yom Kippurim zeh"* and then the elongated line that follows. One doesn't need to be Max Bruch, nor to have a copy of the official cantillation at one's side, to make music *ex tempore* from this.

Whereas the material meaning, dry as any lawyer's *cacoethes scribendi*:

"All vows, prohibitions, oaths, consecrations, oaths sworn when offering sacrifice, pledges made at time of prayer, or any equivalent terms that we may vow, swear, consecrate or prohibit upon ourselves, from this *Yom Kippur* till next *Yom Kippur* (may it come upon us for good) – regarding them all, we regret them henceforth."

An awkward construction, that last phrase, but the words cross cultures only with reluctance.

"They will all be permitted, abandoned, cancelled, declared null and void, without power and without standing. Our vows shall not be valid vows, our prohibitions shall not be valid prohibitions, and our oaths shall not be valid oaths."

What is odd is that this seems to be a derogation of the vows that we're about to make ("from this...till next"), rather than a cancellation of last year's. The Vilna *Ga'on* (Elijah ben Solomon Zalman, 1720-1797) recognised this, and in his liturgy, which many communities follow, altered the phrase to read:

*"Mi-Yom Kippurim she-avar ad Yom Kippurim zeh, u-mi-Yom Kippurim zeh ad...*From last *Yom Kippur* to this one, and from this *Yom Kippur* to the next..."

Which makes more sense, but less effective poetry. For most Jews, I suspect, the latter is what really counts.

Because it's irresistible, I'm listening to Max Bruch's setting of the *Kol Nidre* while I write this (not the best version, which has Pablo Casals conducted by Barbarolli, on *Deutsche Grammophon*; nor the second-best, which Anup Biswas recorded privately for my wife and I some twenty years ago, but on a cassette tape which time sadly hasn't treated well – this version has Maria Kliegel on cello, with the National Symphony Orchestra of Ireland under Gerhard Markson). Bruch wrote the piece, his Opus 47, while he was conductor of the Liverpool Philharmonic Society, on a commission from the city's Jewish community; though it was actually published in Berlin, in 1881, and not in Liverpool, where he stayed from 1880 to 1883. Bruch wasn't of course Jewish, as is apparent from the total lack of connection between his name and the Hebrew word *Baruch*, not to mention the absence of *schmaltz* or *heimische* sentimentality in any of his work, especially that dryly turgid piece of rational constructivism the Violin Concerto in G minor. What Jewish composer ever wrote in G minor anyway (already, *noch*, *nu*), shifting in and out of G major/G minor quite that often? What Jew was ever interested in the fiddle? What Jew ever had middle names like Christian and Friedrich to ensure that no one at the Vienna Opera house, or even remotely connected to it, would mistake the Max for Jewish, let alone the Bruch?

There's the Schoenberg setting, too, of course, though this has never had the popular success that Bruch encountered. It was commissioned by Rabbi Jacob Sonderling of Los Angeles in 1938, and Schoenberg undertook the composition between August 1st and September 22nd, himself conducting the première in Los Angeles on October 4th – I mention the dates only because the festival itself fell precisely at the time the work was finished, yet it was given a secular and not a sacred première. The dates are significant for another reason too - only a month later the *Kristallnacht* in Germany kindled the bonfire in which six million books of life would soon enough be burned.

Schoenberg set the piece for speaker, mixed chorus, and orchestra, allowing the full text to be read. But he didn't like the text, considering it immoral to release a person from those obligations and commitments they had voluntarily assumed during the year. So he modified the text, to indicate that the act of absolution involved only those sinful vows that run counter to Jewish belief in God. An odd arrogance (see *"shichatnu"*), to break a Jewish law in order to uphold a Jewish law. Very difficult music, too.

The text of *Kol Nidre* can be dated at least as far back as the 9th century, for it appears, in slightly different form, in the *Seder* of Rav Amram Ga'on, the very first prayer book as such to be brought out. Amram ben Sheshna was the *ga'on*, or *Talmudic* authority, in Sura in Babylon, and he wrote his prayer book as a *responsum* to the Jews of Barcelona, who had sought his advice on how the liturgy should be arranged. Amram's version confirms that of the Vilna *Ga'on*, several centuries later. It's only those vows made rashly between this and next *Yom Kippur* that we're asking to be cancelled. It's only those vows made rashly before this *Yom Kippur* that we wish to expiate. What we pledged or will pledge sincerely will continue to have value in our eyes and in the eyes of God. What we repent isn't our intentions *per se*, but only the failure of our good intentions, the foolishness of our bad ones. It might have been helpful to add a plausible definition of "sincerely".

The alteration in the text between Sa'adiah and the present today is down to Rabbeinu Tam, or Rabbi Jacob ben Meir Tam, one of Rashi's many grandsons, and the leading *tosafist* in France of his day (he lived from 1100-1171); he was also, incidentally, the first French scholar, Jewish or otherwise, to compose rhymed poetry. Tam argued that past vows had already been nullified by the formula used on *erev Rosh ha-Shana*, and that *Kol Nidre* didn't, anyway, conform to the proper *halachic* procedures for nullifying vows. In his version, which is based on *Nedarim* 23b and does therefore conform to *halachah*, we're not asking in advance for forgiveness of future sins – a kind of credit arrangement not available at Jewish religious banks – but are declaring our hope that this year, unlike previous years, we will neither make rash vows nor leave sincere ones unfulfilled. In place of the clean slate of Amram Ga'on, the naiveté of Tam.

The conclusion of *Kol Nidre*, recited rather than chanted, deliberately prosaic, is the double-prayer that begins *"ve-nislach"* and continues *"selach na"*.

"*Ve-nislach*" is recited three times by the *chazan*, then three times by the congregation.

"May it be forgiven for the whole congregation of the children of Israel, and for the stranger who dwells among them, for it befell the entire congregation through carelessness."

Ah yes, carelessness. The pedestrian run over by the car, because the driver was distracted by his mobile phone. The women and children in the besieged city who were counted as collateral damage. The adultery that might not have happened sober. I can accept and understand the exculpation of unintentional wrong-doing, of benevolent intent gone awry; I have no problem at all with sin performed in obliviousness. But as a result of carelessness?

But the Rabbis say there are such instances. If the *Sanhedrin* rules that something is permitted, and the ruling proves erroneous, but the proof comes only after the something has been done, and the something affects not only he who has performed it, but "the whole congregation...[that] dwells among them..." But does the *Sanhedrin* 's error really count as "carelessness"? Judaism always seeks the side of good over bad, to forgive where it can, to find the cup half-full. But carelessness? Did Jonah's gourd wither and die from carelessness?

Rashi also points out, in his commentary on Numbers 32:6, that if a person breaks a vow which actually wasn't valid anyway, for whatever reason, then he's still guilty of a sin, because in his mind he genuinely believed the vow was valid. Now that's the careful rigour I expect of Judaism.

Nonetheless, given the code of Jewish responsibility, in which "I" must always be extended to include "we", this prayer makes sense. Forgive me my sins, even the careless and the oblivious, but forgive the sins of those others who were affected by my action, who sinned only through my carelessness, my obliviousness. The sin as virus and contagion.

The words of the prayer are taken from Numbers 15:26; the purgative offering for the sin of carelessness is a one-year-old she-goat.

The second prayer, "*Selach na*", is also Mosaic, from the same scroll, Numbers 14:19, when the spies have returned from Canaan and declared "the people is strong that dwells in the land, and the cities are walled and very great, and moreover we saw giants there"; so the dwarfish souls amongst the Israelites "murmured against Moses and Aaron", and wished they'd stayed among the fleshpots of Egypt (I have never understood this phrase: to me fleshpots implies St Tropez, bikinis, *assiettes de fruits de mer*, gambling casinos, film stars – is my memory failing me, or were we not in fact slaves in Egypt?)

And wasn't it ever thus?

In response to God's anger at this pusillanimous funk - "How long will this people provoke me?...I will smite them with the pestilence, and disinherit them..." - Moses prays on all their behalves and bequarters for forgiveness:

"Pardon, I beseech You, the iniquity of this people according to the greatness of Your mercy, and as You have forgiven this people, from Egypt even until now."

"Even until now" is our license to echo Moses. Even until now. Oh yes, it remains ever thus.

In the Book of Numbers we are told simply that, "The Lord said, I have forgiven you, according to your words" – which phrase is once again given the triple-treatment, this time congregation first, *chazan* afterwards. In the original, Moses asks and God accedes, precisely because it's Moses who asks (and perhaps also because, being God who knows everything, this entire foreseen occasion is a part of the divine plan); but in our version the same words acquire entirely different meaning, or at least a very different emotional connotation. The very repetitions give this away. We aren't praying, we're imploring. God who acted for Moses, act for us now. Again – in case He didn't hear. A third time – to alleviate His doubts about our sincerity. A fourth time – to show we're in earnest. But the congregation is only the congregation, not the blue-eyed son; the *chazan* stands surrogate for Moses, perhaps he'll be successful. Perhaps at second try. Perhaps at third.

And we know He will hear us, and He will forgive us, for that's His role, and this is *Yom Kippur*. So we conclude by thanking Him, in advance.

"Blessed are You, O Lord our God, King of the Universe, who has kept us alive, sustained us, brought us to this moment."

Sustained us, from Egypt even until now.

✡

Chapter Three: And It Was Evening

Yom Kippur is the only major festival not to have a second day in the Diaspora. It's also the only one to have as many as five specific services, each with its own *Amidah*. We know from *Ta'an* 4:1 that this was so, even in Second Temple times (in those days *Ne'ilah* still retained its full and proper name, *"Ne'ilat She'arim* - the Closing of the Gates"). Given the nature and scale of the penitence involved in *Yom Kippur*, it's perhaps not surprising that many scholars have seen in the five services of *Yom Kippur* a prelude, even perhaps the source, of the Islamic practise of making *namaz* five times each day. I suspect this is erroneous, but still…the first of the five on *Yom Kippur* is Ma'ariv.

Ma'ariv

After *Kol Nidre*, *Ma'ariv*, the evening service. Like *Shacharit* and *Minchah*, *Ma'ariv* derives from Temple times, but unlike those other two, it wasn't *"avodah"* – a sacrificial rite – but simply the occasion in the evening when the Levites cleaned up the Temple after the daily sacrifices, and the Cohanim dispensed through fire with any sacrificial remains not consumed during the day. After the fall of the Temple in 70 CE, the Rabbis allowed the synagogue *Ma'ariv* to be optional, except for the reciting of the *Shema*, which is requisite at some point after the fall of darkness; but later, probably around the 5th or 6th century CE, it became established as a mandatory rite of prayer.

The structure is that of the everyday *Ma'ariv*, and all the additions for the occasion are the same as those which occur elsewhere on *Yom Kippur*. The service runs as follows:

"She hecheyanu." In some communities *"She hecheyanu"* isn't recited in synagogue, but at home before setting out for synagogue; and not by the men either, but by the women when they light the candles for the living and the dead[7]. In other communities the custom is to recite it on the way to synagogue; in still others it's inserted here, before *"Barechu"*, or held back to the end of *Ma'ariv*.

"Barechu." Two short verses in which God is declared "blessed" – and as such the source of all human blessing - and which constitute an act of summoning the *minyan* for the purposes of praying the *Shema*. There's no responsive *amen* to these blessings, but many congregations recite Joseph

---

[7] See *Hadlakot ha-Nerot* - The Kindling of the Lights, page 45.

Caro's *"Yishtabach"* (*Orach Chayim* 57:1) concurrent to the *chazan*'s *"Barechu"*.

Blessings of the *Shema*. Where the morning *Shema* is introduced by three blessings, in the evening there are four, fulfilling the Psalterer's observation (Psalm 119:164) that "seven times a day I praise You". The first refers to God's authority over nature, the seasons and the cycles of light; the second speaks of His gift of *Torah*; the third returns us to the Exodus from Egypt, and looks forward from there to the final moment of salvation which will be brought by the Messiah; the fourth siblings the *"Modeh Ani"* which we recite when we first wake up, this time praising God for protecting us during the hours of night in which we sleep.

"Shema." I've explored this central credo of Judaism extensively in "A Myrtle Among Reeds"; my accountant, publisher and literary agent all agree that readers would do best to acquire that book and read the explanation there.

The only variation in the *Shema* on *Yom Kippur* is that the second line – *"Baruch shem kavod malchuto le-olam va'ed* – Blessed is the name of His glorious kingdom for all eternity" is recited volubly, where it's usually recited in a whisper. This is because, on *Yom Kippur*, our penitence raises us to the level of the angels, and this line is an angelic insertion for their recitation of the *Shema* in Heaven, though it doesn't in fact appear in the original text, in Deuteronomy 6:4. The ruling for this is given in Deuteronomy *Rabbah* 69.

"Ve'emuna." The last phrase of the morning *Shema* is joined to the opening phrase of the ensuing verse, *"Ve-yatsiv"*, which affirmed God's generosity in bringing us out of Egypt. Similarly with the evening *Shema*, only here the linked phrase is *"Ve-emunah"*, which carries forward that affirmation into a future time of exile, and affirms our confidence that God will repeat His generosity; but rather beautifully it also affirms our confidence that God will repeat that same generosity this very night, and every night, by helping us endure that greatest of all tyrannies, the unconscious period of sleep.

The verse includes phrases from Job 9:10 and Psalm 66:9.

"Mi kamocha." – A citation of Exodus 15:11, "Who is like You among the heavenly powers, O Lord? Who is like You, mighty in holiness, too awesome for praise, performing wonders?", which phrase seems to me proof incontrovertible that Judaism isn't really a monotheistic faith at all, but simply a monistic one; I mean, that we don't regard God as the only "heavenly power", but simply as the "supreme one". After all, why would Moses compare his God to the other heavenly powers, if such creatures didn't exist?

And if the first half of this prayer isn't sufficient, there's always the second half:

"Your children beheld Your majesty as You split the sea before Moses. 'This is my God!' they exclaimed. And then they said, 'The Lord shall reign for all eternity.'" This – rather than any other they might have chosen to worship.

The last phrase is recited by the congregation, before the *chazan* concludes with the observation, quoting Jeremiah 31:10, that "it is further said: 'For the Lord has redeemed Jacob and delivered him from a power mightier than he. Blessed are you, Lord, who redeemed Israel.'"

"*Hashkiveynu.*" The assumption in Judaism is that we recite the *Shema* immediately upon awakening, and last thought at night, in which context the "*Hashkiveynu*" makes more sense than here at sunset, with the long evening still ahead. Still, it is recited here, and the Rabbis can take license to find other meanings in the prayer.

"Lay us down to sleep, Lord our God, in peace; raise us erect, our king, to life" seems perfectly straightforward. Yet *Berachos* 4a contrives to find in it an extension of the "*Mi kamocha*" prayer, and proves it by referring back one stage further to the "*Ve-emunah*" prayer, where future exile and tonight's sleep are joined in a single source of trepidation. Tonight's sleep is as fraught as tomorrow's history. Sadly, the evidence is in favour of the rabbinic interpretation.

The verse includes references to Psalm 17:8 and 121:8, and to Nehemiah 9:31.

"*Ki va-yom.*" "For through this day he will atone for you, to cleanse you; from all your sins before the Lord, you will be cleansed."

The phrase is from Leviticus 16:30, but it's much disputed. As we've seen previously, Hebrew doesn't distinguish, as English does, between lower and upper case. Who, then, is the "he" referred to? The *Cohen Gadol*, performing his acts of extirpation in the Temple? Or God Himself, cleansing us by whitening our pages in the Book of Life? And if it does mean the *Cohen Gadol*, then how can we be cleansed without a Temple – our atonement may prove useless. And if it does mean God, then how can He cleanse us without our making our atonement in the manner He required – through the extirpations of the *Cohen Gadol*. There is irresolvable paradox here. But it doesn't deter us. This is the Jewish response to everything. We don't know, but we do it anyway. Even if it's useless, it can't be completely useless. There will surely be some merit, and therefore some measure of atonement, even in the erroneous?

And finally half-*Kaddish* . Because whenever a section of a service ends, there must always be a *Kaddish* .

✡

Piyyut

Before we begin to explore the texts which are the substance of *Yom Kippur*, let me take a moment to comment on the form, manner and structure of the poetry, so that it will be meaningful as I describe its manifestations.

The origins of *piyyut* are in late Roman and Byzantine Palestine, in the period before the Moslem conquest. The word *piyyut* probably derives from the Greek *poietes*, and as such is a variation of our word "poetry". For the most part the *payyatanim* were cantors or *chazanim*, the men who sang the prayers in synagogue – it isn't the role of the Rabbi to lead prayer services, though it's a fact that many do; any man who knows the words and tunes can lead the prayers; *chazanut* is a lay function. The tradition grew up that a *chazan* would surprise, perhaps even entertain his congregation on a *Sabbath* or a holy day with a *piyyut* written especially for the occasion, elaborating on the nature of the festival or the subject-matter of the *Torah* reading or even a local event of some significance. The earliest of these were probably *ex tempore targumim*, which is to say improvised translations of Bible passages from Hebrew into Aramaic, for the benefit of that vast majority of Palestine's Jews for whom Hebrew was a language as dead as Latin is to us today. It may also be that *piyyut* evolved out of the rabbinic *drasha*, a homily or sermon on the weekly *Torah* reading; in the absence for whatever reason of the Rabbi, the *chazan* would step up and fill his boots, but untrained in the Law would have preferred to make *piyyut* than risk censure for errors in any attempted *drasha*.

Of the earliest *payyatanim*, Yose ben Yose was the laureate; of the middle period, from the 6th to the 8th century, Yannai was the inception (and the first to employ rhyme and introduce his name in acrostics) and Elazar ben Kalir the culmination; and after the fall of Palestine to Islam, when the centre of Judaism switched from Yavneh to Baghdad, *piyyut* acquired a new development altogether that would continue in the mediaeval period in Europe.

Certain features of *piyyut* are in evidence from the very beginning, and Yose ben Yose is the perfect place to go to find them at their best. The use of the alphabetical acrostic, for example, can be found even in those very few instances of poetry in the *Talmud* (the *Kechalot* hymns for example). Quadripartite rhythm, a development of the bipartite form used in many of the Psalms, is also typical; hugely complex, it makes each line of verse out of four equal units, each containing two heavily accented words; and in the most complex the acrostic is run through either two or all four of the units. *Piyyut* from the outset tended to avoid rhyme, which is understandable given the nature of Hebrew grammar; because it uses regular suffixes that are endlessly repetitive, rhymed verse is doomed to the tedium of feminine endings, pronouns, past tenses and nominal contrivances, salvageable only by geniuses such as Bialik and Halevi, intolerable in anybody else's hands. Later, when rhyme became the fashionable mode, it avoided the problem of the dead-hand of grammar by the construction of elaborate monorhyme verses; speaking entirely personally, because I regard all poetry as intended to be sung, or at least chanted, and not read as though it were prose upon the page, I find the rhyming *piyyut* much less satisfactory, because forcing language into rhyme within the narrow parameters available in Hebrew does awful damage to the rhythms of the verse, thus undermining singability. But this is a matter of taste.

The length of any poem was defined by the pattern of the acrostic, though often acrostics are doubled, tripled or even quadrupled to expand the length, or to show off the poet's virtuosity. The language of *piyyut* is borrowed from the Biblical sources (not the *Talmudic* because, remember, the *Talmud* was written in Aramaic and all liturgical poetry except the *Kaddish* is in Hebrew); but once *piyyut* begins it becomes self-referential to a point of incest and inbreeding, and even if not on the same scale as Shakespeare, whom Harold Bloom accredits with coining more than a thousand new words, neologisms abounded.

What the *payyatanim* appear to have loved most though, with a joy that is truly Joycian, was the potentials in the permutations of the acrostic. Closing verses built on the author's acrostic signature became emblematic, and many give not only the signature but the father's name, the town of residence, his occupation when not writing poetry, and on two famous occasions the invocation to "be strong", the Hebrew "*chazak*" that is chanted threefold at the completion of the reading of any of the Five Books of Moses.[8]

Piyyut was not written for its own sake, as other poetry may have been; it was written specifically for liturgical purposes, and it was needed because, right up until the early Middle Ages, Judaism really had no liturgy by any meaningful definition of the term. Until the destruction of the Second Temple in 70 CE, Jewish worship was entirely about sacrifice of the first fruits, whether vegetal or animal, and the ceremonies were accompanied by the orchestrated singing of specific Psalms, plus a number of what we call prayers but which were not really prayers at all. The *Shema* is a credo, a

---

[8] See pages 91 and 126.

statement of our monotheistic faith and a recounting of the list of our primary obligations: to teach our children, to wear *tsitsit*, to lay *tefillin*, to put up *mezuzot*. The *Aleynu* likewise details our duties and responsibilities and functions really as a daily personal reminder. The *Amidah* comes closest to prayer, being a series of benedictions, conveyed upwards from Man to God, thanks in advance for his fulfilling a number of our requests. The *Kaddish* in its four forms is a hymn, not a prayer. Prayer in the sense of a personal outpouring of spiritual and religious feeling, the individual dialogue with Self and God, does not exist until the *payyatanim* began to create it, and it is not insignificant, in my view, that the publication of the first prayer books, starting with that of Rav Amram Ga'on in Babylonia in the 9th century, are coincident with the publication of the first *kedushtot*, a *kedushta* being a sequence of *piyyutim* on a connected liturgical theme, culminating in a rhymed prose *kedushah*, and inserted into the *Amidah* on *Sabbath*s and festivals. Essentially the prayer books that we have today, both daily *siddur* and festival *machzor*, are the *piyyutum*, differentiated as *Avoda*, *Kerova* and *Yotser*, and completed by the residual psalms and hymns and credos of the Temple period.

✡

Amidah

In principle an *Amidah* is an *Amidah* – the recitation of the Eighteen Benedictions. But nothing is ever quite that simple. For one thing, there are actually Nineteen Benedictions, even in a regular *Amidah* (see "A Myrtle Among Reeds"). For another, only the morning repetition holds firmly to the recitation of the Benedictions; all other occasions add paragraph upon paragraph of further text, or even, as in this *Ma'ariv* of *Yom Kippur*, fail to recite the full Eighteen Benedictions.

Though the tune is different, the opening is familiar, the Blessing of the Patriarchs, with the same additional verse – "*Zachreynu*" – as we have sung at *Minchah*. "*Gevurot*" is likewise familiar and, as in *Minchah*, "*Mi kamocha av ha-rachamim*" is appended before "*Ve-ne'eman*". The third blessing, "*Kedushat ha-shem*", commences, but then the *Amidah* appears to go awry. Where a normal weekday *Ma'ariv Amidah* continues the regular blessings, *Yom Kippur* substitutes an entirely different set of verses, which don't reflect the remaining benedictions in any shape or form, but which come under the heading "*Kedushat ha-Shem* – the Holiness of God's Name".

"*U-ve-chen ten pachdecha*" is the first addition, a text composed by the greatest of all Babylonian *amora'im*, Rabbi Abba Arikha, known simply as "Rav – the wise one". Personally ordained by Judah *ha-Nasi*, he founded the academy at Sura in the 3rd century CE, and, with his friend and colleague the physician-astronomer Samuel who was head of the Nahardea academy, began a series of written dialogues that would establish the Babylonian *Talmud*. Rav's *halachah* reflects that of Israel, where Samuel was the expert on Jewish civil law and on the customs of the Babylonian communities; it's the melding of these dichotomies, the dialectic of their affable disagreements, which provides the Socratic base for *Talmud*; but this isn't relevant to the liturgical fragment we have here. Rav extols the greatness of God, and calls on all of God's creation to form a single, harmonious community, bound by the divine laws – a view that would be shared by Antigone, but not, perhaps, by Creon.

"*U-ve-chen ten kavod*" continues the same theme, asking God to bless those who do indeed follow the divine laws, asking Him to grant those blessings promised in the words of the regular *Amidah* – restoration of the Temple and Jerusalem, peace, health, prosperity, the ingathering of the exiles, and of course the Messiah.

"*U-ve-chen tsaddik*" borrows a phrase from Job (5:16), "Iniquity will close its mouth"; this, alongside the other events that will accompany God's fulfilment of His promises, lead to the concluding verse, "*Ve-timloch*", which place God in the utmost heights of power, universal ruler of a perfect cosmos (c.f. Psalm 146:10). Liturgy thus transpires to have been rhetoric too, an argument stated, formulated, developed, expounded, perorated, always within the form and terms of prayer. But prayer as thesis. The harnessing of the rational and scientific mind to faith. It can be done.

The final verse is "*Kadosh atah*", which places a blessing upon God in the name of the preceding thesis, and thereby brings to a liturgical conclusion what requires a liturgical conclusion. Prayer may be thesis, but it must first and last be prayer.

✡

The next thirteen blessings do not appear on this occasion. Instead, as on *Shabbat* and at all festivals, the middle section of the *Amidah* comprises four paragraphs, three familiar on all equivalent occasions, the last specific to *Yom Kippur*, speaking as it does of forgiveness. The theme of the four paragraphs is the "holiness of the day", or, in Hebrew:

Kedushat ha-Yom

"*Atah vechartanu*…You have chosen us from all the people; You loved us and found favour in us; You exalted us above all the tongues and You sanctified us with Your commandments. You drew us close, our King, to Your service, and proclaimed Your great and Holy name upon us."

"*Va-titen lanu*…and You have given us, Lord our God, with love this Day of Atonement for pardon, forgiveness and atonement, and to pardon all our iniquities on it, a holy convocation, a memorial of the Exodus from Egypt."

These two verses are self-explanatory. The three levels denoted here – pardon, forgiveness and atonement – reflect the three concepts already outlined, of *mechilah* (pardon), *selichah* (forgiveness) and *kapparah* (atonement). The reference to Egypt is worth a passing mention however: it's held in Jewish tradition that Moses received the second set of laws and came down the mountain with them on *Yom Kippur*, thereby obtaining final redemption for the sin of the Golden Calf. Tradition also tells that, in the seventh year, the year of the jubilee when all slaves were freed, the date of liberation was *Rosh ha-Shana*, and because this was also the date of the beginning of the Days of Awe, the liberated slaves would remain with their former masters an additional ten days, to share with them the festivities, to prepare with them for the fast of *Yom Kippur*. Then, on *Yom Kippur* itself, the *Sanhedrin* would sound the *shofar* for the jubilee, and at that alarum the liberated would go home. The reference to Egypt reflects the formal liberation from slavery of the Jews themselves.

"*Eloheynu…Ya'aleh* - Our God…may there rise". Prayers to remember not only us, but all those who came before us; and especially those who gained merit before us, because merit too is contagious, and we would be happy if some were to pass across to us.
The closing phrase is from Nehemiah 9:31.

"*Eloheynu…mechal* – Our God, pardon". This is the only one of the four paragraphs of "*Kedushat ha-yom*" which has a history in Temple times, it being one of the eight blessings uttered by the *Cohen Gadol* after the reading of the Law on *Yom Kippur*. In calling on God directly to wipe clean our slates, it incorporates verses from Isaiah (43:25 and 44:22) and Leviticus (16:30). Note again the uncommon use of *Yeshurun* as a synonym for Israel.

✡

So we return to the more familiar text of the *Amidah* with the Temple Service paragraph "*retseh*" and its subsequent "*ve-techezeynah*", after which the thanksgiving "*Modim*" is completed with an additional verse for *Yom Kippur.*

"*U-chetuv* – and inscribe all the children of Your covenant for a good life."

Next "*Shalom rav*", the prayer for peace, which also contains a specific addition for *Yom Kippur.* "*Be-sepher chayim* – in the Book of Life...", whose ending is contested by the different rabbinic schools; some insist on "*Baruch atah adonay, ha-mevarech et amo yisra'el ba-shalom*", while others favour the simpler "*Baruch atah adonay oseh ha-shalom*". No explanation is given by either party – it comes down to issues of custom and practice. Both sides however agree that after the *baruchah* all should say the closing "*yehiyu le-ratson* – may the expressions of my mouth and the thoughts of my heart find favour before You, Lord, my rock and my redeemer". Beautiful lines, from Psalm 19:15.

✡

And so we come, for the second time, to the *Vidu'i* , identical in every way to the *Vidu'i* of *Minchah*, save one difference. At *Minchah*, *Vidu'i* provided the end of the individual's recitation of the *Amidah*, after which the *chazan* took the community through the whole prayer a second time; at *Ma'ariv* there is no repetition.

✡

Selichot

We have foresworn all our oaths in *Kol Nidre*. We have confessed our sins in the *Vidu'i* . Now, in order to move on to full atonement, we have to say sorry in order to seek forgiveness.

Until now much has been chanted, or spoken. With the *Selichot* we move to singing. Only those who have participated can understand the significance of this change of form, the deepening of our emotional plane as we move up or down the scale. One can speak with almost no emotion, reciting, if not mechanically, then certainly prosaically. To chant brings in the body, for no one chants standing entirely still, and whether they indulge the full *shockeling* – swaying backwards and forwards from the knees – or merely the gently rhythmic fidgeting of wallflowers at the discotheque, it still deepens. And then there's singing, in which the mind, and the body, and now also the soul, are fully engaged, because we sing, not from the throat like pop stars, not from the diaphragm like opera divas, but from the very gut, from the solar plexus, the inner sun that turns its countenance to shine upon us. And nowhere more so than in the gloriously antiphonous "*Ya'aleh*".

For "*Ya'aleh*" the Ark is opened and the congregation stands. In the common version, the prayer is taken word by word, the *chazan* leading, the congregants responding. The form of the hymn is complex. Each line is symmetrical. Each line is chronological. And as a whole it forms an alphabetical acrostic once again, only this time, cabbalistically, in reverse (the Cabbala teaches that, when a man believes he has reached the full extent of his understanding, he should go back to the beginning and learn how much he still doesn't know).

> May our supplications rise from the evening,
> and may our cry come from the morning,
> and may our praise find favour by the evening.

Eight verses, in which only the subject of each line changes, not the structure, nor the intent: the evening of the first line being now, the *Ma'ariv* at the start of *Yom Kippur*, the evening of the last line being soon to come, the time when *Yom Kippur* is done and our atonement is complete. And of course we should not forget that a Jewish "day" begins in the evening, not the morning, with the moonrise, not the sunrise, with Yah, the sacred number fifteen of the full moon.

✡

The second of the *Selichot* is "*Shema tephillah*", which is also used as an introductory meditation to the daily *Selichot*. Where most of the *Selichot* find their authorship amongst the *amor'aim* and *ga'onim* and *rishonim*, the great scholars of early and mediaeval Judaism, "*Shema tephillah*" is essentially an anthology of psalmic soundbites, augmented by other Biblical allusions, through which the authority of God is overwhelmingly acknowledged, and the children of Israel urged to worship Him. The textual sources are as follows (quotations are given as open text, allusions in brackets):

"You who...will come." Psalm 65:3
"All flesh...O Lord."(Isaiah 66:23)
"They will come...Your Name." Psalm 86:9
"Come!...our Maker." Psalm 95:6
"Enter His gates...His Name." Psalm 100:4
"Behold...bless the Lord." Psalm 134:1-2
"Let us come...His footstool." Psalm 132:7
"Exalt the Lord...He is holy!" Psalm 99:5
"Exalt the Lord...our God." Psalm 99:9
"Prostrate yourselves...on Earth." Psalm 96:9
"As for us...in awe of You." (Psalm 5:8)

"We will prostrate…beyond your Name." (Psalm 138:2)
"Lord God of Legions…surrounds you." Psalm 89:9
"For who…the angels." Psalm 89:7
"For you…O God." Psalm 86:10
"For great…Your truth." Psalm 108:5
"The Lord is great…unfathomable." Psalm 145:3
"For the Lord is great…heavenly powers." Psalm 96:4
"For a great…heavenly powers." Psalm 95:3
"For what power…deeds and power?" Deuteronomy 3:24
"Who would not…none like You." Jeremiah 10:7
"There is none…great with power." Jeremiah 10:6
"Yours is a…Your right hand." Psalm 89:14
"Yours is the day…and the sun." Psalm 74:16
"For in His power…are His." Psalm 95:4
"Who can express…His praise?" Psalm 106:2
"Yours, Lord…every leader." 1 Chronicles 29:11
"Yours is the Heaven…You founded them." Psalm 89:12
"You established…You fashioned them." Psalm 74:17
"You crushed…the mighty rivers." Psalm 74: 14-15
"You shattered…upon the water." Psalm 74:13
"You rule…You calm them." Psalm 89:10
"Great is…His Holiness." Psalm 48:2
"Lord…Who is God." Isaiah 37:16
"God is feared…surround Him." Psalm 89:8
"Heaven will…holy ones." Psalm 89:6
"Come, let us sing…out to Him." Psalm 95:1-2
"Righteousness…countenance." Psalm 89:15
"For together…in multitudes." Psalm 55:15
"For His is the sea…fashioned it." Psalm 95:5
"For His is the soul…human flesh." Job 12:10

The method, of quoting Biblical verses in reverse order, is commonplace in *piyyut* of this kind. Given that the poet is seeking to construct a logical paragraph out of a set of disparate, organically unconnected fragments, there's no reason for not taking them in any order that may please; only, because it's the Jewish habit to seek explanations for every written line, and because the writers know that other scholars will do this to their own work, can we really allow a writer to escape with the defence that "I happened to come across the lines in that random manner" or "I didn't mean anything by it"? Even if it's true, it isn't permissible.

✡

Are the "Thirteen Attributes of Mercy" a part of the *Selichot*, or an intermission? Or are they, with "*Ya'aleh*" and "*Shema tephillah*", all three introductory meditations? There's much dispute in all directions of this particular compass, though I fail to see how "*Ya'aleh*" can be represented as anything but magnetic north. I propose to let the controversy slip through these pages. Readers may dance on the pin-head in their own time, if they're so minded.

Before the "Thirteen Attributes of Mercy" three introductory verses, the first two written by Yose ben Yose, the earliest known liturgical poet after the fall of the Temple (4th, possibly 5th century CE). Many even regard him as the founder of *piyyut*, the tradition of liturgical poetry. When the *genizah*, the burial-ground for any Jewish manuscript in which the name of God is mentioned, was unearthed in Cairo, and literally thousands of Jewish manuscripts recovered from *She'ol*, Yose's name appeared on more scrolls and papyrus rolls than any other.

"*Darchecha eloheynu*", the first verse, refers back to Exodus 33:13, where Moses pleaded with God after the sin of the Golden Calf: "Now therefore, I pray, if I have found grace in Your sight, show me now Your way, that I may know You, that I may find grace in Your sight; and consider that this nation is Your people." Here, employing Moses' prayer as a springboard, Yose says "It is Your way, our God, to delay Your anger, against people both good and evil – and this is Your praise."

The verse is recited by the *chazan*, then repeated by the congregation, as happens again in the following verse, "*le-ma'ancha*":

"Act for Your sake, our God, and not for ours; behold our state, destitute and empty-handed."

These verses in fact belong elsewhere – as the alternating chorus and refrain to Yose's immense poem "*Amnam ashameynu* – alleviate our guilt". "*Amnam*" contains a quadruple acrostical poem – which is to say, sequences of four lines, each beginning with the same letter of the alphabet, commencing with four *alephs* and ending with four *tavs*. However the full version of the poem is almost never recited; at most, the verses up until the letter *yud*, the tenth sequence of quatrains; and then the final quatrain, *tav*. Many congregations do in fact recite that first part now, before embarking on the "Thirteen Attributes of Mercy"; and even those congregations which do not recite "*Amnam*" still utter the "*darchecha eloheynu*" and "*le-ma'ancha*", as well as the "*ta'aleh*", the final quatrain of "*Amnam.*"

✡

Shelosh-Esrey Midot ha-Rachamim - The Thirteen Attributes of Divine Mercy

This is the heart of the *Selichot*, both for itself and because it contains that most riveting of all liturgical fragments, sung out of Exodus 34:6-7: "*Adonay, adonay, el rachum ve-chanun*", from which the Thirteen Attributes are deduced. According to Rabbi Yochanan[9] (*Rosh ha-Shana* 17b), Moses was convinced that the sin of the Golden Calf was so momentous that even he couldn't successfully intercede with God to mitigate against destruction. So he prayed the lines in Exodus 33:13 mentioned above, and – according to Rabbi Yochanan – God appeared to Moses in the guise of a *chazan* and wrapped in a *tallit* (a person and an article that would actually have been meaninglessly unrecognisable to Moses), in order to teach him the Thirteen Attributes of Mercy. "Whenever Israel sins," God then told Moses, "have them recite this in the correct order, and I will forgive them." This is lousy theology but wonderful *Midrash*.

The Thirteen appear repeatedly in *Selichot* and are always prefaced by the verse "*el melech yoshev al kiseh rachamim* – O God, King, who sits on the throne of mercy", a prayer which itself enumerates most of the Thirteen Attributes.

But not formally. Formally – which is to say, in the opinion of Rabbeinu Tam, in *Talmud Tractate Rosh ha-Shana* 17b, the generally accepted view - they are:

The name of God, in the form of the Tetragrammaton, YHVH, which defines God as the Creator and contains implicitly the state of Man before the Fall, to which we always have the possibility of returning.

The name of God, repeated in the same form, a delay in the line which allows God time for mercy.

The name of God, given in the Canaanite El by which the patriarchs knew Him, denoting His power over Nature, including human nature, including the evil inclination within human nature, which God gave us, and for whose use He must therefore be merciful.

"*Rachum*" or compassion, the fourth word in the line.

"*Chanun*" or graciousness, the fifth word in the line.

"*Erech apayim*", slow to anger.

"*Ve-rav chesed*", abundant in kindness.

"*Ve-emet*", truth.

---

[9] Yochanan ben Zakkai was the head of the Sanhedrin at the time of the destruction of the Temple (70 CE). It was he who negotiated the surrender of Jerusalem with the Romans, receiving as his part of the bargain the rabbinic yeshiva at Yavneh, where he would begin the creation of the Jerusalem Talmud.

"*Notser chesed la-alaphim*", preserver of kindness for thousands of generations.

"*Noseh avon*", forgiver of iniquity.

"*Va-phesha*", forgiver of wilful sins.

"*Ve-chata'ah*", and forgiver of errors.

"*Ve-nakeh*", He who cleanses.

After the Thirteen there is always a short prayer for forgiveness, which follows the example of Moses (Exodus 34:8-9) who did the same when God did indeed forgive the sin of the Golden Calf. In this case it comes in five short verses:

"May You forgive our iniquities and our errors…Give ear…As a father…Forgive, please…Incline your ear…"

The first is recited by the *chazan*, the second by everyone together, the third by the *chazan*; the last two are sometimes recited responsively, sometimes in silence, a variation of custom and practice between synagogues. The third verse, "*Ke-rachem av* – as a father" is another compound of verses from the Psalms (in this case 103:13, 3:9, 46:8, 84:13 and 20:10). The fourth verse, "*selach na* – forgive, please", was Moses' plea for forgiveness (Numbers 14:19) after the return of the spies from the land of Canaan, when the whole people expressed its lack of faith in the capacity of God or Moses to take them safely into Israel. The closing line is quoted from Numbers 14:20: "And the Lord said, 'I have forgiven according to your words – *salachti ki-devarecha*'". The fifth verse concludes with a reference to the Book of Daniel, 9:18-19.

✡

Selach, na – Forgive, please

Out of Moses' cry for forgiveness comes the next *piyyut*, another alphabetical acrostic, its authorship unknown. It is recited, standing before an open Ark, responsively, the first verse led by the *chazan* and repeated by the congregation, the remainder led by the congregation and repeated by the *chazan*. At its conclusion the Ark is closed, but once again the "*el melech yoshev al kiseh*" is recited, still standing, as prelude to the second recitation of the Thirteen Attributes.

"*Al tavo* - do not enter into judgement with us", follows, a request for God to delay His final decision – we have not, after all, even begun our asking for forgiveness. We are barely into the first hour of *Yom Kippur* – there remain another twenty-four, and only at the very end, we pray, should

God make up His mind about us.

"*Al tavo*" replaced "*ha-azinah* – give ear", after the previous recitation of the Thirteen Attributes; like then, "*ke-rachem* – as a father", follows; but the next version of "*selach na*", which collects the spy-verses of Numbers 14:19-20 with the cited fragment of Daniel (9:18-19), though recorded in most prayer books, is in fact omitted by most congregations. Why then are they there? Because Rabbi Yochanan, the principle voice in defining this section of prayer, argued (in *Yerushalmi Berachos* 5:1) that we should always hold two verses in our mouths, both of which begin "*adonay tseva'ot*" (one from Psalm 46:8, the other from 84:13); they are included here in "*ke-rachem*", but their context isn't made specific by that verse; by adding the references in "*selach na*" they become contextualised, and as such completed; there is, however, no need to state them.

✡

Amnam Ken

The date is September 3rd 1189, the day on which King Richard I, the Lion-Hearted, set the crown of England upon his lion's mane at Westminster Abbey. The chronicles of Roger of Wendover record how:

"Duke Richard, when all the preparations for his coronation were complete, came to London, where were assembled the archbishops of Canterbury, Rouen and Trèves...the archbishop of Dublin, with all the bishops, earls, barons and nobles of the kingdom. Proceeding to the altar, Duke Richard swore, in presence of the clergy and people, that he would observe peace, honour and reverence all his life, towards God, the holy Church and its ordinances, and he swore that he would exercise true justice towards the people committed to his charge."

It wasn't more than minutes before he had the chance to prove these oaths. Jewish delegations had come from all over England, but weren't allowed inside at the ceremony. What precisely happened isn't clear, but at the moment where he announced a general amnesty for all those held in gaol, a jostling began outside, with Christians turning upon Jews wherever they could find one. This jostling quickly turned to rioting, and by the end of the ceremony the whole of London Jewry had been sacked. The King, whose day, according to Roger of Wendover, ended with "wine flowing along the pavement and walls of the palace", clearly couldn't tell that much of that red wine had been transfigured into human blood. He did indeed send Ranulph de Glanvil, his Chief Justice, to protect the Jews and end the riots. But Glanvil's task ended in failure, "for there never was such a massacre of Jews in England as upon this day".

In fact, there was, there were, repeatedly. That day was just the start of it.

There followed further anti-Jewish outbreaks in the spring of 1190, wherever there was plunder to be looted. Christian mobs demanded death or baptism as well as cash. At Dunstable the whole community accepted baptism. At Lynn the massacres were attributed to foreign sailors. At Stamford the Jews took refuge in the castle, a futile act because it was the Sheriff, Gerard de Camville, who personally led the pogrom. At Bury St Edmunds, Abbot Samson expelled all who weren't vassals of St Edmund, but fifty-seven Jews had already been murdered. At Colchester, Thetford and Ospringe Jews were also murdered, though at Lincoln Bishop Hugh gave them his protection. But it was in York that the Jews were worst affected.

York, or Yorvik, was the northern capital of England. After the death of Aaron of Lincoln, Josce and Benedict of York had become the two principal elders of the Jews. King Richard's post-coronational departure for the Crusades left the Jews unprotected, and York was the prime target. Where elsewhere pillage and murder left Jews alive but plundered, at York the whole community died. First the mob burned the home of Benedict, the owner having already died while fleeing the riots at the time of the coronation. Josce's house was next, but he'd already taken refuge with his valuables at the Royal Castle, gathering with him as many Jews as could take refuge there. But to no avail. The clergy joined the assault, one Praemonstratensian with a banner crying "Destroy the enemies of Christ" while the ramparts were assailed. After several days of battle, on the advice of Rabbi Yomtob of Joigny, Masada was emulated by means of a knife, the last two men alive of the entire community being Josce and Yomtob, of whom the latter slew the former, and then took his own life. Those who survived the communal suicide were massacred, and all records of debts owing to them were then burned. The number of Jewish dead in York has been counted up at almost fifteen hundred. Later King Richard sent Geoffrey Rydle, Bishop of Ely and Chancellor of the Kingdom, to punish the perpetrators of the York massacre. Among those charged were no less than ten of the most important barons, but most of the perpetrators had already fled, under the leadership of one Richard Malebisse, a name well given - it means "Evil Beast" in English. Nonetheless, the presence on the list of so many noble names may well suggest the motive for the attack upon the Jews was money, not religion, for all these barons were in debt to Jews for land and trade and buildings in which they were committed. Of those charged or persevered, not a single one paid with his life.

Rabbi Yomtob of Joigny, whose *halachic* decisions are recorded in the writings of Mordechai ben Hillel, was a leading Biblical exegesist who engaged in numerous anti-Christian polemics, and wrote an elegy on the martyrdom of the Jews of Blois in 1171. He had only come to York as late as 1180, persuaded there by Josce, and it's reckoned that he wrote the "*Amnam Ken*" in York. Based once again on Moses' plea following the sin of the spies, it focuses on God's answer – "*salachti*" – using that single word as a refrain at the end of each of its eleven pairs of alphabetically acrostical, rhymed couplets. The poem is recited standing, with the Ark open, and once again it's followed by "*El melech yoshev*", and by the Thirteen Attributes.

✡

Ki Hineh

So much Hebrew poetry is formulaic, in the way that the Elizabethan sonnet, the Japanese Haiku, are formulaic. My stating this isn't a criticism, merely an observation: poetry, after all, is the verdict, not the intention. "*Ki hineh*" is another such. Built in quatrains, the first line expounds a simile for Man's relationship to God; the second, in a parenthesis, describes the way in which God uses that relationship to further the objectives of Creation; the third completes the first and applies a positive epithet to God in consequence; the fourth is a refrain, identical at the end of every stanza, reminding God that our relationship is also covenantal, and that His part of the covenant is to safeguard His people, in this case specifically against "the Accuser". The piece comes in seven stanzas – a number which emphasises its holiness.

The source of the first simile – "like clay in the hands of the potter" - is Jeremiah 18:6. The pattern is established: man as the material, God as the artisan. In the ensuing verses we are stones in the hand of the cutter, axe-heads to the blacksmith, anchors to the sailor, glass to the blower, curtains to the embroiderer and finally silver in the hands of the silversmith. A good relationship this, creative material to skilled craftsman. If I cannot be a poet, at least let me be a poem. If I cannot create, at least let me be a force for someone else's creativity. I like "*Ki Hineh*".

I should like, also, to know who wrote it, so that I could tell his story, and make him an anecdote in the hands of the scholar-historian, and so complete the cycle. But sadly the name is lost; as, almost certainly, are a further sixteen verses: the verses we have seem to follow the pattern of an alphabetical acrostic (we have the scriptural root, then verses whose key-word – stone, axe-head etc – are *aleph, gimmel, hey, zayin, yud*, and *kaph*). Would some modern *payyatan* like to do for "*Ki Hineh*" what Derek Cooke has done for Mahler's 10th? It's so precisely formulaic, it shouldn't be difficult.

✡

Zechor rachamecha

The Ark is closed, and again *"El melech"*, again the Thirteen Attributes, and then *"Zechor rachamecha"*, the collection of verses which, admittedly in a slightly different order, end the *Selichot* on most fast days. It pleads for God to recall His covenantal promises to the patriarchs, to have mercy on their offspring, to end our exile and return us to a rebuilt Jerusalem, and especially, because that's the purpose of the prayer, to grant forgiveness. Following that other formula with which we're now familiar – in secular poetry it's known as a cento - it's constructed entirely from scriptural quotations, the texts here being Psalm 25:6, 79:8, 106:4 (by allusion, not direct quotation), 74:2, 137:7, 102:14, Exodus 32:13 and Deuteronomy 9:27. Like all these prayers, we plead our case not just in Heaven but specifically in the Heavenly Court, and like all good lawyers arguing before a judge, we need a case. Here it's made threefold: our antiquity; the fact that He has redeemed us previously; the Temple in which we used to worship Him and hopefully will do so again. Added to this, God should forgive us because of the affliction of Jerusalem by the Edomites, which is to say the Romans who destroyed the Temple and Jerusalem, took us out of the land of our antiquity, and refused to redeem us. It makes a compelling case: the challenge to God, in a world dominated by Rome, to prove Himself greater than Jupiter and the Tiberian theocracy, by His actions towards His chosen people. Irrefutable, one would have said.

It's hard at times to distinguish poetry from prayer. Even the *piyyut* contains much that's liturgical, while often the prayers are full of form and language such as we expect from poetry. In the lines that follow *"zechor rachamecha"* there is no question.

"Al na taseh aleynu chatat, asher no'alnu va-asher chatanu – please, do not reckon for us as a sin, those things we did foolishly and those things we did carelessly and without intent."

This is prayer in the sense of pleading (the verb from which we also have the noun "plaintiff"), asking God for something specific. The words are said twice, first by the *chazan*, then the congregation, as are the lines that follow.

"Chatanu tsureynu, selach lanu yotsreynu – we have erred, our Rock; forgive us, our Creator."

"Hen ya'avir zadon lim'shugah, ki le-chol ha-am bishgagah – behold, He transforms wilful sin into mere error, because the entire people has acted carelessly."

In some congregations *"chatanu"* is repeated after *"hen ya'avir"*.

Then, reciting together, *"Zechor lanu"*, an immense cry to God, full of scriptural references and allusions, to remember us, to have mercy on us, to restrain Himself from destroying us for our o so many sins. We are sorry. We have lived all year on the kinesis of neurosis – the dynamic power of guilt which pervades all Jewish thought and action. Now, on this day, beating our breasts, fasting, pleading, all our accumulated guilt pours out. God, we are sorry. And do You question the sincerity of our regret? Okay, question it now – but surely, when we reach the end of this twenty-five hour apology, surely You won't be able to question it any more? So remember us, have mercy on us, restrain Yourself from destroying us. We are, truly, truly, sorry.

The references in *"Zechor lanu"* are from Leviticus 26:42, 45, 44 – a misordering which leads some authorities to question the organisation, and even the completeness, of the text as we now have it – then Deuteronomy 4:31, 30:6, 30:3,4, 4:29, Isaiah   43:25, 44:22 and 1:18, Ezekiel 36:25, Leviticus 16:30, and finally Isaiah 56:7.

✡

Shema Koleynu – Hear our voice

The Ark is re-opened for *"Shema koleynu"*, yet another compilation, this time recited with consciously increased passion, to provide the sequence of *Selichot* with an appropriate emotional crescendo. The theme is our dependence upon God's wanting us to continue as good Jews, and thus His having a vested interest in granting us forgiveness. It's another extremely good legal case: a plea-bargain for rehabilitation and community service instead of the statutory stoning, burning, strangling and beheading. At least this gives a man the chance to get it right next year. And encourages the other sinners too, unlike that theory favoured by the French, that *"il faut de temps en temps tuer un amiral pour mieux encourager les autres"*.

"Shema koleynu" is the opening phrase of one of the Eighteen Benedictions recited every morning of the year, and that opening phrase is also the opening phrase here. But afterwards the text is completely different. Its construction involves a citation from Lamentations 5:21, and then allusions to Psalms 5:2, 19:15, 51:13, 71:9, 38:22, 86:17 and 38:16. The text is unusual in making so many allusions rather than directly quoting; I can find no explanation amongst the Rabbinic writings as to why this might be so.

✡

The Ark is again closed and the congregation seated. *Selichot* continues

74

with "*Al ta'azveynu*". We are entitled to ask: why so many versions of the same plea for forgiveness? The answer is twofold. On the one hand, our prayers are bound in time as well as in intention – frankly, we need multiple versions to fill up the twenty-five hours, since we can't just sit and stand in silence and expect God to forgive us. But that's only the flippant answer. More seriously, it's an issue of detail, and in explaining it we return to the Heavenly Court of Law and our role as barrister in our own defence; and indeed, in defence of all Israel simultaneously. We are asking forgiveness, but there are many counts, many pleas, many vindications, many mitigating and extenuating circumstances, many precedents, many witnesses; many sins too, each of which, like charges in a court of civil law, must be taken individually, and each of which is entitled to be argued, on its own merits, down to the most infinitesimal of detail.

So, here, we are making our plea in terms of God's response. By denying our plea, He would be forsaking us, casting us off, even perhaps humiliating us; it might even be that to deny forgiveness would, by inference, nullify His covenant with us. All this needs to be taken into account before a judgement can be made. This is less an appeal to the judge than to the jury.

And then there's the intent behind our confession and our asking for forgiveness. Are we not owning up, and therefore deserving of better treatment than he who sins and denies he's done the deed, or denies that the deed he's done is even sinful? Should we not be granted better treatment, in order to praise us for our honesty, and give value to the act of owning up? And are we not owning up because we're genuinely sorry (though we know we'll sin again, and repent again, next year)? Are we not yearning to return to *Torah*, and if we're forgiven are we not more likely to fulfil that yearning, than if we're spurned and scorned with unforgiveness.

For your sake, God. Not for our sake. Forgive us, pardon us, atone for us. "*Selach lanu, mechal lanu, kaper lanu*".

That last line sung, another of several refrains that will recur and recur throughout the day of *Yom Kippur*, sung, chanted, recited, if necessary howled.

The closing phrase of "*Al ta'azveynu*" is given in most texts in the singular: "*Ve-salachta la'avoni* – may you pardon *my* guilt"; however I've seen texts in which this is written "*Ve-salachta la'avoneynu* – may you pardon *our* guilt." I suspect that both are correct.

"*Al ta'azveynu*" was recited for us by the *chazan*; the song "*Ki anu amecha*" which follows is either sung responsively, each line a chiasmus of which the *chazan* sings the first half and the congregation the second, or else sung by the whole congregation together to what is virtually a pop melody in the tempo and timbre of "Bridge Over Troubled Water".

The source of "*Ki anu amecha*" is *Shir ha-Shirim Rabbah* 2:16, where the parallel relationships between Man and God are made explicit. Most of these echo the poetic similes in "*Ki hineh*", and form the basis of this text:

We are your People – You are our God
We are your Children – You are our Father
We are your Servants – You are our Master
We are your Congregation – You are our Portion
We are your Heritage – You are our Lot
We are your Sheep – You are our Shepherd
We are your Vineyard – You are our Watchman
We are your Handiwork – You are our Shaper
We are your Friend – You are our Beloved
We are your Treasure – You are our God
We are your Designated – You are our Designated

There's something slightly disappointing about the repetition of God in the first and then the penultimate line, as though the author ran out of metaphors; but more than compensated by the lovely star-crossed symmetry of the close, in which Romeo-Man and Juliet-God (or should that be the other way around?) are shown to be a marriage made in Heaven.

In the Hebrew, grammatical construction makes every line-ending, including the chiasmi, rhyme monometrically (*eloheynu, adoneynu, malkeynu* etc).

We are brazen but You are compassionate and gracious
We are obstinate but You are slow to anger
We are filled with iniquity but You are filled with mercy
We – our days are like a fleeting shadow, but You are eternal and Your years never end

These last four verses, which allude to Psalmic passages (144:4, 102:28 and 88:3) don't have the same feel as the first set of verses, and it isn't simply the change from objective to subjective qualities (sheep, friend, vineyard – brazen, obstinate, sinful). It's also the structure, which seeks palpably to imitate the echo-line pattern of the Psalms; it's the textual allusions; it's also the cumbersome prose, which lacks any of the charm, let alone the sophistication and refinement, of the poetry of "*Ki anu amecha*". As though Jeffrey Archer had tried to finish an unfinished work by W.B. Yeats.

✡

Selichot - Confession

What – yet another *Vidu'i*? But of course – this, do I have to keep reminding you, is *Yom Kippur*. There's a *Vidu'i* in the *Amidah*, and now there's a *Vidu'i* in the *Selichot* as well – what use an asking for forgiveness without a formal confession of the sins we're asking forgiveness for?

Did I mention before that there's a solemn position in which a person should stand to recite the confession? Head and body slightly bowed, in what the Rabbis call "submissive contrition". Not leaning for support on anything, not even the seat in front of you, but still standing, still not prostrate. This is Jewish submission, after all, not Islamic.

The same paragraph begins the confession on this occasion as previously – "*Eloheynu tavo lephanecha*" though now "*ana* – please" is added, to give weight to the prayer. Once again the "*Ashamnu*", the right fist beating the left side of the chest on each admission; once again "*Sarnu*". But then this *Vidu'i* begins to differ from previous confessions, and again the difference lies in the deepening. Until now we've only admitted our sins; now we admit that it's our sins that have prevented us from being saved. Sin, in other words, isn't an event *per se*, committed, then rendered up to oblivion. Human actions for good or bad take place in time, and are burdened down with repercussions. This is weighty indeed.

But weightiness is, sadly, next to ponderousness. Where the first paragraph makes its profound point, and then moves on, the second paragraph indulges in what it takes for philosophising, but is only a lengthy exercise in passing platitudes. "What are we? What is our life? Are not all the heroes nothing before You?" Sentence upon sentence of it. "The pre-eminence of man over beast is non-existent for all is vanity. Surely everything has been revealed?" Perhaps it's just the rhetorical style that grates on me, but I feel like I'm listening to some armchair truth-seeker on "Thought For The Day", with nothing to tell me about Life, God or the Universe, but that peculiarly pious and sanctimoniously unctuous voice in which the vacuous always splutter their banal truisms. Ecclesiastes, besides, has already written this poem, and written it better.

It's mercifully brief however. After it, "*Atah meyvin*", though this isn't recited in every synagogue; a *piyyut* of double alphabetical acrostics, written by Rabbi Eliyahu ha-Zaken, the brother-in-law of Chai Ga'on, who led the Pumbedita Academy at the end of the 9th century, when it transferred to that epicentre of human civilisation, the Baghdad of Caliph Haroun al-

Rashid.

Follows "*Shimcha me-olam*", a brief introductory prayer to what is now the main pillar of confession. As before, "*Atah yodeyah*", then "*Al-chet*" with its refrain after the 10th and 16th verses and at the end; "*Ve-al chata'im*", another added prayer – "*Ve-atah rachum*", and then a series of scriptural prayers specific to this *Vidu'i*, treating of the theme of purity through several Biblical figures. David...Micah...Daniel...Ezra.

This done, we call again on God not to forsake us – "*Al ta'azveynu*" as before, but a variant text from the one we recited just a handful of pages earlier; and concluding with "*Amcha*".

Once more the text becomes open to variations and options. Two *piyyut* are available here, for those who wish to utter them. The first is "*Adonay menat chelki*", a sequence of chiasmic double-stiches, each beginning "*Adonay hu*" and declaring an attribute of God. The second is "*Meyuchad*", which is essentially a draft version of the "*Aneynu*" prayer that we will be reciting almost immediately afterwards.

Next "*El rachum shemecha*", yet another alphabetic acrostic, though when the alphabetical acrostic runs out at *tav* the verses keep on piling up, by arbitrary initial letter; this one calling on God to act, and cataloguing all the reasons why He should do so: for the sake of Your truth, Your law, Your kindness, Your Oneness, and so forth. Legal language. The barrister trumping the prelate – but both inhabiting the same rabbinical gown.

And then, as I mentioned only a line or two back, the glorious "*Aneynu*". Yet again an alphabetic acrostic, but this one beaten like a mantra on the percussion of the human soul.
"*Aneynu adonay aneynu* – answer us, Lord, answer us" Every phrase begins and ends "*aneynu*", and often there's only a single word, at most a very short phrase, in between. "*Aneynu eloheynu aneynu. Aneynu avinu aneynu. Aneynu boreynu aneynu. Aneynu go'aleynu aneynu...*" and on, through almost thirty of these phrases, pounding, pounding, *aneynu, aneynu*, like a son beating at his father's door, stay with me and comfort me it's dark tonight, calling and calling until, father, guide me through the chasm of another smoky night, "*aneynu dayan almanot aneynu, aneynu, aneynu*", answer, father, answer, until, eventually, at last, He surely must.

But still He doesn't. And so we try a slightly varied tack. Instead of the mantraic "*Aneynu*", a more gentle call, practically obsequious.
"He who answered Our father Abraham on Mount Moriah, may He

78

answer us – *hu ya'aneynu*."

One has to keep on trying.

"He who answered his son Isaac when he was bound on the altar – may He answer us."

Calling, not directly to the Father, but indirectly, calling to history, calling to sacred memory, calling to past action, as though it's this action that will be repeated, now, and by pure chance include us as well, conferring atonement by contagion of good-will.

"He who answered Jacob at Bethel, Joseph in prison, Joshua at Gilgal, Hezekiah in his illness…" lists of these names…"Daniel in the lion's den, Ezra in exile…" all of them so familiar, so known, that surely, surely, because the grammar is ambiguous, "*hu ya'aneynu*", may He answer us, "*hu ya'aneynu*", He *will* answer us.

It isn't working though. Not yet. Twenty-five hours we were told, and it's not yet three. Why do we expect him to answer so soon? Have we become impatient, like Job? But we go on asking anyway.

And by yet a third method now. If appealing to history doesn't work, appeal to His good nature. And if Hebrew doesn't work, try Aramaic.

"*Rachamana de'aney la-aniyey* – the merciful one who answers the poor…" ah we know these attributes of mercy well, for we've sung them several times already, "*adonay, adonay, el rachum ve chanun, rachamana recham alan* – merciful one have mercy upon us", now, urgently, and soon.

But not that soon. Another twenty-two hours from now.

Yet the pace is building, the intensity, the desert heat, the flies and the mosquitoes, the sexual passion, the sweat, the burden of guilt, the whole gamut of human emotion, building, building. And at its climax – always, always: this:

"*Avinu malkey-ey-ey-nu. Avinu malkey-ey-ey-nu. Avinu malkeynu. Avinu malkeynu…*"

This is the greatest of all the Hebraic mantras, forty-three verses in all[10], each one starting exactly as I've transliterated it here, sung slowly, lugubriously, one of those melodies that can only be sung with the eyes closed and the torso rocking and the fringes of the heart stroking the stretched jawbone.

---

[10] Or possibly not 43. See page 175.

79

"Avinu malkey-ey-ey-nu. Avinu malkey-ey-ey-nu. Avinu malkeynu. Avinu malkeynu chatanu lephane-e-e-cha..."

It really doesn't matter what the words mean. The Ark is open once again and we're standing, weary already from the hours of prayer and fasting, desperate for rest and water, but denied it, as the Bedouin of Abba Moses were denied it as they crossed the outer wilderness in search of the atonement of Law and land. Our Father, Our King, do all these things for us that we are listing, be all these things that we are naming, hear all these sins we are confessing, but mostly, listen to our *kavanah*, our undiminished and untamed intensity. We who do not need to flagellate ourselves with whips, as the fanatics do, because we are whipping ourselves with song, and the heart winces more potently than flesh. *"Avinu malkeynu eyn lanu melech eleh atah."*

"Avinu malkey-ey-ey-nu. Avinu malkey-ey-ey-nu. Avinu malkeynu. Avinu malkeynu..."

But it's still too early. Not yet the full, sung version; not yet all of the three-and-forty verses – that can only be sung once, last hymn of all, at the very close of the fast day, in the final moments before sunset. For now, merely, a hasty cantation, the first half-dozen lines and then, in a rapid undertone, the verses merely uttered, so fast the intensity is muffled, stifled, brought to the point of ending. But it doesn't end. There's still the last verse of all, and that we may sing, even now, at *Ma'ariv* of the eve before.

"Oseh imanu tsedakah ve-chesed ve-hoshi'ey-ey-ey-nu."

It's the strangest song in all the world. A song that ends, not on the tonic, not even on the dominant, but on the relative minor of the sub-dominant, so that you feel you must, you simply must, start it again (and in the Reform movement the temptation proved irresistible; there, the closing line is sung, repeatedly, joyfully, again and again, until a tonic is found. But a tonic is a kind of resolution. And surely resolution here is far too early? If the resolution is even ours to make.)

✡

After *"Avinu malkeynu"*, recite Psalm 24, though whether the Ark is closed or left open is a matter of local custom, as is the decision whether to let the *chazan* recite the Psalm, or have it read responsively by *chazan* and congregation. It's really an issue of mood, not orthodoxy: decisions of this sort should be determined by the ambience a community wishes to engender. Try it. You'll find that some *chazanim* make *kletzmer* of it, others read it like a Shakespearean sonnet; some congregations *shockel* and *daven*, others appear to be reciting the words of an oath of allegiance with which they're not terribly familiar. Ambience is as central to *Yom Kippur* as faith.

Why Psalm 24? Because it awards prosperity to the sincere.

Why is this also ironical? Because Psalm 24 is the Psalm which the Rabbis recommend (*Shabbos* 119a), for those who wish to say Grace before a meal.

✡

Full *Kaddish*

Because we've reached the end of a section of prayer, so there must be a securing *Kaddish* , full because we have also reached the end of the whole service, and because the mourners' *Kaddish* , which is due next, can't stand alone. A full *Kaddish* , which also requires a Psalm before it, and then an intervening prayer, as two forms of the *Kaddish* can't stand immediately back-to-back.

So, after the full *Kaddish* , the *Aleynu* (see "A Myrtle Among Reeds"), with the optional addendum of "*Al tira* – do not fear sudden terror, or the holocaust of the wicked when it comes. Plan a conspiracy and it will be annulled, speak your piece and it will not stand, for God is with us. Even till your old age, I remain unchanged, and even till your ripe old age, I shall endure. I created you and I shall bear you. I shall endure to rescue you."

Powerful words, which I put into the mouth of my war hero Bernhard Aaronsohn more than twenty years ago in "The Flaming Sword" – though I seem to recall translating it slightly differently. Words combined from Proverbs 3:25, Isaiah 8:10 and 46:4.

Then the Mourners' *Kaddish* , which is properly called the Orphans' *Kaddish - Kaddish Yatom -* and because a *Kaddish* requires a text afterwards, Psalm 27, which is recited every morning and every evening from the new moon of the month of *Elul* – the month preceding *Rosh ha-Shana* and *Yom Kippur* – until the festival of *Shemini Atseret*, which falls on the 8th day of *Sukkot* (Tabernacles), just thirteen days after *Yom Kippur*. The recitation is required by a commentary of the *Talmudic* Rabbis, which identifies the language of the Psalm with the rigours of the festival: "the Lord is my light" being the illumination of our sins on *Rosh ha-Shana*, "the Lord is my salvation" being our atonement on *Yom Kippur*. Of the same spurious order, I recall once finding a work of dubious literary criticism in my university library, which demonstrated from textual evidence that Macduff, Angus, Lennox and the King of England were actually the four riders of the apocalypse, Macbeth the Lord of the Underworld, and the whole of Shakespeare's play an allegorical representation of the Book of the Revelation of St John the Divine.

The Mourners' *Kaddish* , as is customary, is recited for a second time, at which point the service may end, though in most congregations the singing – on this occasion to a measured tune – of "*Adon olam*" is customary, and if *Yom Kippur* falls on a Friday, of "*Yigdal*" as well.

✡

It's customary in many communities to conclude the two and a half hours of *Kol Nidre* and *Ma'ariv* with a recitation of the first four Psalms – though I'm not convinced that this is entirely appropriate – and then whichever fragment of the "Song of Unity" belongs to the day of the week on which the fast falls that year.

The "Song of Unity", or "*Shir ha-Yichud*", was probably written by Shmuel ben Kalonymos, somewhere between 1120 and 1175, in Speyer in Germany, where his family had lived since emigrating there from southern Italy in the 9th century. One of Jewry's most distinguished mediaeval families – almost a dynasty – they provided a surfeit of rabbis, poets, philosophers and scientists, including their most significant, from the Provençal branch of the family, Kalonymos ben Kalonymos, also known as Ben Me'ir ha-Nasi, who translated numerous scientific works from Arabic into Hebrew and Latin in the early 14th century, and who provided me with a loose source for Izak fils l'Eveque in my novel "The Persian Fire".

Rabbi Shmuel – he of the "Song of Unity" – was known as "*ha-Chasid*" because of his attachment to the ethics of the Cabbala, and it was from his "Song of Unity" that the "*Chasidei Ashkenaz*", the "Pious Germans" found their inspiration and endurance through the ordeals and persecutions of the Crusades. The leader of the "*Chasidei Ashkenaz*" was Shmuel's own son Yehudah.

The "Song of Glory" or "*Shir ha-Kavod*" follows, but not in all communities. Like the father, so the son, for this is Rabbi Yehudah ben Shmuel's poem, compiled from personal meditations and fragments of scripture (Psalm 113:2; 1 Chronicles 16:36; 29:10-11; Daniel 2:20; Nehemiah 9:5 et al). Known popularly by its opening phrase as "*Anim zemirot*", it's always recited with the Ark open, and with *chazan* and congregation alternating verses. Most communities end their *Sabbath* morning services each week with younger members of the community, not yet of *Bar Mitzvah* age, leading the singing of "*Anim Zemirot*".

✡

And what now? The prayers are done, and it's only two and a half hours past sunset, another eight, nine hours perhaps, another twelve in some parts of the world, before the sun comes up again and we may commence *Shacharit*, the morning prayers. What do we do now? We can't go for a meal to pass the time, nor read a book, watch television, make love, relax in a warm bath; and we're Jews, who suffer quickly from withdrawal symptoms when we're deprived of our addiction to perpetual mental stimulation. Sleep – yes, a slow walk home, and bed; that's one option. A night of study in the Rabbi's house – another option. By whatever means, we wait, wrapped in our hunger like a prayer shawl, for the dawn.

✡

Chapter Four: And It Was Morning

Shacharit

Even for the very orthodox, who keep all the many fast days that occur throughout the Jewish year, waking up on the morning of *Yom Kippur* is different from waking up on any other morning – assuming, that is, that one is waking up, for many will have chosen to stay awake all night, studying the laws of *Yom Kippur*, the "*Mishnayot Yoma*", reading and discussing other sacred texts.

The normal morning practices apply (see "A Myrtle Among Reeds"), from "*Modeh ani*" upon awakening, through "*Reyshit chachma*" and the donning of the *tsitsit*, but the manner of performing the rituals and saying the blessings is necessarily altered. With "*Reyshit chachma*", for example, there's a strict limit as to how much water may be poured over the hands on *Yom Kippur*, because technically there's a prohibition against washing.

So we arrive at *shul*, and don the *tallit*, and if we didn't sing the "Song of Unity" at *Ma'ariv*, we sing it now (each day has its own fragment, but remember, the Jewish day begins at night, the day of *Yom Kippur* began last night), and after it the fragment of the "Song of the Day" appropriate to that day of the week (though some congregations wait to sing the Song of the Day before the reading of the Law). "Today is the ...[th] day of the week, on which the Levites in the Holy Temple would recite:

Sunday – Psalm 24
Monday – Psalm 48
Tuesday – Psalm 82
Wednesday – Psalm 94:1 – 95:3
Thursday – Psalm 81
Friday – Psalm 93
Shabbat – Psalm 92

If a mourner is present, the Mourners' *Kaddish* is recited after the "Song of the Day", and Psalm 27 completes it, with the option of appending either "*Adon olam*" or "*Yigdal*", or indeed both, though it's rarely done.

✡

All of this is terribly preliminary, as though those present need to be kept occupied while the remainder of the congregation stagger in, hungry and tired, to start the day itself. Where *Shacharit* really begins is now, with the Morning Blessings, *"Al netilat yadayim"* for those who may have forgotten the washing of the hands at home, *"Ropheh kol bassar"*, which acknowledges what Swift so neatly satirised in his ode to Celia, the fact that Almighty God created Man with a heart, a soul, a mind – but also a bowel. *"Ha-melamed Torah"* is weightier – it's forbidden to study or recite any passage of the *Torah* until this blessing has been made, and with it *"noten ha-Torah"*. Follows the Priestly Blessing, the beautiful *"Yevarechecha"* with which Christian readers will no doubt be familiar:

> "May the Lord Bless you and keep you
> May He turn His face to shine on you and be gracious unto you
> May He reveal Himself to you and bring you peace."

taken from Numbers 6:24-26 and reminding us again that Elohim was once a sun-god, consort to the moon-goddess Yah. And then the two *"Elu devarim"*, the first a listing, from *Mishan Pe'ah* 1:1 of those five "precepts that have no fixed measure", namely the leaving of a corner of a field for gleaning by the poor, the offering of the first fruits of the harvest, pilgrimage to Jerusalem, acts of kindness towards others, and finally, pertinently here, the study of *Torah*; the second from *Shabbos* 127a, an inventory of those precepts whose fruits are enjoyable in this world and for which reward is also given in the world to come, namely: respect for one's parents, acts of kindness towards others, early attendance morning and evening at a house of study, provision of hospitality to guests, visiting the sick, providing a dowry for a bride, escorting the dead to their burial place, absorption in the act of prayer, arbitration between two parties who are in strife; and the study of *Torah*, it is re-emphasised, is equivalent to them all.

The last of these preliminary blessings is *"Elohay neshama"*, a thanksgiving for the creation of the individual soul, and the surprising statement of faith in the resurrection of souls – surprising, because it's theologically controversial to say the least.

Those blessings are recited by each member of the congregation individually. The next set of blessings is led by the *chazan*, with the congregation merely adding its *amen* – all, that is, save the women's blessing, which the women recite aloud and where the men respond *amen*. These are the Fourteen Blessings, discussed in "A Myrtle Among Reeds", as are those that follow: *"ha-ma'avir"* and *"yehi ratson"*, the *Akeda* service with its partial recitation of the *Shema* and the account of the laver or morning offerings. This lengthy passage is concluded with the recitation of the Rabbi's *Kaddish*, Psalm 30, which serves as an introductory Psalm to *"Pesukei d'Zimrah"*, and a second recitation of the Mourners' *Kaddish*, bringing all the preliminaries for *Yom Kippur* to a conclusion.

✡

"*Pesukei d'Zimrah*" is explained in full in "A Myrtle Among Reeds". Here, the opening passages are regular, "*Baruch she-amar*" and "*Hodu l'adonay*", all the way to "*Ki gamal alay*". At this point there would normally be "*Mizmor le-todah*" but this is never recited on *Yom Kippur*, *Pesach* or the intermediate days of festivals. In its place we follow the *Shabbat* pattern for "*Pesukei d'Zimrah*", reciting Psalm 19, "*La-menatseyach*", Psalm 34 "*Le-David*", Psalm 90 "*Tephillah le-Moshe*", Psalm 91 "*Yoshev be-seter elyon*", and Psalm 135 "*Halleluyah*", all of these led by the *chazan* while the congregation remains seated. For Psalm 136, "*Hodu l'adonay ki tov*" the congregation now stands, reciting the refrain "*Ki le'olam chasdo*" at the end of every stich.

Psalm 33, "*Ranenu*" comes next, then Psalm 92, "*Mizmor shir*", of which the first two verses are sung, the rest recited. Psalm 93, "*Adonay malach*", completes this section of Psalms, with a closing prayer of special intensity, "*Yehi chevod*", which, alongside *Ashrey*, recited next, brings us back into cohesion with the daily "*Pesukei d'Zimrah*", which is always followed by the sequence of closing Psalms, 146 through 150, the Psalms which Maimonides identified as being the "real" "*Pesukei d'Zimrah*".

"*Baruch adonay le'olam*" calls us to our feet once more, and we remain standing through the ensuing readings: "*Va-yevarech David*" from 1 Chronicles 29:10-13, "*Atah hu*" from Nehemiah 9:6-11, the magnificent song of Moses at the Red Sea, from Exodus 14:30-15:19, and the compendium of scriptural passages which make up "*Nishmat*".

The ending of "*Nishmat*" on *Yom Kippur* is slightly different from that of regular *Shabbat* recitals of the prayer, and different again from that of the pilgrim festivals. Normally, on the three festivals, the *chazan* who will lead the main prayers for *Shacharit* takes over from the *chazan* who has led up until now, after "*Shem kodsho*" at the start of "*Ha-el be-ta'atsumot*"; on *Shabbat* the change is two lines later, at the start of "*Shochen ad*"; but on *Yom Kippur* the change comes midway between these two, the second *chazan* taking over after "*Be-norotecha*" where the key-word "*Ha-Melech* – the King" is first mentioned. The significance is entirely in the words. "*Ha-el be-ta'atsumot*" suggests the omnipotence of God, and the three pilgrim festivals, Passover, *Shavu'ot* and *Sukkot*, all involve journeying to the Temple in Jerusalem, to pay tribute with the first fruits of the seasonal harvest to the deity; in addition, all three festivals were inaugurated in the passage from Egypt to Mount Sinai, when God showed his omnipotence most clearly. "*Shochen ad*", by contrast, means "He who abides forever", which eternity is expressed in the Creation, whose culminating pinnacle is the *Shabbat*.

"*Ha-Melech*" is simply "the King", and it's the jurisdiction of the king who lives and dies, who sits in judgement, who punishes, who receives clemency. "*Ha-Melech*", then, for *Yom Kippur*.

One other small change. Through the rest of the year He is described as "*Ha-Melech ha-yoshev al-kiseh ram ve-nisa* – the King who is seated on His high and exalted throne", but now the definite article is dropped, so that "*yoshev*" switches from being a mere participle to a fully-fledged verb: this is not a figurative description of God's role, but an active description of His state; not the frieze or tableau, but the physical act of sitting on the throne of judgement. He is there *even now*.

Even as he approaches the *amud*, the *chazan* begins chanting the wordless melody which sets the ambience for "*Ha-Melech*", increasing the volume gradually until the opening word is practically howled. I like the description of this given in the *Sepher ha-Chayim* of Reb Shlomo Kluger - the early 19th century Rosh Beit Din of Grodi in Galicia, whose commentaries on the *Shulchan Aruch*, *Orach Chayim* and *Chochmas Shlomo* are almost as famous as his contention that homosexuality is an effect of nature not of nurture - where the howl is given the capacity to drive away accusers from the throne of God. "It is like someone taken captive by bandits," he writes, "who force him to accompany them through the royal city. When the victim comes within earshot of the palace, he screams out 'O King', and the bandits, fearing the King's wrath, flee in panic, leaving him behind, in safety."

The commandment in "*Shochen ad*" is to "sing joyfully before the Lord". And so we do.

> By the mouth of the upright you shall be exalted
> By the words of the righteous you shall be blessed
> By the tongue of the devout you shall be sanctified
> And in the company of the holy you shall be praised.

This is the literal meaning of the text, but it needs retranslating, not because the meaning is obscure in any way, but because the Hebrew text contains a pair of vertical acrostics, placed within the words, which spell out the names of the patriarchal couple Isaac and Rebecca.

> By the **li**ps of the upright – **re**vered you shall be
> By the word**s** of the righteous – **bl**essed shall you be
> In the **la**ng**ua**ge of the devout - **c**onse**cra**te shall you be declared
> And in the **c**ompany of the holy – **h**eralded shall you be

By no means a perfect transculturation, but I've tried to keep the formal pattern, where Isaac is formed vertically from the initial letter of the second word of each line, and Rebecca from the third of either five or six letters in the third word.

In the normal *Shabbat* version, Isaac occurs as here, but the words which form Rebecca are, alas, in an entirely different order, spoiling the anagram.

The song ends with *"u-ve-mak'halot."*

✡

The Fifteen Expressions of Praise

"Yishtabach" is recited standing (see "A Myrtle Among Reeds" for details.) The Ark is then opened and *"Shir ha-ma'a'lot"* recited responsively. At its end the Ark is closed, and half-*Kaddish* sung. We now begin the blessings before the reciting of the *Shema.*

Begin with *"Barechu et adonay ha-mevorach"*, as always, with the congregation responding as always *"Baruch adonay ha-mevorach le-olam va'ed"*. Except when the Ark is opened, as it is now for *"Baruch...amar va-yehi"*, these passages should all be recited seated.

"Selach le-goy kadosh be-yom kadosh, marom ve-kadosh – forgive the holy nation on the holy day, O exalted and Holy One' – recited by the *chazan*, then the congregation. As is:

"Chatanu tsureynu, selach lanu yotsreynu – we have erred, our rock; forgive us, our moulder' – words we've already used this morning. These words give the appellation *"yotsrot"* to all the *piyyut*im appended in this section of the service; *piyyut*im appended during the recital of the Eighteen Benedictions are called *"krovets"*, from the initial letters of *"Kol rinah ve-yisra'el be-ahaley tsadikim* – the sound of rejoicing in the tents of the righteous", the text from Psalm 118:15 which is understood to describe them.

The meditative *piyyut "Az be-Yom Kippur"* which comes next is yet another double alphabetical acrostic – authorship alas unknown. Once again, as with all these lengthy exercises in spiritual reflection, I do not propose to set the text here, nor to paraphrase it into journalese for the purposes of commentary; nor, indeed, to offer commentary. The reader will find the texts in any *Yom Kippur* prayer book and is warmly encouraged to read them there, whether in *shul* on *Yom Kippur*, or at home in the quiet of an evening.

Now we must make a distinction. The text bifurcates here. When *Yom*

Kippur falls on a *Shabbat*, or when it falls on a weekday, we go by very different routes to arrive at the same point: the reciting of the *Shema*. On weekdays the starting-point is *"Ha-me'ir"*; on *Shabbat* we follow *"Ha-kol yoducha"*, *"El adon"*, and *"La-el asher Shabbat"*, which is more or less the pattern for daily and *Shabbat* services that do not coincide with *Yom Kippur*. *"El adon"* – guess what – is alphabetically acrostic (though once again there's a *seen* line where there ought to be a *samech*). *"Ha-me'ir"* is not, initially, acrostical, but becomes so from *"El baruch"* in the third verse until *"tamid"* in the penultimate – has someone edited the text, oblivious to the original author's structure?

The forks make a handle at *"Titbarach tsureynu"*. Then the customary procession of *"Et shem ha-el"* before the first recitation of the great angelic chant *"Kadosh kadosh kadosh, adonay tseva'ot, melo kol ha-arets kevodo* – holy holy holy is the Lord God of hosts; the whole world is filled with His glory"*. And then, where usually the *"Kadosh"* is merely chanted, today the Ark is opened for the magnificent full *"Kedushah"* based on the phrase *"Baruch shem kavod malchuto* – blessed is the name of His glorious kingdom"*: words which we recite only silently during the year, but are permitted to recite out loud on *Yom Kippur*.

Yet another alphabetical acrostic – and it's time to give the simple explanation why. When God made the Universe, He did so with the power of the word – the *logos*, in the Greek of St John. "Let there be light – and there was light" – the magical, shamanistic power of language. To transform an idea into speech brings it into existence. To say the word God, for example, or Hope; Love - or Hatred.[11] And how are words formed? By the conglomeration of seemingly arbitrary, even random letters, into the perfect unity and harmony of a meaningful word. To pronounce the letters of the alphabet in order is to make of them another perfectly harmonious form, and to invoke, in the very act of writing, the creative impulse, the dynamic and kinetic force itself, the power implicit in the deity. For a Jew, to write is always more than just to write; it's also to participate in the act of permanent Creation through the power of the Logos. And what exaltation then, to write a paean to the divinity!

The Ark is closed and we recall – depending on which version is your synagogue's custom and practice – how the *Ophanim* and the *Chayot* raise

---

[11] Husserl's school of Phenomenology developed this into the existentialist conviction that consciousness must mean consciousness of something, and that, therefore, by refusing to admit the existence of that phenomenon, it can not exist. This provides the faithful with the final ontological argument: to pronounce the word God brings God into existence, even if God does not actually exist.

themselves towards the *Seraphim*, or how the *Chayot* sing, the *Cherubim* glorify, the *Seraphim* rejoice, the *Erelim* bless...either way, orders and hierarchies of the angels in Heaven, as ineffable and as inexplicable as the Land Surveyor K's attempts to comprehend the roles of Klamm and Barnabas and Schwartzer.

"Baruch kavod adonay mimkomo."

Each of these refrains belongs to the familiar *"Kedushah"*, but here they're taken a phrase at a time, and elaborated with poetry. *"Le-el baruch"* follows, as always, referring back to the previous *"El baruch"*; then the normal daily *"Ahavah rabah"* which leads to the full recitation of the *Shema*, in the normal daily manner, but including the *"Baruch shem kavod malchuto le'olam va-ed"* out loud...linked as always to *"Va'yatsiv"*...kiss the *tsitsit* on *"U-le'olmay olamim"*..."*Al ha-rishonim"*..."*Ezrat"*...and the preparations for the *Shemoneh Esreh* with *"Tehilot le-el elyon"*, *"Adonay yimloch le-olam va'ed"*, and finally, standing, *"Tsur Yisra'el"*. There's nothing to merit commentary on here: this is simply what we do every morning, repeated with only that tiny, angelic alteration, on *Yom Kippur*. Those who attend regularly know what to do; those who only ever attend synagogue on *Yom Kippur* plus weddings, *B'nei Mitzvah* and funerals, should follow the crowd.

✡

Shemoneh Esreh

The Eighteen Benedictions recited now are identical to the *Amidah* described in *Ma'ariv*[12], until the *"Shalom"* prayer. Where in *Ma'ariv* we recited *"Shalom rav"*, at *Shacharit* we recite *"Sim shalom tovah"*. In terms of meaning the two are almost identical; the essential difference is their relationship to the Priestly Blessing, for *"Shalom rav"* may be said at any time, but *"Sim shalom"* alludes directly to that blessing, and so may only be said during a service that will also contain the Priestly Blessing – as *Shacharit* will.

The *Vidu'i* attached to this *Shemoneh Esreh* again repeats that of *Ma'ariv*. However, at *Ma'ariv* the *Shemoneh Esreh* was recited only once, but at *Shacharit* it's recited twice, the first time by the individual privately – which is to say, in a just-audible undertone – the second time congregationally, led by the *chazan*. Only the *chazan*'s repetition is far longer, far more elaborate, than the individual recitation.

---

[12] See page 13.

The Ark is opened for the opening paragraph of *Avot*, which is here the customary text; it's followed by *"Mi-sod"*, which is an introductory statement by Rabbi Elazar ha-Kalir to his liturgical *piyyut* *"Emeycha"*. (Cabbalists have come to believe that Elazar was the son of the great Rabbi Shimon bar Yochai, the favourite pupil of Rabbi Akiva, the spiritual leader of the Bar Kochba Revolt against Rome in 135 CE. When the rebellion against Rome ended in tragedy, and Akiva with three of his fellow sages was martyred by the Romans, Shimon and his son Elazar took refuge in a cave, where they remained for thirteen years, studying the hidden, or secret, *Torah*, the *"Torat ha-Sod"*, which later became known as Cabbala. Unfortunately this has no historic base. When Moses de Léon wrote the Zohar, the definitive text of mediaeval mysticism, he attributed it retrospectively to Shimon, for reasons obvious to anyone who has just read this account; and at some point along the way Eliezer, Shimon's actual son, became confused with Elazar, who was an Italian Jew of the late 6th century CE. Most of the *piyyutim* in this *Shemoneh Esreh* and that of *Musaph* come from the stylus of Elazar ha-Kalir; Cabbalistic legend holds that many were written while he was in hiding with his "father" in the cave.)

"Emeycha" is another alphabetical acrostic, after which the Ark is closed; it's followed by *"Imatsta"*, again an alphabetical acrostic, and ends with the *"Zachreynu"* and the *"Melech ozer"*, completing *Avot*, the first blessing.

Gevurot, the 2nd of the eighteen benedictions, starts with the *"Atah gibor"* of daily practice. Its interjectory *piyyut* is *"Ta'avat"*, again *aleph*-acrostical; after which the brief phrase *"Ad yom moto"* leads into *"Enosh mah yizkeh"*; *"Ad yom moto"* is repeated, and *"Mi kamocha"* returns us to familiar territory. But we're not yet done with *Gevurot*. A further *piyyut*, *"Ichadeta yom zeh"*, *aleph*-acrostical again, is followed by *"Yimloch adonay"*, and then the Ark is opened for the sentence by sentence responsive recitation of *Atah hu eloheynu"*, which is yet again *aleph*-acrostical. The phrase *"Chay ve-kayam nora u-marom ve-kadosh"* brings the curtains of the Ark together as the doors close.

Supplication is now the mood. *"Ana selach na* – we beg you, forgive now" deepens and extends it. The form of the *piyyut* is immensely intricate. Each verse is written as a double stich followed by a congregational response, the first two stiches always four words long, the response line either three or four. The initial letters of both the first and second stiches, in parallel to each other, spell out acrostically the phrase *"Meshullam ben-Rabbi Kalonymos chazak* – may Meshullam the son of Rabbi Kalonymos be strong", which reveals the authorship of the poem but also echoes the prayer recited at the completion of the reading of any of the Five Books of Moses, *"Chazak*

chazak ve-nitchazek"; the initial letters of the response line are simply what we're now beginning to think of as the dull and standard alphabetical acrostic. Before and after the verses containing the name Kalonymos and the word "*chazak*" the "*Ana selach na*" is repeated.

"*Melech shochen ad*" follows, again containing Meshullam's name acrostically, as does "*Melecha ma'azin*", which follows. "*Eder*" is a double alphabetical acrostic, but carries no author indication. "*Ana elohim chayim*" is still more complex. Written in quatrains, the first line runs an alphabetical acrostic from *aleph* to *tav*, the second reverses this, running its acrostic backwards through the alphabet from *tav* to *aleph*. The third line is non-acrostical. The fourth is a refrain, "*Ve-atah ke-rachum selach lanu*". There is little argument that the *payyatanim*, especially those of the European renaissance though it's mostly true of the Babylonians and Palestinians of the Roman era, held the technicalities of the writing in as high a regard as they did the spiritual intent. A *payyatan* is always a poet as well as a liturgist.

"*Ha-yom yikatev*" leads to "*Ayumah ba-har*", verse triplets in which each stich reveals the alphabetical acrostic, until the immensely rich last verse. Here both the first two letters of each stich continue the alphabetical acrostic in the first two lines; and in the last line, using the same double-pattern, give us the name Yoseph, which is generally believed to be Yoseph ben Isaac ibn Avitur, a Spanish-born Talmudic scholar of the 10th and 11th century, who was forced to leave his home in Cordoba; he travelled to Egypt, Babylon and Israel, leaving behind more than three hundred *piyyutim*, plus commentaries and responsa.

Most references to ibn Avitur call him ibn-Shatanash, a nickname which he ascribed to his great-grandfather, "who wielded great power in Spain, even the power of life and death" – "*shot-enosh*" in Hebrew meaning "the scourge of man". But in fact neither ibn Avitur, nor ben Avitur, nor even ibn Avisur, all of which are variants I've seen, are correct. He signed himself quite simply Yoseph ben Isaac he-Sephardi, and sometimes more simply still Meridi, after his birthplace Merida. Yoseph was head of the Jewish community in Cordoba until the community split in two rival camps, both sycophanting for the support of Caliph al-Hakim II; Yoseph lost and was forced to flee; until his supporters overthrew Chanoch ben Moshe and invited Yoseph back. Yoseph declined the invitation, stating, somewhat surprisingly, that "from Spain to Babylonia there is no scholar so worthy as Rabbi Chanoch" and insisting that his vanquisher resume his rightful role. In Babylonia Chai Ga'on refused to meet him, although in Palestine Shmuel ha-Cohen, and in Egypt Shemariah ben Elkanan, the respective heads of those communities, welcomed and befriended him; Shemariah even went so far as to defend Yoseph publicly against his detractors. He died in

Damascus, but the date of his death isn't recorded.

"*Ha-yom yikatev*" is now repeated, with "*u-ve-chen*".

The next *piyyut* is *Ach atim*" again *aleph*-acrostical, with the line-by-line refrain "*Ki atah rachum le-chol po'al*".

The Ark is opened for "*Imru l'elohim*". This is composed in a most unusual form. The opening line is the eponym, followed by a quatrain whose initial letter is an alphabetical acrostic, and a fifth line which leads by way of an elongated hyphen – almost unprecedented in Hebrew – to an epithetical conclusion. "*Imru*" is itself an acronym: it stands for "*El melech rachum ve-chanun* - the king, merciful and gracious', which makes it self-referential to the Thirteen Attributes ascribed on *Yom Kippur*; and the final four stiches of the poem contain an initial-letter acrostic on the name Meshullam, leading us once again to that same author. However, this isn't the whole richness of Meshullam's poetic layerings, for in building the initial letter acrostic of each set of stiches he hasn't simply found any word that met his need, but has built, literally stich by stich, a tapestry (the pun is awful, but what other term would do?) of Biblical references – more than eighty of them in total through the poem (eat your heart out, T.S. Eliot!), mostly from the Psalms and Prophets and *Torah*.

Just to make matters more complex, the poem is recited responsively, the congregation leading and the *chazan* giving the reiteration, and although the eponym is placed at the start of each stanza, the opening "*Imru l'elohim*" is silent, allowing the phrase to come at the end of each stanza, giving a formal "*halleluyah*", or its equivalent, as continual peroration – not Meshullam's intention, but a rather neat trick.

"*U've-chen*" is once again repeated, but with variations on the words this time, and the Ark is left open, so that "*Ma'aseh eloheynu*" may follow without pause. "*Ma'aseh*" like "*Imru*" is treated as an acronym: "*Melech elyon shar ha-olam*", at least according to the *Machzor Kol Bo*, a late 15th or early 16th century compendium of Jewish ritual and civil laws, whose author is unknown, but which usually knows about these esoteric mysticisms. In form "*Ma'aseh*" parallels "*Imru*", the eponym repeated with each stanza, supported by a quatrain containing the alphabetical acrostic and a concluding fifth stich, leading through an elongated hyphen to an epithetical peroration. The acrostic runs out, however, at the end of the fifth stanza, the twentieth line – two letters short of a full acrostic (might that phrase, I wonder, enter the language as an idiom?). The Ark is closed, the final stanza changes "*Ma'aseh eloheynu* – the work of God" to "*Ma'aseh*

93

enosh – the work of Man", reverses the letter order of the acrostic, and repeats the letters *kuph* and *reysh*, so that form and content balance each other, just as Samuel Beckett always said they should.

The Ark is reopened for the three lines *"Aval ma'aseh eloheynu"* which complete the poem, and complete the acrostic too, giving the *sheen* and *tav* at last.

The Ark is re-closed, another version of *"U-ve chen"* leads to the next *piyyut*, *"Asher omets tehilatecha"*, alphabetically acrostical of course, as are all of the next six.

"Al Yisra'el emunato" extends the motif of *"u-ve chen"*, on this occasion opening with *"U-ve chen tenu oz le'elohim* – and so, attribute might to God", and continuing with a phrase that becomes a mantra through the remainder of the poem: *"Al Yisra'el* – upon Israel'. Twenty-two phrases all open with those same two words, and are completed by a single word, acrostically from *aleph* to *tav*, denoting the "majesty", "purity", and "pleasantness" that God bestows, His kingdom and His presence. The opening descriptor, *"ga'avato"* precedes the acrostic and alludes to Psalm 68:35, "You are awesome, God, in your sanctuaries. The God of Israel gives strength and power to his people. Praise be to God!"

"Eyn kamocha be-adirey" is not recited in all synagogues. Some recite *"Aphsi eretz"* in its place, others skip straight to *"U-ve chen ne'adercha"*. Those who do recite it will recognise immediately the two phrases whose line-by-line repetition provide its structure: *"Eyn Kamaocha…ve-eyn ke-ma'asecha"* being the song that accompanies the regular opening of the Ark for taking out the scrolls and reading from the Law. On this occasion the two phrases are extended to provide epithets and sobriquets for God, the first half of each stich placing God in the heavens above, the second in the depths below, to convey His universality in physical space.

The Ark is opened for *"Ha-aderet"* which completes the intention of *"Eyn kamocha"* by describing the universality of God's attributes in time. What was probably the original text of *"Ha-aderet"* is found in the *"Heichalot"* (*Heichalot Rabbati* 26), a collection of mystical writings from the early Cabbala, which focus in an almost Dantesque manner on how to achieve heavenly ascent through the *heichalot* (heavenly palaces) and what to expect there; or else teach men how to draw down angelic spirits in order to interact with them and gain their help. Alongside *Heichalot Rabbati* there are also *Heichalot Zutarti*, and a 6th-century version of the apocryphal Book of Enoch, upon which the Mormon faith is founded; as well as hundreds of small documents, many little more than fragments.

The Ark is then closed again for *"Na'amirach"*, though here too many congregations choose to skip. As with every *piyyut* at this phase of prayer, a variant of *"U-ve chen"* prologues the poem, where the acrostic is placed at the second letter of every word, though not as was done just now in *"Ha-aderet"*, where each acrosticated word began with the definite article.

Having set out once more the attributes of God, and what He can do for us, it's now of ourselves that we speak, declaring what we intend to do for Him, praising Him with reverence, blessing Him with insight, and on through the full alphabet of good intentions that conclude with yet another version of *"U-ve chen"*, on this occasion sourced in Psalm 99:5.

Like *"Eyn kamocha"* a moment ago, *"Romemu"* alludes to the taking out of the *Torah* scrolls for reading, and in so doing raises the emotional intensity of prayer in a manner that's really rather cheap and tricksy, the kind of device employed by Hollywood to have us weeping in our seats: the sentimentality of familiarity. *"Romemu"* runs its acrostics through a split stich that is in fact a mediaeval version of the psalmic echo-line: initial letter of the second word of the first half of the line, initial letter of the third word of the second half of the line.

The phrases *"Le-yoshev"* and *"Zeh el zeh"* follow, each one stated first by the *chazan*, then repeated by the congregation, after which the Ark is again opened for *"Le-vohen levavot"* and closed afterwards. Once again it's the structure of the poetry that fascinates, the imposition of discipline upon the writer, the self-conscious constriction within the prison of form — I can imagine today's *payyatanim* expressing themselves with equal satisfaction, though less spirituality, in the writing of computer programmes or the setting of Sudoku puzzles.

But we must also recognise that this was the mediaeval Jewish world prior to Dante. That is significant. It was a Jewish *payyatan*, Immanuel of Rome, who taught Dante the sonnet, and whose own poetic forms led Dante to the complexity of *terza rima*. Within the elaborate intricacies of these *piyyut*, we can detect one of the first flowerings of the European Renaissance.

Another version of *"U-ve-chen"* completes this section and leads into the *Kedushah*. The standard *Yom Kippur Kedushah* is perfectly acceptable, though some communities prefer the extended version which involves four *piyyutim* composed by that same Rabbi Elazar ha-Kalir whom we met earlier, introduced by the responsive *"Kakatuv"*: *"El be-rov etsut"*, *"Tamid"*, *"Eleycha ve-adeycha"* and *"Eleycha teluyot"*

Whichever version you may have followed, the service continues with a form of the *Kedushah* that is fundamentally a *Musaph Kedushah*. Based on the *Pirkei d'*Rabbi Eliezer, in which Eliezer narrates the angelic praises, it includes the opening line of the *Shema* and the angelic additional line, again following the custom (*Chullin* 91b) that on *Yom Kippur* we are on a par with the angels and so should pray as they pray. In the *Musaph* of *Shabbat*, where the *Shema* is also added but without the angelic lines, we are permitted to combine our tributes to God with those of the angels, but not to echo them as equals.[13]

The construction is thus "*Na'aritsecha*", "*Le-dor va-dor*", "*Chamol*", "*Be-eyn melits*", "*Od yizkor lanu*", "*U-ve-chen yitkadesh*" and finally "*Toosgav*". These are followed by three paragraphs, each beginning "*U-ve-chen*", and then the verses "*Ve-timloch*" and "*Kadosh*", before we begin the section known as "Holiness of the Day": "*Atah bechartanu*", "*Va-titen*", "*Eloheynu*", "*Zechor rachamecha*" and "*Zechor lanu*", which include references to Isaiah 5:16, Psalms 25:6, 79:8, 74:2, 137:7 and 102:14, Exodus 32:13 and Deuteronomy 9:27, as well as allusions to Nehemiah 9:31 and Psalm 106:4. The verse preceding "*Zechor lanu*" - "*Al na tashet*" - refers to Numbers 12:11, and "*Zechor lanu*" itself is laced with scriptural allusions, particularly from Deuteronomy and Isaiah.

The Ark is opened for "*Shema koleynu*", yet another compendium of scriptural references, on this occasion entirely out-takes from the Psalms; and closed again immediately afterwards.

Two verses, both commencing with the word "*Eloheynu*", prepare the next recital of "*Ki anu amecha*" and a closing verse, "*Anu azey panim*"; and then, once more, the *Vidu'i*: "*Eloheynu...anu*", "*Ashamnu*", "*Sarnu*", "*Hirshanu*", "*Eloheynu*", the optional *Atah meyvin*", "*Shimcha me-olam*" and lastly "*Atah yodeya*". Followed by the full confession of "*Al chet*", "*Ve-David*" and "*Al-tira*".

"*U-mey'ahavatcha*" once again plays with the acrostical forms (only four pairs of letters are used acrostically: *aleph-bet*, *zayin-chet*, *mem-nun* and *sheen-tav*), but goes further than any previous *piyyut* in that it's at once liturgical poetry and a *D'var Torah* – a rabbinic sermon – upon itself. It's not certain who wrote the *piyyut*, but the style and form suggest once again Rabbi Meshullam ben Kalonymos. Here, he alternates the words "day" and "today" line by line, building an *aleph-tav* acrostic in the "day" lines and a *tav-aleph* acrostic in the "today" lines, each pair separated by a scriptural commentary commencing with the repeated "as it is written", and making

---

[13] Rabbi Eliezer ben Hyrcanus (80-118 C.E.) was a disciple of Rabbi Yochanan ben Zakkai and a teacher of Rabbi Akiva; however the Pirkei is now thought to have been an 8th century attribution rather than an authentic work by Eliezer.

reference to all parts of the *Tanach*.

The verse that follows, *"Ahalelcha"*, appears to be incomplete. This is discernible precisely through the acrostic, which runs smoothly from *aleph* through to *vav*, but then jumps to *kuph* before completing the alphabetic correctly. What happened to the middle verses? Were they never written? Or were they lost? The refrain, *"Mi el kamocha"* is taken from Micah 7:18-19, which is also the text used as *Haphtorah* on *Shabbat Shuvah*, the *Sabbath* of Repentance that falls between *Rosh ha-Shana* and *Yom Kippur*, so it's almost to be expected that some *payyatan* would use the phrase.

"Ta'avur" continues the *chazan*'s repetition of the *Vidu'i*, then *"Eloheynu"*, then the familiar closing to the repetition, first recalling the Temple Service with *"Retseh"* and *"Ve-techezeynah"*, giving final thanksgiving with the *"Modim"*; this latter recited aloud by the *chazan* while, in theory anyway for I've never heard it yet, the congregation recites in an undertone its own variation, the so-called *"Modim d'Rabbanan"* or Thanksgiving of the Rabbis – I say "so-called" because it neither makes reference to the Rabbis nor is recited by them. The explanation is actually quite simple: the text anthologises a number of well-known sayings of the *Talmudic* sages, so the term *"Modim d'Rabbanan"* is really an adjective and not a noun.

A version of *"Avinu Malkeynu"* follows, not the long song that we still eagerly anticipate, but one which leads to the special *Yom Kippur* phrase "U-ketuv le-chayim tovim kol beney Yisra'el – inscribe all the children of Your covenant for a good life'; and then the Priestly Blessing, *"Sim shalom tovah"* with the second *Yom Kippur* phrase *"Be-sepher chayim…u-le-shalom"*; and now the long *"Avinu malkeynu"*, though we're still not permitted to sing it fully, line by line, from start to finish (and on *Shabbat* it may not be sung at all; not even recited). As at any juncture in the act of worship, the Full *Kaddish* is recited to complete the phase.

✡

Removal of the *Torah* from the Ark

Congregations which didn't begin the service with "Song of the Day" should recite it now, following it with Psalm 27, a reflection of the custom in Temple times (*Tamid* 7:4, *Rosh ha-Shana* 31a) that the Levites would sing one Psalm each day, appropriate to the significance of that day, as part of the Temple service – and from that significance, which is in every context cosmological, as from the chronology of the Creation story itself, we are able to discern which of the seven planetary deities ruled the heavens in the days before Judaism became monotheistic. The custom, introduced by Nachmanides (*Ramban*, Exodus 20:8) of naming the days numerically towards *Shabbat* was probably a mediaeval attempt to remove the final vestiges of that polytheism.

For the rest, consequent upon a recitation of the Mourner's *Kaddish*, "*Ayn kamocha*" is not on this occasion sung, but rather "*Atah hareyta*", which joins a phrase from Deuteronomy 4:35 with others from Psalms 86:8, 145:13, 10:16, Exodus 15:18 and Psalm 29:11 to give praise once more to the mighty attributes of God. The familiar "*Av ha-rachamim*" follows, after which the Ark is opened for the *chazan* to take out the *Torah* scroll from which the Law will be read, and a second person to take the second scroll for *Maphtir*. Simultaneously the congregations sings "*ve-yehi bi'nso'a ha-aron*". The two stand, facing the congregation, holding the Scrolls, the two Ark-openers framing them. The Thirteen Attributes of Mercy ("*Adonay, Adonay, El rachum ve-chanun*") are sung – *midrashic* tradition holds that God Himself taught this prayer to Moses, after the incident of the Golden Calf - the meditation "*Ribbon shel olam*" is recited (in some congregations Psalm 121 is inserted first), and the verse "*Va-ani tephilati*" repeated three times. "*Berich shemey*", though it appears in most prayer books, is but rarely spoken. The *chazan* sings the opening line of the *Shema*, which is then repeated by the congregation; slightly raising the scroll, the *chazan* recites "*Echad eloheynu*", the closing phrase on this occasion augmented with the additional epithet "*nora* – awesome" between "*kadosh*" and "*shemo*". The *chazan* then faces the Ark, bows with the scroll, and sings the "*Gadelu*" before turning – to the right please – and carrying the *Torah* to the reading desk by way of the congregation, allowing those who wish to do so to step forward and kiss the hem of the cloak that garbs the scroll, in the ancient manner of honouring a king. Both scrolls are paraded together in this manner, "*Lecha adonay*" being sung all the while, and the accompanying meditations "*Al ha-kol*" and "*Av ha-rachamim*" (not the same "*Av ha-rachamim*" as previously).

Amongst the honours bestowed whenever the Law is read, second after the carrying of the second scroll on festivals, is that of the "*gelilah*", he who will now undress, and later re-clothe the *Torah* scroll. Later he will be formally called, and blessed, but for now he will have been forewarned of his honour by the *gabbai*, and will have stepped forward while the scroll is being paraded. Only the first scroll is undressed at this stage, and as soon as it is done, from a seat behind the *bimah*, it's brought to the *bimah* and set down. Hopefully (never the case in my *shul*) the correct place will have been found before the service, as rolling a *Torah* can be a difficult and time-consuming process: it isn't like finding a page in a book.

In some synagogues there's no distinction, except linguistic, between the *amud* and the *bimah*, the same desk serving for both prayer (the function of the *amud*) and the reading of the law (the function of the *bimah*).

Once the scroll has been set down, the congregation resumes its seat, and the *gabbai* summons a Cohen to the first portion of the Law, using the traditional formula *"Va-ya'azor…"*, followed by the blessing of the *Torah* – *"Baruch she-natan…chayim kulchem ha-yom"*. Traditionally the *"oleh"* (the person called) will touch the parchment with the fringe of his prayer shawl at the point where the reading commences, before reciting his own blessings.

The *chazan* then chants, directly from the *Torah* scroll, while the *oleh* follows the text, but not with his finger – direct human contact isn't permitted – rather with the finger of a silver pointer known as a *yad*. Chanting from the *Torah* is known is Yiddish as *leyning* (different from the chanting of prayer, which is known as *davening*). It's an extremely difficult art, because not only is the Hebrew written without any vowels, but it's also sung to a complex cantillation, for which the score isn't provided. Those amateurs, dilettantes and general incompetents (such as myself) who cannot fulfil this task satisfactorily, may be grudgingly excused for chanting from the *Chumash*, a special version of the text which provides both vowels, punctuation and cantillation.

After the portion is complete, the *oleh* touches with his *tallit* the last word read, and says the closing *barucha;* the next *oleh* is then called, the previous *oleh* blessed. A prayer for others is available at this moment, allowing the *oleh* to offer special solicitations for, say, someone sick, or in advance of a forthcoming birth or marriage; and then the next portion is chanted. Since mediaeval times the custom of including monetary pledges has become common for any person given the honour of an *aliyah*. But a pledge isn't permissible on *Yom Kippur*, for a pledge comes under the category of *Nidre*, and we've annulled all *Nidre*. In place of the normal *"Ba'avur she nadir"* therefore, the formula *"Ba'avur she yiten"* is used *(Beitzah* 36b) – "for he will make a contribution".

Provided there's a Cohen present for the first *aliyah*, the second *oleh* is always a Levite; if there's no Levi, a second Cohen substitutes; the remainder may be chosen at the *gabbai*'s pleasure or where honour is deserved (or a donation to the synagogue roof-repair fund generously offered). On *Shabbat* there are seven portions; on *Yom Kippur* only six. On *Shabbat*, we read the next section from where we left off last week, in a fixed order that starts and ends at *Simchat Torah*, a fortnight after *Yom Kippur*. On *Yom Kippur* itself the most appropriate fragment of *Torah* is chosen, which is Leviticus 16:1-34.

✡

The Reading: Leviticus 16:1-34

This is the text that gives us the concept of the *Azazel*, the scapegoat so fundamental to the ancient sacrificial ceremonies of *Yom Kippur*, though in fact the goat wasn't ritually slaughtered, as was customary with Jewish sacrifice, but merely cast out, sometimes into the desert and sometimes over a cliff; and in all probability the name *Azazel* refers to the many places to which goats were despatched, rather than the goat or the act of sacrifice itself.

Yoma 6:4, a tractate of *Mishnah*, tells us that the Babylonians would pluck the hair of a goat before driving it away; we know from other sources that this happened at the feast of *Akitu*, the New Year, and that the goat was dedicated to Ereshkigal, the goddess of the abyss. The Babylonians and their predecessors the Akkadians both regarded despatching a goat in this manner as a cure for sicknesses of various sorts; in some cases the goat was tied to the patient's bed, in order that the sin responsible for the sickness be transferred contagiously; the goat was then taken into the desert and decapitated or left to die – the early Hebrews, like their middle eastern neighbours, regarded the desert as the habitat of daemons, so that sending the goat into the wilderness wasn't a deportation but a repatriation, and as such understood as the white magic of propitiation.

The same tractate (*Yoma* 4:1-2) describes the process by which the High Priest would draw lots to determine what was "*L'Adonay*" and what was "*L'Azazel*"; if the goat was selected for expulsion a thread of crimson wool was bound around its throat and the animal taken to the gate to wait until the "*Ish Itti*" (c.f. Leviticus 16:21) or designated man, who had to be of priestly status, was ready to take the goat up to the cliff, and push it over, backwards. Height and backwardness ensured that the goat was well dismembered before reaching the sandy bottom. But this only applied to the Jerusalem rituals.

The thread of crimson wool is interesting. Perez' brother Zerach came out of his mother's womb (Genesis 38:30) and had precisely such a thread wrapped round his wrist, to show he was technically the first-born; though how this connects to *Azazel* remains obscure. More pertinently, we know the Hittites fought off the plague by making crowns of coloured wool and binding goats with these, sending the goats into enemy territory so that, again, the sickness be transferred contagiously.

The *D'vei* of Rabbi Yishmael[14] regarded the goat-ritual as an atonement

---

[14] See page 142 and also chapter 7 of "A Myrtle Among Reeds".

for the acts of the fallen angels, specifically Uzza and Aza'el (*Yoma* 67b), whose names, they claimed, had become mixed up. The First Book of Enoch, some fragments of which were discovered at Qumran and form part of the Dead Sea Scrolls, but most of which has survived only in Ethiopian translations, treats *Azazel*, or Aza'el, as one of the leaders of the angels who desired the daughters of men (Genesis 6:1-4), and taught the skills of manufacturing weaponry and ornaments (Genesis 8:1-2). Almost certainly we should read Aza'el as correct and regard any connections with the *Azazel* as merely the consequences of post-Biblical dyslexia.

[1] The Lord spoke to Moses after the death of the two sons of Aaron who died when they drew too close to the presence of the Lord. [2] The Lord said to Moses: Tell your brother Aaron that he is not to come at will into the Shrine behind the curtain, in front of the cover that is upon the ark, lest he die; for I appear in the cloud over the cover. [3] Thus only shall Aaron enter the Shrine: with a bull of the herd for a sin offering and a ram for a burnt offering. — [4] He shall be dressed in a sacral linen tunic, with linen breeches next to his flesh, and be girt with a linen sash, and he shall wear a linen turban. They are sacral vestments; he shall bathe his body in water and then put them on. — [5] And from the Israelite community he shall take two he-goats for a sin offering and a ram for a burnt offering. [6] Aaron is to offer his own bull of sin offering, to make expiation for himself and for his household. [7] Aaron shall take the two he-goats and let them stand before the Lord at the entrance of the Tent of Meeting; [8] and he shall place lots upon the two goats, one marked for the Lord and the other marked for Azazel. [9] Aaron shall bring forward the goat designated by lot for the Lord, which he is to offer as a sin offering; [10] while the goat designated by lot for Azazel shall be left standing alive before the Lord, to make expiation with it and to send it off to the wilderness for Azazel. [11] Aaron shall then offer his bull of sin offering, to make expiation for himself and his household. He shall slaughter his bull of sin offering, [12] and he shall take a panful of glowing coals scooped from the altar before the Lord, and two handfuls of finely ground aromatic incense, and bring this behind the curtain. [13] He shall put the incense on the fire before the Lord, so that the cloud from the incense screens the cover that is over [the Ark of] the Pact, lest he die. [14] He shall take some of the blood of the bull and sprinkle it with his finger over the cover on the east side; and in front of the cover he shall sprinkle some of the blood with his finger seven times. [15] He shall then slaughter the people's goat of sin offering, bring its blood behind the curtain, and do with its blood as he has done with the blood of the bull: he shall sprinkle it over the cover and in front of the cover. [16] Thus he shall purge the Shrine

of the uncleanness and transgression of the Israelites, whatever their sins; and he shall do the same for the Tent of Meeting, which abides with them in the midst of their uncleanness. [17] When he goes in to make expiation in the Shrine, nobody else shall be in the Tent of Meeting until he comes out. When he has made expiation for himself and his household, and for the whole congregation of Israel, [18] he shall go out to the altar that is before the Lord and purge it: he shall take some of the blood of the bull and of the goat and apply it to each of the horns of the altar; [19] and the rest of the blood he shall sprinkle on it with his finger seven times. Thus he shall cleanse it of the uncleanness of the Israelites and consecrate it. [20] When he has finished purging the Shrine, the Tent of Meeting, and the altar, the live goat shall be brought forward. [21] Aaron shall lay both his hands upon the head of the live goat and confess over it all the iniquities and transgressions of the Israelites, whatever their sins, putting them on the head of the goat; and it shall be sent off to the wilderness through a designated man. [22] Thus the goat shall carry on it all their iniquities to an inaccessible region; and the goat shall be set free in the wilderness. [23] And Aaron shall go into the Tent of Meeting, take off the linen vestments that he put on when he entered the Shrine, and leave them there. [24] He shall bathe his body in water in the holy precinct and put on his vestments; then he shall come out and offer his burnt offering and the burnt offering of the people, making expiation for himself and for the people. [25] The fat of the sin offering he shall turn into smoke on the altar. [26] He who set the Azazel-goat free shall wash his clothes and bathe his body in water; after that he may reenter the camp. [27] The bull of sin offering and the goat of sin offering whose blood was brought in to purge the Shrine shall be taken outside the camp; and their hides, flesh, and dung shall be consumed in fire. [28] He who burned them shall wash his clothes and bathe his body in water; after that he may re-enter the camp. [29] And this shall be to you a law for all time: In the seventh month, on the tenth day of the month, you shall practice self-denial; and you shall do no manner of work, neither the citizen nor the alien who resides among you. [30] For on this day atonement shall be made for you to cleanse you of all your sins; you shall be clean before the Lord. [31] It shall be a Sabbath of complete rest for you, and you shall practice self-denial; it is a law for all time. [32] The priest who has been anointed and ordained to serve as priest in place of his father shall make expiation. He shall put on the linen vestments, the sacral vestments. [33] He shall purge the innermost Shrine; he shall purge the Tent of Meeting and the altar; and he shall make expiation for the priests and for all the people of the congregation. [34] This shall be to you a law for all time: to make atonement for the Israelites for all their sins once a year. And Moses did as the Lord had commanded him.

The reading is divided into six portions. When the last is done, the *Torah* scroll is closed and covered, though not yet dressed, and half-*Kaddish* recited. Two *olim* are now called, one to raise the *Torah* scrolls and turn a full circle holding them up, so the congregation may sing "*Ve-zot ha-Torah*"; the second is the *gelilah*, he who will now re-clothe the Scroll. While this is happening a second person chosen for *gelilah* will come forward to undress the second scroll, which is now placed on the *bimah*. An additional *oleh* is called to the reading of this additional fragment of the law, known as "*Maphtir* – additional". On *Shabbat* it's the final verses of the week's portion chanted again; on *Yom Kippur* it's a quite separate fragment of Law, the inauguration of *Yom Kippur* itself, in Numbers 29:7-11.

> [7] On the tenth day of the same seventh month you shall observe a sacred occasion when you shall practice self-denial. You shall do no work. [8] You shall present to the Lord a burnt offering of pleasing odor: one bull of the herd, one ram, seven yearling lambs; see that they are without blemish. [9] The meal offering with them — of choice flour with oil mixed in — shall be: three-tenths of a measure for a bull, two-tenths for the one ram, [10] one-tenth for each of the seven lambs. [11] And there shall be one goat for a sin offering, in addition to the sin offering of expiation and the regular burnt offering with its meal offering, each with its libation.

For those of us engaged upon the act of fasting, this passage is at once torturous and relieving. The smell of roasting meat pervades the text, reminding us of our hunger, tantalising us with rich gravy. But it's only words (and the vast majority of the congregation sadly don't understand the Hebrew anyway); for those who came to celebrate *Yom Kippur* at the Temple, two thousand years ago, the sacrifices were entirely physical.

The process for *Maphtir* is the same as for the other readings. The *oleh* is called, kisses the foot of the parchment with the fringe of his *tallit*, recites his blessings, follows with the *yad*, kisses at the end, recites his second blessing, receives his own blessing (or "*Mi she berach*" as it's called), has the opportunity to offer a special prayer of his own, for a sick member of his family, or a special occasion, or a journey. But instead of now returning to his seat, he waits, for the *oleh* of *Maphtir* is always the *chazan* of *Haphtorah* – the greatest and most demanding of all honours in the synagogue.

But before he can embark on this, the second scroll must be lifted by a second person called to this task – "*hagba'ah*" in Hebrew; again with "*Ve-zot ha-Torah*" sung; after which the second *gelilah* may re-clothe it. Both scrolls are held on the laps of their *hagba'ah olim* while the *Haphtorah* is chanted.

The origin of the tradition of *Haphtorah* is as obscure as many of the prophetic texts included in its annual cycle. Tradition maintains that the practice was introduced in 168 BCE, when the Seleucid king Antiochus IV Epiphanes forbad the reading of the *Torah*; a typical stupidity by an autocratic ruler, who tend to the view that prohibition will lead to extinction, whereas history shows us that prohibition generally leads to secret substitution, and through the clandestine a strengthening of the very conviction which the autocrat sought to destroy. The secret substitution in this case was a passage from elsewhere in the Bible – for it was only the Five Books of Moses that were prohibited, and by careful selection a passage could always be chosen that reflected on the banned text. When it was the autocrat and not the faith that found extinction, the tradition of *Haphtorah* was so embedded it was agreed not to abandon it. The earliest recorded reading of the *Haphtorah* is in 70 CE, in the presence of Rabbi Eliezer ben Hyrcanus.

Unlike the reading of the Law, the *Haphtorah* can only be chanted from the *Chumash*, synagogue copies of which provide the *Haphtorot* alongside the readings from the *Torah*, because there are no scrolls in existence for the latter sections of the *Tanach*. Cantillation, however, is quite different, and while each sentence of *Torah* has a melody attached to it, it's the other way around for *Haphtorah*, where a consistent rhythmic melody is sung unchanging, and the words of each verse must be made to fit.

Before the chanting of the *Haphtorah*, the *chazan* sings a special blessing which is of profound significance. In *Pirkei Avot*, the Ethics of the Fathers, a section of *Mishnah* studied every *Shabbat* afternoon between Passover and *Shavu'ot*, we read that "Moses received the *Torah* at Mount Sinai and handed it down to Joshua. Joshua gave it to the Elders of the Tribes, the Elders to the Prophets, and the Prophets gave it to the Men of the Great Assembly." The Rabbis, then, have superceded the Prophets in spiritual authority. But here we are, listening to the instruction of the Prophets? What status does it have, what possible validity, if authority has been transferred? Do we follow the edicts of deposed kings and defeated Prime Ministers? "Blessed are you, O Lord our God, King of the Universe, who has chosen good Prophets and was pleased with their words, which were uttered with sincerity. Blessed are you, O Lord, who chooses the *Torah*; Moses, his servant; Israel, his nation; and the Prophets of truth and righteousness." Then the words of the Prophets are as authoritative as those of the *Torah*, even when they criticise the words of the *Torah*, even when they disagree implicitly with the teachings of the Rabbis. Authority in Judaism isn't cemented in dogma, but grown in the intensity of engaged debate.

The *Haphtorah* for *Yom Kippur* is taken from Isaiah 57:14-58:14.

[14] And it will be said, "Build up, build up, prepare the way, remove every obstacle out of the way of My people." [15] For thus says the high and exalted One Who lives forever, whose name is Holy, "I dwell on a high and holy place, and also with the contrite and lowly of spirit, in order to revive the spirit of the lowly and to revive the heart of the contrite. [16] "For I will not contend forever, nor will I always be angry; For the spirit would grow faint before Me, and the breath of those whom I have made. [17] "Because of the iniquity of his unjust gain I was angry and struck him; I hid My face and was angry, and he went on turning away, in the way of his heart. [18] "I have seen his ways, but I will heal him; I will lead him and restore comfort to him and to his mourners, [19] Creating the praise of the lips. Peace, peace to him who is far and to him who is near," says the Lord, "and I will heal him." [20] But the wicked are like the tossing sea, for it cannot be quiet, and its waters toss up refuse and mud. [21] "There is no peace," says my God, "for the wicked."

Isaiah 58: [1] "Cry loudly, do not hold back; raise your voice like a trumpet, and declare to My people their transgression and to the house of Jacob their sins. [2] "Yet they seek Me day by day and delight to know My ways, as a nation that has done righteousness and has not forsaken the ordinance of their God. They ask Me for just decisions, they delight in the nearness of God. [3] 'Why have we fasted and You do not see? Why have we humbled ourselves and You do not notice?' Behold, on the day of your fast you find your desire, and drive hard all your workers. [4] "Behold, you fast for contention and strife and to strike with a wicked fist; you do not fast like you do today to make your voice heard on high. [5] "Is it a fast like this which I choose, a day for a man to humble himself? Is it for bowing one's head like a reed and for spreading out sackcloth and ashes as a bed? Will you call this a fast, even an acceptable day to the Lord? [6] "Is this not the fast which I choose, to loosen the bonds of wickedness, to undo the bands of the yoke, and to let the oppressed go free and break every yoke? [7] "Is it not to divide your bread with the hungry and bring the homeless poor into the house; when you see the naked, to cover him; and not to hide yourself from your own flesh? [8] "Then your light will break out like the dawn, and your recovery will speedily spring forth; and your righteousness will go before you; the glory of the Lord will be your rear guard. [9] "Then you will call, and the Lord will answer; you will cry, and He will say, 'Here I am'. If you remove the yoke from your midst, the pointing of the finger and speaking wickedness, [10] And if you give yourself to the hungry and satisfy the desire of the afflicted, then your light will rise in darkness and your gloom will become like midday. [11] "And the Lord will continually guide you, and satisfy your desire in scorched places, and give strength to your bones; and you will be like a watered garden, and like a spring of water whose waters do not fail. [12] "Those from among you will rebuild the ancient ruins; you will raise up the age-old foundations; and you will be called the repairer of the breach, the restorer of the streets in which to dwell. [13] "If because of the Sabbath, you turn your foot from doing your own pleasure on my holy day, and call the Sabbath a delight, the holy day of the Lord honourable, and honour it, desisting from your own ways, from seeking your own pleasure and speaking your own word, [14] Then you will take delight in the Lord, and I will make you ride on the heights of the earth; and I will feed you with the heritage of Jacob your father, for the mouth of the LORD has spoken."

Isaiah is at odds with the Rabbinic tradition that came after him, and with the *Torah* that came before him, because he emphasises the intrinsic over the extrinsic. In Isaiah's world, we don't fast to make atonement to God, but within ourselves; but wanting God to see, and to approve our doing so, for we always have a child-parent relationship with God, and what child can bear to act without parental audience? But Isaiah makes a metaphor out of fasting, reflecting in it both the material and the spiritual drought; he rebukes Israel, not for fasting inappropriately but for failing to make the act of fasting antithetical: it must lead back to the taking-in of food, in the same way that it was itself a lapse from eating; and the act of sinning therefore a learning exercise that will lead back to the act of doing right. Breaking the fast is as sacred as the abstention, because for all our *selichot*, we know that we're going to return to doing wrong.

I find this really extraordinary. *Yom Kippur*, not as a day of mourning, of lugube and lamentation, but as a fast for freedom, an abstention that liberates the body with the soul. Even through the soul. This is confirmed in Leviticus 25:9-10, which tells us that in the Jubilee year the *shofar* was sounded on *Yom Kippur* precisely to testify the setting-free of slaves, and the restoration of land to its ancestral owners. Atonement, then, as an act of purgation, of making clean, of the soul as well as of the slate. Isaiah hints in these lines at the fulfilment of the eighteen blessings in the *Amidah* (light, health, righteousness, reward); but in his form of atonement, the entire process is personal and internal. One can achieve atonement *even without God's forgiveness*. It's about our own forgiveness of ourselves.

✡

At the end too there are specific, much longer blessings, recited by the *chazan* of *Haphtorah*, because it's never enough to have read the sacred scriptures, not even to have read them aloud in synagogue. To read is to perform a sacred duty, and each act of sacredness requires sanctification.

✡

Yekum Purkan

On *Sabbath* only, and not in Sephardic synagogues, two prayers are added, the first written for the welfare of the students in the academies of Israel and Babylon, their teachers, their judges, and their lay leaders, the second a more general prayer for the welfare of the congregation as a whole. Both are in Aramaic, and both clearly belong to the Babylonian exile, but neither appears in the published manuscripts until mediaeval times, the first in the *Machzor Vitry*, the second in the *Rokeyah* of Eleazar ben Yehudah of Worms, around 1200. Both prayers begin with the same phrase, "*Yekum purkan* - may salvation arise"; the first conveys echoes of the *Kaddish d'Rabbanan*, the second of the traditional "*Mi she beyrach*" which itself constitutes the third section of this fragment.

✡

Yizkor

Recited on the last day of Passover, the second day of *Shavu'ot*, *Shemini Atseret* and on the Day of Atonement[15], *Yizkor* is a most beautiful set of prayers recited in commemoration – the name means "He shall remember" – for close relatives deceased. In fact, *Yizkor* isn't the correct name for the service, which should be "*Hazkarat Neshamot* – the mentioning of the souls", but as so often in Judaism the formal name has been forgotten, and in its place the prayers are known by the first word uttered, which in this case is *Yizkor*.

The prayer is amongst the most ancient still in use; in 2 Maccabees 12:39-45 we can read how Judah ha-Maccabee and his warriors prayed for the souls of their fallen comrades and brought offerings to the Temple as an atonement for those sins they must have performed before their deaths, sins inexorable to a warrior, even though they were considered justified by the necessity of defending Judaism against the Greek aggressor.

---

[15] In the Sephardic rituals, it is recited in the evening, before *Ma'ariv* rather than in the morning after the reading of the Law.

It was from these verses that the *Talmudic* Rabbis took their cue, insisting that the meritorious deeds of the descendants may serve to atone for the sins of the ancestors, a logical inversion of the Biblical mandate that allows the sins of the fathers to be visited upon the sons, even to the third and fourth generations of those who transgress God's Law. What cuts one way, the Rabbis argued, must perforce cut the other also (*Hor* 6a; *Sanhedrin Yerushalmi* 10:4, 29ff; *Sif Deut* 210 are just three of many instances in *Aggadah*, but the primary source for *Yizkor* is *Midrash Tanchuma, Ha'azinu*). Not all the mediaeval Rabbis accepted the ruling however. Around 1000 CE Chai Ga'on and his pupil Nissim ben Jacob pronounced their opposition both to the reciting of *Yizkor* and to the giving of charity on behalf of the deceased, insisting that only those deeds performed by a man himself, during his own life, could be brought as evidence in the Divine Court. Good or bad, he must be judged on his own merits, and not redeemed by the kindness of posterity.

The argument raged only for a short while. As so often in philosophical and theological argument, history provided the syllogism. The First Crusade was launched in 1096, and as the redemptors of Jerusalem for Christ marauded across Europe in search of Infidel to burn or quarter, Jews good or bad found themselves standing in the Heavenly Dock somewhat in advance of their expectation, and without the time to make right their sins. From that date through to the middle of the twentieth century, the pogroms, persecutions, banishments and holocausts persisted without pause, and community after community found itself inscribing ever more names of martyrs in the *Yizkor-buch*, the "*kunteres*" – the death rolls. In time, the names of martyrs were augmented by the names of those who died by other causes, natural or unnatural, and *Yizkor* was enshrined as custom and tradition.

Only those who will recite *Yizkor* should remain inside the synagogue; those who have even one parent still alive will generally depart, returning with the recitation of "*Av ha-Rachamim*".

Custom and tradition also require that no service begins where it's meant to begin, but is always prologued by additional Psalms and meditations. So, today, we recite a short anthology of Psalmic verses (144:3-4; 90:6; 90:12; 37:37; 49:16; 73:26) culminating in that verse from Ecclesiastes (12:7) which declares that "thus the dust returns to the ground as it was, and the spirit returns to God who gave it". Psalm 91 is read in full, and then *Yizkor* commences: "May God remember the soul of…" Six versions of the same prayer may be uttered, the first for one's father, the second for one's mother, the third for a near relative (and within this a male and a female variant), the fourth for one's extended family, the fifth for martyrs, the sixth, added only in the last half-century, for the fallen soldiers of the Israel Defence Force.

"May God remember the soul of...who has gone on to his/her world; because, without making a vow, I shall give to charity on his/her behalf. As reward for this, may his/her soul be bound in the Bond of Life together with the souls of Abraham, Isaac and Jacob, Sarah, Rebecca, Leah and Rachel, and together with the other righteous men and women in the Garden of Eden..."

These verses include a repeated pledge of alms, but alms may not be given in the synagogue, especially on a holy day. A *tsedakah* box no doubt sentries the outer hall (cheques should be crossed please and a credit card number noted on the back as guarantor). The custom derives from *Orach Chayim* 621:6. It's essential that the pledge be fulfilled before next *Yom Kippur*, because a pledge in Hebrew is a *"neder"*, and, as we know, *Kol Nidre*, all our vows or pledges, are annulled next *Yom Kippur*. However, just in case, we don't use the word *"neder"* in *Yizkor*, but an eccentric syntactical construction, *"ba-avur she-bli neder eten tsedakah ba-ado* – therefore, without actually making a vow, I pledge to give to charity on his/her behalf", which gets the giver off the consequences of failing to fulfil, whilst still committing him/her to the fulfilling.

I am particularly fascinated by the appearance of the matriarchs in *Yizkor*, for modern Progressive Judaism has introduced them into the *Amidah*, to the sound of much wailing and gnashing of teeth amongst the Orthodox; and yet here is the living testimony to the validity of their inclusion, deep-rooted in the ancientness of Judaism.

And on the subject of Progressive Judaism, the Reform movement has created its own version of *Yizkor*, which is recited only on the last day of Passover and here, on *Yom Kippur*, though not actually here, but later, in the *Minchah* service that precedes *Ne'ilah*. A shortened version of the traditional text is elaborated with Psalm 23, and a selection of poems by the Malagan poet and philosopher Solomon ben Yehudah ibn Gvirol, Abu Ayyūb Suleiman ibn Yahya ibn Jabirūl as he's known in Arabic; the man who introduced Neo-Platonism into Europe and provided a key bridge for Greco-Arabic scholarship to enter Europe, primarily through the later work of Aquinas. As well as Gvirol, Reform includes poetry by Yeudah Halevi and Bachya ben Joseph of Saragossa, likewise brethren of that golden age of Jewish history, when Moslem and Jew lived side by side, in relative peace if not actual eqality, in mediaeval North Africa and Spain. Another source of mourning, the death of that great amity.

Further prayers, known as *"El maleh rachamim"*, the same as are recited at

Ashkenazi funerals, are also recited now, an appendix to the *Yizkor* though they follow at once and the separation isn't necessarily apparent: for an individual, male and female versions; for a group; for martyrs – specifically the martyrs of the Nazi Holocaust; a *"Mi she beyrach"* for the Rabbi. Finally the *"Av ha-Rachamim"*.

As noted previously, *Yom Kippur* is properly known as *"Yom ha-Kippurim"*. Not the Day of Atonement but the Day of Atonements. Why the plural? Because, the Rabbis tell us, and *Yizkor* provides the proof, we are atoning for our own sins on this day, but we are also atoning for the sins of the deceased.

Throughout this the *Torah* scrolls have been held at the *bimah*. The conclusion of *Yizkor* is the recitation of *Ashrey* – yet *Ashrey* may also be regarded as, properly, the opening of *Musaph* - at whose end the *chazan* takes the *Maphtir Torah* on his right arm, recites *"Yehalelu"* and leads *"Hodu al erets"* and Psalm 24 (Psalm 29 if the fast falls on a *Shabbat*) while taking the scroll back to the reopened Ark. As the two scrolls ae set back into their houses *"U'venucha"* is recited; then the Ark is shut, the curtain closed and the *Shacharit* service is complete.

✡

110

Chapter Five: The Eighth Day

"Today is the eighth day, but where is God?"

"God is resting."

"But God rested yesterday."

"And He is resting again today. And tomorrow. And the day after to-morrow. And for all days to come. For God's task was the Creation of the Universe, and on the sixth day it was done."

"Yes, it was done. But He cannot simply rest. He remains responsible for what He has created."

"No. He has completed Creation, and He is Creation, and that is the end of God. But as the very final act of Creation He said: 'Let us make Man in our own image and likeness, and let Man bear responsibility for the fish of the sea and the birds of the air and the animals that walk the earth, and every living thing.'"

Today is the eighth day of Creation, and Man is wondering why God still sits at rest.

Today is the eighth day of Creation, and God is wondering why Man still sits at rest.

Today is the eighth day of God.

Today is the first day of Man.[16]

✡

Musaph

In Biblical times, when the dialogue with God was achieved primarily through sacrifices in the morning and the afternoon, an additional ceremony of sacrifice was appended on certain sacred festivals: *Sabbath*, the new Moon, the three Pilgrim festivals (Passover, *Shavu'ot* and *Sukkot*), *Rosh ha-Shana*, and now, here, on the Day of Atonement. *Tosef* Ber 3:3 and *Sukkot* 53a both tell us that, even in Temple times, the additional sacrifice, the *Musaph*, was performed to the accompaniment of prayers, and we can deduce from the text of the liturgy that was given formal authority to replace the sacrifices after the Temple fell, what prayers these must have been: the *Amidah* of course at their centre.

Judaism was once based in cultic sacrifice. Then the Prophets argued that God didn't want our sacrifices, but only our obedience. The Romans came, and the Temple where the sacrifices were performed was ruined. What should become of the sacrifices now? Orthodox Judaism adopted prayer, as a form of substitution. Reform Judaism accepted the absence of the

---

[16] From my collection of stories "The Captive Bride".

Temple, the impossibility of sacrifice, the lack of appetite to re-establish it, the legitimacy of the Prophetic rejection – and adopted a silence that denotes obedience. In Reform Judaism, there is no *Musaph*.

Prayer services in Judaism generally require a *minyan*, a quorum of ten adult males; but the *Musaph* service is an exception. While the Rabbis have declared the *Musaph* to be obligatory, and indeed to have the same eminence as *Shacharit* itself, they have also declared (*Ber* 30b, *Shulchan Aruch*, OH 286:2) that it's equally acceptable to *daven Musaph* individually or within a quorum. No reason is afforded.

Nor is the timing of *Musaph* fixed. In most synagogues, *Musaph* follows *Shacharit* without a break; but this is not obligatory. On the other hand, to delay consistently beyond the seventh hour is considered a transgression (*Ber* 4:1, 26b et al); and on this of all days we wouldn't wish to add one more transgression. And besides, what use have we for *haphsakah*? We have neither eaten nor drunk for more than half a day now – no need for the washroom. And though not eating and not drinking inclines us to a coffee break, it isn't permitted. Bravely, then, we struggle on. Half way across the zigzags of our personal wilderness, *Musaph* is a point well beyond Sinai, and our spies are beginning to think ahead to possibilities of tea, whether with milk or honey.

So we begin, prologued by *"Hineni he-ani"* and then, in some congregations, the silent meditation *"El melech na'eman"*, before a *"chetsi-Kaddish"* formalises the transition from *Shacharit* to *Musaph*.

✡

Individual *Amidah*

The *Musaph Amidah* on every occasion varies the regular *Amidah*; on *Yom Kippur* there are distinctions specific to the festival. The first benedictions are identical to the ones we just recited in *Shacharit*: *"Avot"* with its added *"Zachreynu"*; *"Gevurot"* with its added *"Mi kamocha"*. *"Kedushat ha-Shem"* is much extended from the regular daily *Shacharit*, but only in the same way it was already extended for *Shacharit* of *Yom Kippur*. Where *"Kedushat ha-Yom"* is normally just two lines, here it's considerably protracted; *"Atah vechartanu"* and *"Va-titen"* are added, followed by *"U-miphney chata'eynu"*, with *"U-ve-assur"* before the regular *"Eloheynu…mechal"*, the two *"Avodah"* prayers – *"Retseh"* and *"Ve-techezeyna"* - and the *"Modim"* into which is inserted the additional phrase *"U-chetuv le-chayim tovim kol beney Yisra'el"*. The prayers for peace are as in *Shacharit*. The *Vidu'i* is identical to that recited in *Shacharit*. The recitation is considerably longer than this short paragraph describing it.

✡

Chazan's repetition of the *Amidah*

Much dispute over who should recite the *Amidah*, which is why there are both individual versions, for private prayer within the *minyan*, and communal repetitions. Much dispute, too, over who should recite the communal repetitions. In Ashkenazi synagogues, the *chazan* generally recites it all; Sephardi communities prefer to let the congregation join in with the *chazan* for the first three verses, and then leave the *chazan* to perform alone.

"*Avot*" commences it, as always, and with the Ark open, but this time only the opening of the opening, the first paragraph as far as "*Shemo be-ahavah*"; at which point "*Mi-sod chachamim*" is added and the Ark then closed.

"*Shoshan emek ayumah*", which follows, is a beautiful acrostical *piyyut*, like "*Avot*" itself believed to have been written by Rabbi Elazar ha-Kalir, the sixth century CE *Tanna*. Kalir means "cake", and the probably incorrect nickname derives from an 11th century *Talmud*ic dictionary known as the "*Aruch*", compiled by Rabbi Nosson of Rome and much beloved of Rashi and his grandsons; Nosson (no doubt because he had read the Cabbalistic legend, recounted on page 91, which confuses this Elazar with Eliezer the son of Shimon bar Yochai) tells that Elazar was a mystical precursor of the Cabbalists, who learned a sacred formula by which cakes baked with certain phrases on them would imbue the eater with great wisdom, a eucharism not normally associated with Judaism. In fact, Nosson got it completely wrong, and not only historically, as evidenced by the text of "*Esah de'i*" which follows shortly[17], in which Elazar uses his own name acrostically to construct the poem.

The acrostic is not, for once, alphabetical, but uses the phrase "*Shabbat shabbaton*" – an epithet for *Yom Kippur* found in Leviticus 16:31 - taking each letter four times before taking the next letter.

> *Shoshan emek ayumah, shabat shabaton lekayamah,*
> *Shoresh ve-anaph suyemah, shavim yachad letsayemah*

The title, "The Rose of the Valley", is understood to be a double allusion to the "Song of Songs", first through the use of echo in the acrostic, which translates as "*Sabbath* of *Sabbaths*", secondly through the floral link to chapter two, verse one of that lovely Canaanite wedding song borrowed by

---

[17] See page 114.

the Hebrews as an expression of God's love for His people Israel. But this latter seems to me incongruous, partly for the reason just given, which makes it surely inappropriate. But mostly because the original doesn't speak of a Rose of the Valley at all, but of the Rose of Sharon, and of the lily of the valleys; and goes on to state that, "as the lily among thorns, so is my love among the daughters", which phrase may well have been in Rabbi Abba bar Zabda's mind when he construed the phrase "A Myrtle Among Reeds".

"*Zachreynu*" and the final phrase of "*Avot*" complete the first set of benedictions.

"*Gevurot*", the second set of benedictions, is likewise augmented by *piyyut*. After "*Atah gibor*" "*Yom mi-yamim hucham*", again by ha-Kalir, again acrostical, this time using the phrase "*Yom Kippurim*" in precisely the same fourfold manner as "*Shabbat shabbaton*" previously, and like that *piyyut* deploying biblical references liberally, presumably because many *payyatanim* were great constructors of labyrinthine prayers, no doubt great engineers and logicians and mathematicians of language, but also, sadly, lousy poets, for whom plagiarism wasn't an issue, because one is never a plagiarist who piously reuses for the purposes of prayer the words of God, or Moses or the Prophets.

"*Enosh*", the third of ha-Kalir's *piyyut*im, is available, though few congregations choose to recite it, preferring to recite the "*Mi kamocha*" straight away, and then move on to his fourth *piyyut*, "*Tsepheh*", again a fourfold construction, this time using the phrase "*Tsom he-Assur* – the Fast of the Tenth". It's his least successful work; all too often he can't find a suitable word, particularly to take the *seen* (Hebrew does not offer a huge number of words beginning with this letter), and so he falls back on the cheat we've already noticed, of deploying the identical-sounding letter *samech* as a substitute.

After "*Tsepheh*" the two-line "*Yimloch*", and then ha-Kalir's immensely complex *piyyut* "*Esah de'i*". In most prayer books the three rotating refrains are printed before the poem, but shouldn't be recited until their time is due, within the *piyyut* itself. As I've already pointed out, this *piyyut* is constructed around the name Elazar bey-Rabbi Kalir – "*bey*", which means "son of", on this occasion, rather than "*ha*", which means "the", as Nosson would have us imagine – with the odd numbered letters doubled and the even numbered letters used only once. The *piyyut* is written in triplets, with the three refrains alternating between verses.

The same happens with ha-Kalir's next *piyyut*. The two verses printed first in the prayer book are not yet read (they too contain the acrostic of his name, once in each verse), but serve as alternating refrains for "*Eyn aruch*", which is an alphabetical acrostic.

The next *piyyut*, "*Al tizkor*" is thought not to be by ha-Kalir, though who its author actually is remains a mystery. The same is true of "*Ach omrim*", which is likewise alphabetically acrostical.

We return to ha-Kalir for "*U-ve-chen imru le'elohim*", which is recited standing before the open Ark. The *chazan*'s repetition in *Shacharit* also contained a long prayer with "*Imru le-elohim*" as its refrain, but the main text, though likewise alphabetically acrostical, is verbally different. So also the text of "*Ma'aseh eloheynu*", during which the Ark is closed and reopened for the single verse which refers to Man, not God.

Should the Ark remain open or now be closed for "*Asher eymatecha*"? Some do, some don't, some leave it out completely. The resolution lies in local practice. Once again the authorship is unknown. Whether open or closed for the *piyyut*, it should be closed by the time we recite "*Le-yoshev*" and "*Elu le-elu*", and then re-opened for what is not in fact the start of *Kedushah*, though we say "*U-ve-chen...*" which is the introductory prayer for the *Kedushah*, anyway. What actually comes now is:

U-netaneh tokeph

The story of Amnon of Mainz is known only at third-hand. Isaac ben Moses of Vienna, a 13th century writer, quotes Ephraim ben Jacob, a 12th century writer, who describes Amnon as "a leader of his generation, wealthy, of distinguished ancestry and pleasant appearance." The legend is thus, at the very least, apocryphal – but where is it written that apocryphal legends can't also be authentic?

According to the legend, the Bishop of Mainz tried repeatedly to persuade Amnon to accept Christianity, knowing that, as the leader of the community in Mainz, to proselytise one was to proselytise all. Pressed on more than just an intellectual front, Amnon requested three days to make his mind up, but he failed to appear at the appointed time, and only did so at all when brought under arrest.

"Why did you not appear at the appointed time?"

Amnon's answer contained multiple layers of complexity. He pleaded guilty, asking that his tongue be cut out – for not having refused to attend at all.

"Not your tongue, but your legs, which failed to bring you at the required hour."

Amnon's legs were amputated, and for good measure his arms as well, with salt poured onto the wound.

But he did not die of his lacerations. He was carried home, and managed to join the community in synagogue on *Rosh ha-Shana*. While the *Kedushah* prayer was being recited, Amnon interrupted, asking that he be allowed to say a special prayer that he'd written, in which he sanctified the name of God, reasserting his refusal to accept forced conversion to that barbarism posing as a religious faith called Christianity. The prayer he recited was "*U-netaneh tokeph*". On finishing his utterance, he died.

Three days later, Rabbi Kalonymos ben Meshullam dreamed a dream, in which Amnon appeared to him and taught him the words of "*U-netaneh tokeph*", asking him to write it down and circulate it among the communities of the Diaspora, so that all Jews could recite it, every *Rosh ha-Shana*, as we still do, even in Ladino translations in some Sephardi *shuls*, and now on *Yom Kippur* as well as *Rosh ha-Shana*.

Only, sadly, though the legend of Amnon's refusal and mutilation is all-too-true, the authorship of the *piyyut* is not. Archaeologists rummaging among the *genizot* of Europe and North Africa have found versions of the text dating right back to the Roman era. Amnon may well have recited it; what he didn't do was write it.

✡

The majesty of the judge is only part of the equation; there's also the nature of the judgement. "*Be Rosh ha-Shana yikateyvun, u-ve-yom tsom kippur yeychateymun...*" in Aramaic, the inventory of punishments available to the Master of the Universe, not quite the version sung by Leonard Cohen in his beautiful "Who By Fire", but near enough.

Not that punishment is inevitable; or rather, for the line isn't as it first seems, not that punishment is improper. "*U-teshuvah...ha-gezeyrah* – but repentance, prayer and charity may remove the evil of the decree!" Most Rabbis interpret this line to mean that, through fasting, prayer and acts of charity, we may persuade God to punish us more gently, even to alleviate the punishment altogether. But this I think is wrong – or at least, it misses the main point. Each one of the punishments available to God also comes under the category of sin; thus we always hear the argument against capital punishment, that to kill a man who has committed murder is to make the state its own enemy. How can God punish a man for sin, by committing a sin? Through our *Vidu'i* we acknowledge God's right to punish us, for we have sinned wilfully; through our fasting, prayers and acts of charity we exonerate God for any sin that may be committed in the act of punishing.

"*Ki ke-shimcha*" and "*Ve-atah hu*" complete this section, after which the

Ark is closed for "*Eyn kitzvah*", a statement of the eternity of God, and a prologue to the arrival of the angels; for we're about to raise ourselves to the same level as the angels, a privilege afforded us today, and only today, in the reciting of their *Kedushah*.

✡

The *Kedushah* for *Musaph* of *Yom Kippur* recited in most synagogues is in fact the standard *Shabbat* and festival *Kedushah*, though there is an enhanced version, authorship unknown, which includes a four-part *piyyut* comprising both a double alphabetical acrostic ("*Amnah yom yom*") and a double reversed alphabetical acrostic ("*Talpiyot marom*") – the kind of high-diving-board gymnastics in which mediaeval Jews were forced to compete, being disbarred from the squash and golf clubs of their fellow Christians.

The regular *Kedushah* consists of an opening phrase, "*Keter yitnu*", in which the angels place a formal crown upon the head of the King of Heaven, and thereby take Judaism into a territory that remains completely alien to me, the realm of Zoroastrianism, which the exiled Jews of Babylon acquired and brought back with them upon return to Israel under Ezra and Zerubabel; and which, of course, we know became significant, for it was precisely the priests of Zoroaster, the Magi, who were believed to have brought the symbols of the triple-goddess, myrrh for Miriam-MorYah, gold for Sarah-Asherah and frankincense for Devorah the bee-goddess of the Underworld, to the cradle of the Christian Messiah - or Tammuz, the Corn-God of Bethlehem-Ephratah, the "House" (Temple) of the Corn God of the Euphrates, as they must have presumed him to be – in the "manger" in Bethlehem. But I'm raising controversies and potential blasphemies that don't belong in this text.

After the "*Keter*", the phrases are conventional, focused upon the triplet "*Kadosh, Kadosh, Kadosh*", with an optional Cabbalistic meditation after "*ayeh*". "*Le-dor va-dor*", "*Chamol*", "*U-ve-chen*", "*Od*", and "*Be-eyn*" are all recited with the Ark still closed, but it's opened for "*Ha-ochez be-yad*", a variation on the customary form of *piyyut*, in that this one uses an alphabetical motif, but not acrostically, sewing it into the stiches rather than pricking the openings of the lines. Each phrase begins "*Ve-chol ma'ameenim she-hu* – all believe that He is…", and is recited by the congregation first, the *chazan* repeating. Although the attributes of God are all scripturally based, they are none of them on this occasion direct quotations.

At the conclusion of the *Kedushah*, the Ark is closed.

✡

"*Tushgav*" is taken from Zechariah 14:9, a statement of monotheism in a time when the battle wasn't with atheism but with polytheism; which is to say, when the Prophets railed against too many gods, whereas now they rail against a preference for none at all.

"*Ana be-ko'ach*" is an optional appendix here, but it's one that no mystic with a conscience could possibly leave out. Its author, Nehunya ha-Kanah, was a student of Yochanan ben Zakkai, the Rabbi who single-handedly rescued Judaism from the flames of the Temple when he persuaded Titus to keep open the *yeshiva* at Yavneh. Nehunya was himself the teacher of Rabbi Yishmael, whose rules for the interpretation of *Torah* are explained in the companion to this volume, "A Myrtle Among Reeds"; the most important book ever written on Judaic Law (his I mean, not mine), as it defined the formulae by which a moral meaning or an actual law may be construed out of the reading of the text, leading thereby to the six hundred and thirteen commandments that provide the republic of Judaism with its written constitution to this day – an exercise known technically as hermeneutics.

The text has much occupied Cabbalists for many centuries. It promulgates that the "*Ana be'ko'ach*" is built around a sequence of fifty-two initial letters that are encoded within the first forty-two words of the Book of Genesis. This isn't immediately obvious when you look at the text, but that's because you don't know how to look at the text through the correct prism, and are likely blinded by your own scepticism in addition. The Cabbalists explain that there is a seven-sequence combination of letters within the code, which takes us to the time of Creation. Each time we meditate on a particular sequence, we are returned to the original uncorrupted energy that built the world. The "*Ana be'ko'ach*" corresponds to the seven days of the week. Each sentence also corresponds to a particular heavenly body. By performing the "*Ana be'ko'ach*" meditation, we enrich our lives with unadulterated spiritual Light and positive energy. Many children believe the same to be true of a visit to Disneyland or the grotto of Santa Claus.

As with the *Amidah* of *Shacharit*, the phrase "*U-ve chen*" is used formulaically to introduce a succession of prayers and meditations, many of them repetitions from the *Shacharit* service. Three verses on this occasion, "*U-ve chen ten pachdecha*", "*U-ve chen ten kavod*" and "*U-ve chen tzadikim*", of which the third borrows a phrase from Job (5:16) that seems to allude to the most ancient form of sacrifice, in which El the bull-god was believed literally to eat the meat of sacrifice, and to be propitiated by the smell of roasting meat and boiling gravy, and to close his mouth to indicate when he was satisfied. Psalm 107:42 – "The upright saw this and rejoiced; all wickedness shut its mouth" – nuances the same concept.

"*Ve-ye'etayu*", which follows, is yet another acrostical *piyyut*, authorship unknown, one which begins each phrase with what appears to be the use of the *Vav* Consecutive, the *Vav Ha-hipuch* in Hebrew, but in fact is simply the prefixing of the future tense with an ungrammatical conjunctive. The acrostic comes afterwards.

"*Ve-timloch*" and "*Kadosh*" lead into "*Kedushat ha-Yom*", which commences with "*Atah vechartanu*", then "*Va-titen*" (additional phrases exist here for when *Yom Kippur* coincides with *Sabbath*).

"*U-miphney chata'eynu*" is one of the great arguments, not so much against Reform Judaism, as for a reform of Reform Judaism. Nor is it the words of the text, which simply provide yet one more anagram for the thesis of the day, that sin requires repentance and here we are repenting. Reform Judaism has no *Musaph* service, and even if it did, "*U-miphney chata'eynu*" is precisely the sort of mediaeval platitudinising it would leave out. But "*U-miphney chata'eynu*" is also one of the great operatic moments in the *Yom Kippur* liturgy, and though Reform has many arias, and many outstanding *chazanim* and *chazanot* to sing them, leaving out "*U-miphney chata'eynu*" is like perfoming Bizet's "Carmen" without "Habanera", or Verdi's "Rigoletto" without "La donna è mobile". Even as I write these lines I'm listening to Cantor Josef Rosenblatt, from his album (do Cantors have "albums", like hip-hop singers and jazz bands?) "Masterpieces of the Synagogue, Volume 2" (RCA Camden, CAL 507 K3WP-1806). Very fine. Very pleasing. There's also a version by Alberto Mizrahi which you can hear on-line, at the wonderfully named "Oi-Tunes.com".

And afterwards, "*U-ve-assur*", a verse which leaves me wondering what historical circumstance must have occurred, to introduce into the liturgy the very portion of the scriptures that has just been read, as *Maphtir* in the *Shacharit* service minutes earlier. Was it another moment like the introduction of the *Haphtorah* in Greek times, when anti-Semites forbad the reading of the Law, and the prohibition was circumscribed by inserting the text unnoticed at this point? It would be fascinating to know.

✡

Aleynu

The Ark is opened for the start of the rendition of the credo, but closed after "*Ha-adamah*", no doubt for a good reason, though I've been unable to ascertain one anywhere. It's then reopened at "*Va-anachnu korim u-mishtachavim* – so we bend our knees and bow*".

The act of prostration was the ancient mode of prayer, and no less than thirty-three examples can be found in the Bible, of which the most famous are Abraham in Genesis 17:3, when God appeared to him to tell him Sarah was pregnant, and Numbers 20:6, when Moses and Aaron saw the "glory of God" in the entrance to the *Ohel Mo'ed,* the Temple of Meeting. Prostration was the norm then, and still is, for a Moslem – flat upon the ground, face down. In Temple times it was still the norm, though by then it had been fenced around by strict laws. Leviticus 26:1 forbids prostration upon hewn stone, at least with outstretched arms and legs; a lesser form of prostration may be acceptable, if one can imagine it. Rama, Orach Chayim 131:8 and Mishnah Berurah 40 extend this to floors that are not of hewn stone, and forbid kneeling of any kind on a stone floor; those who wish to prostrate themselves must do as Moslems do, and place a prayer mat of some sort beneath themselves. I believe this is an error; or at least it manages to miss the point. It isn't the coldness of the stone that was the problem for Leviticus, but its being hewn, and so extending it to any other stone is plain irrelevant, and covering the stone just hides from the eyes what is clear knowledge in the heart. It's the hewn nature of the stone that matters, the *"even masu ha-bonim haita la rosh pinah",* the stone rejected by the builder which has become the chief cornerstone of the Temple (Psalm 118:22). Why did they hew stone in Biblical times? To build a sacred place. We may not kneel on hewn stone because it's sacred. Perhaps if we compromised, and knelt upon a prayer-shawl, it would become admissible?

And in fact this is precisely what takes place in many communities, and it's entirely admissible. This is because a second school of thought rejects the Leviticus argument, insisting that the Rabbinic prohibition was a response to the rituals of heathen cults, who worshipped on stone floors in places like Stonehenge and Carnac – "for they bow to vanity and emptiness and pray to a god who cannot help them" is Isaiah's take on this, in chapter forty-five, verse twenty of his great book. Alongside the prayer shawl, straw, green leaves, even plain cloth, are perfectly acceptable.

Why does any of this matter anyway? Because the text does indeed require us to prostrate ourselves, though most modern translations wilfully mistranslate it. In Hebrew the text is clear: *"Anachnu korim u-mishtachavim"* – for which "we bend our knees and bow" is sufficient for *"korim",* but omits *"u-mishtachavim"* entirely: "we prostrate ourselves" is unequivocal. The *Aleynu* is recited daily, at the conclusion of every service of worship, but while most people do indeed bend their knees slightly, and make a small rocking movement forwards, fulfilling *"korim"* quite satisfactorily, the *"mishtachavim"* was long ago abandoned. Until this moment. At *Musaph* of

Yom Kippur, when this phrase is reached, we kneel down on the floor, and bow from the waist, until our heads touch the prayer-mat or the carpet; a posture that may well be an extended genuflection but is still not the full-fedged prostration; that would require pressing the whole body flat upon the floor. Why do we do it now? Why do we do it now, but not do it properly? Why do we not do it at all, at any other time? Matters of tradition, which generally amount to little more than doing things incorrectly because we've always done them incorrectly. The truth is, we don't prostrate ourselves because of our dignity, and our fashionable clothing, and not for any theological reason; but we don't like to admit this, so I shall cease there. And why, in that case, do we almost do it correctly now? For an equally bad quasi-theological reason: we are as the angels on this day, and apparently this is how they pray in Heaven. How do we know? From the Book of Daniel, which unfortunately we also know was a work of literary fiction that probably shouldn't have found its way into the Bible, where all texts are to be regarded as literal and historic. And does it matter anyway? Followers of Maimonides and some Yemeni Jews prostrate themselves on innumerable occasions through the year. God hasn't yet struck them down for doing so, nor the rest of us for not doing so, though there have been occasional reports of head colds and other chills, which may or may not be connected with the stone.

So the Ark is reopened, and all kneel, and prostrate themselves, for "*Ve-anachnu korim...*"; after which the congregation rises. The Ark stays open until "*ayn od*", and the second verse of the *Aleynu* – "*al ken nekaveh*" - is omitted.

✡

"*Eloheynu*" forms a prologue to the Temple Service, which is the absolute heart of *Yom Kippur*. The prayer is generally known, not by the "*Eloheynu*" that opens it, but as "*Heyeh im ha-pipiyot* – be with the mouths", the second phrase. The translation doesn't sit well with me: in full "Our God and God of our forefathers, be with the mouths of the agents of Your people, the Family of Israel..." simply doesn't make sense. The normal plural for mouth is "*piyot*", but this double construction "*pipiyot*" mirrors many others in the scriptures, of which "*Elohim*" is the best known; the proper plural for "*el*" should be "*elim*", thus allowing "god" to become "gods"; but the multiple plural "*Elohim*" conveys something still larger, a universal Omnideity, the monotheistic construction that all Gods are One. In a similar manner "*mey*", which is a drop of water, becomes "*mayim*" in the plural, but is also regarded as a multiple plural when it conveys its broader meaning of "the elements" (as in Genesis 1:2). However, in the case of "*pipiyot*", interpretation isn't that simple. For one thing, there's only one occurrence of "*pipiyot*" in the entire Bible, in Isaiah 41:15, and there the word doesn't mean "mouths" at all, but is in fact a metaphorical device for describing the toughness of that newly invented iron instrument, the double-edged sword: "*Hineh samtich le morag charuts chadash, ba'al pipiyot; tadush harim, ve tadok, u-geva'ot ka mots tasim* - Behold, I will make you a new sharp threshing instrument having teeth: you shall thresh the mountains, and beat them small, and shall make the hills as chaff."

We can only wonder if the use of the term in this prayer is intended, not to call on God to "be with the mouths", but rather to insist that those who speak the words of penitence and supplication do so with the toughness of iron, and not the tenderness of flesh. The remainder of the text supports this.

✡

The Ark is reopened briefly at "*Ochilah*", then closed for "*Amits ko'ach*", the first phrase of the Temple Service in Ashkenazi synagogues; Sephardim conduct a very different service.

✡

The service performed by the *Cohen Gadol* in Biblical times has already been detailed in a previous chapter. What we have now is not the event, but the description of the event, and not always the description of the event, but mostly the description of the spiritual significance of the event; and that spiritual significance was very different for the Babylonian or Sephardi community, which had gone into exile from Israel in 586 BCE, at the time of the destruction of the First Temple, had chosen not to return with Ezra and Zerubabel at the time that Cyrus of the Medes assisted in that venture, and who had therefore already spent four hundred years building alternatives to Temple worship, and living substitutions to the Temple liturgy, by the time that Titus' army burned the Temple in Jerusalem in 70 CE. The Babylonian *Talmud* was already well under way; the great *Yeshivot* were long established. But for the Jews of Israel taken into Roman slavery, building again in Europe over the next thousand years…

✡

Avodah – Temple Service (Sephardi)

The Sephardi service commences with "*Atah konanta*", a *piyyut* believed to have been written by Yose ben Yose[18], though *Tashlum Abudarham* questions this and places the text earlier even than Yose. Yose was probably born in the *yishuv* in Palestine, among the small number of Jews who remained after the Roman destruction, somewhere at the end of the fourth or the beginning of the fifth century CE. Saadiah Ga'on regarded him as one of the great poets of antiquity, and certainly he's the first known author of *piyyut*. He's sometimes given the sobriquet "*ha-yatom* - the orphan", an assumption made from his patronymic, for it's most unusual for a father and son to bear the same name. Many *Talmudic* commentators ask if he was the High Priest Yose ben Yose, or did two men have the same name? Both answers are unlikely, the former because there were no High Priests in the 4th and 5th centuries.

"*Atah konanta*" first appears in the *siddur* of Rav Amram Ga'on, the head of the *yeshiva* in Sura in the late 9th century who was the first to collect the liturgy in a formal manner, and publish it as an advisory on how to pray. This text precedes the Ashkenazi *siddurim* by several centuries.

Not unusually, "*Atah konanta*" is an alphabetical acrostic; more unusually, after the line-by-line acrostic is complete, but the poet found that he had more to say, a second *piyyut* is appended, rather than distinguished as a separate poem, reversing the acrostic, allowing each line to expand into full paragraphs through which the Temple Service is recounted almost prosaically...and then interrupted after the *hey* line, to allow three verses supplementary to the *piyyut* to be introduced, the first of which, "*Ve-chach haya omer*" is recited by the *chazan* and repeated by the congregation, the second of which, "*Ve-ha-Cohanim*", is one of those many occasions that I referred to earlier, where Sephardim are unconcerned about the coldness or the hewnness of the stone, but kneel and then prostrate themselves in the ancient manner, on this occasion prompted, logically enough, by the word "*U-mishtachavim*". The third interjected verse, "*Ve-aph hu hayah*" is then recited by the *chazan* and the congregation together, before Yose ben Yose's *piyyut* is resumed...and then interrupted again after just two verses, for a second paragraph beginning "*Ve-ha-Cohanim*", though on this occasion there are specific instructions not to bow at "*U-mishtachavim*", which to me is incomprehensible. Following this, the last two verses of the *piyyut* are at last achieved, and as before "*Ve-chach haya omer*" is recited by the *chazan* and repeated by the congregation, followed by a third "*Ve-ha-Cohanim*", this

---

[18] See pages 59 and 67.

time with full genuflection and prostration, and a repetition of *"Ve-aph hu hayah"*.

Why do Sephardim prostrate themselves on two stipulated occasions, but not on the third? I have no answer.

For those unaccustomed to the Sephardi form of worship, there's an almost mathematical precision and symmetry in the structure of this service, of a joyful and serious but also of an intellectually playful nature, which renders it quite different from Ashkenazi forms of worship. I make no value judgement between the two; I merely point out.

✡

"Achar Vidu'?", the *piyyut* that follows, is once again an alphabetical acrostic, and once again more prose than poetry, for its goal isn't to inspire through the spiritual, emotional or psychological power of language (the main difference between a book and a movie and the reason why the latter will never finally replace the former), but simply to recount the events in the Temple during the ceremonies of *Yom Kippur*, all of which, anyway, we already know, from staying up all night to study the *"Mishnayos Yoma"*. Once again the *piyyut* is constantly interrupted; after verse *tet* for *"Ve-chach hayetah tephilato"*; after verses *yud*, *lamed*, *mem* and *nun* for *"Ve-chach hayah moneh"* ('and so the High Priest would count, One, one plus one, one plus two...one plus seven'); after verse *tzade* for yet another *"Ve-chach haya omer"* recited by the *chazan* and repeated by the congregation, followed as the familiar pattern is now by *"Ve-ha-Cohanim"*, once again this time with full genuflection and prostration, and a repetition of *"Ve-aph hu hayah"*. The last four verses of the *piyyut* continue uninterrupted, but don't manage to complete the account of the High Priest's performance, which suggests that some of the text may have been lost. *"Achar kalato"* attempts to do this, but it strikes me that there's enormous scope in all this section of the liturgy for some modern *payyatan* to come along and construct a more effective poem, one that manages to tell the whole tale in a single construction from *aleph* to *tav*, or if it must be three poems, then three poems that sub-divide the fragments logically, and function coherently within their own poetic form. How can we expect God to answer our petitions, if we speak to Him in broken sentences?

✡

The latter sections of the Temple Service, at least in the Sephardic tradition, return us to another familiar pattern, that of the verses beginning with the word *"U-ve-chen"*. The first occurrence precedes a *"Yehi ratson"* prayer – Leonard Cohen's name cropping up for the third time in this book, as it's from this prayer that he took his song "If It Be Your Will". Cohen didn't accomplish an alphabetic acrostic however, as this *piyyut* does, though once again it's *piyyut* of indifferent quality, for the strict pattern of the first eight verses, where one attribute of the year is noted, is suddenly extended to two attributes in verse *tet* (9), as it is to three in verse *kuph* (19), to two again in *sheen* (21) and to an entire essay in the final verse. A good editor would surely have insisted on one attribute per verse, or if more needed to be included, then a logical mathematical pattern to accommodate the extras. Form and content need to be one. The structure of the act of worship is undermined by so much sloppy verse. This matters especially in this of all prayers, for this is the one which incorporates the very prayer uttered by the High Priest in the Temple.

Two more verses commencing "*U-ve-chen*" lead to the responsive "*Mareh Cohen*", an exemplary alphabetical acrostic which uses the *Kaf*-Comparative – "Like" - as the opening letter of each line, and makes the acrostic on the second letter. And finally a great cacophony of unharmonic noises as "*Kol eleh*" and "*Ashrey ayin*" encourage the congregation to offer the repetition of the closing lines of each paragraph without waiting for the *chazan* to complete it. Are we in such a hurry to get the aroma of the Temple sacrifices out of our starved nostrils? Clearly the poet was in such a hurry, for his placement of the acrostic, randomly through the verses albeit in alphabetic order, suggests the work of one fulfilling an obligation rather than participating in a joyful act.

✡

Technically the Temple Service ends here, but the next part of the *chazan*'s repetition actually extends it. "*Aval avonot avoteynu*", followed by "*U-mey-rov*", "*Tachphu*" and "*Tanot*" all remind us that what we've just read is History, that remembering what's gone is all we have, but can still be made significant, that today we're contrite about our sins because it's those sins that caused the destruction of the Temple and are preventing the final redemption. This is an atavism that I simply can't accept. My personal sins, performed last Tuesday afternoon, or on the Friday before that, are responsible for the Messiah not yet being here, despite the fact that here I am in *shul* today, asking for atonement from those sins? And where is the credit balance on this financial statement (the Hebrew word for this – "*cheshbon*" – allows this pun: the word means both a moral and a financial reckoning)? Where is the acknowledgement of my good deeds, which may even outweigh my bad ones? Where is the recognition that my good deeds may actually be speeding the arrival of the Messiah?

The *chazan*'s repetition concludes now with a series of prayers, each calling on God to be merciful and to accelerate salvation. "*Al ta-as*" plays creatively with the alphabetic acrostic, running *aleph* to *lamed* forwards and *tav* to *mem* back, in alternating stiches. "*Ke-to-im*" simply inverts the process, starting at the end with *tav* and ending at the start with *aleph*; a *piyyut* of similes on this occasion, using the second letter of each word because the first, each time, is once again the *Kaf*-Comparative – "like". "*Im ta-inu*" is another failed attempt at linguistic complexity – each letter of the acrostic in alphabetical order, but twice, not once; except that, on seven separate occasions, the second time simply doesn't happen. "*Ta-avat*" is effective as a reverse alphabetic acrostic, "*tomar*" is in conventional order *aleph* to *tav*, but it uses the vocative form, so that each word that's acrosticalised begins with the letter *tav* and the acrostic is on the second letter – this is beginning to look like showing off. "*Orcha*" is likewise an alphabetical acrostic, *aleph* to *tav*. "*Ophel*" pulls off an almost flawless triple alphabetical acrostic, gaining full marks for artistic quality but losing a point for technical merit because on several occasions the *payyatan* has had to resort to second letter initialisation when he couldn't find a suitable first letter. "*Titen*" and "*ta'inu*" conclude the *piyyut* in this section of the *chazan*'s repetition, "*Titen*" again on the second letter of a vocative and with a reverse alphabetical acrostic; and then the section itself ends with "*Mah nedaber*" and "*Zechor rachamecha*". This is Olympianism par excellence!

✡

Avodah – Temple Service (Ashkenazi)

The pattern of the Ashkenazi service mirrors that of the Sephardi, but the opening *piyyut* are different.

"*Amits ko'ach*" was written by Rabbi Meshullam ben Kalonymos of Lucca. It consists of a complex, multiple alphabetical arrangement: the first four stiches a quadruple alphabetical acrostic, but only as far as the letter *nun*, at which point the *piyyut* becomes elongated, the letters *samech* and *ayin* requiring eight stiches apiece (though yet again we find a single *seen* where *samech*s must have run out in Meshullam's mediaeval thesaurus); the letters *peh* through *sheen* requiring twelve stiches each, and *tav* an astonishing twenty-four. The *piyyut* then ends, unusually though not uniquely for Meshullam[19], with a ten line acrostic spelling out "*Meshullam bey Rabbi Kalonymos chazak* – Meshullam, the son of Rabbi Kalonymos, may he be strong".

---

[19] See page 91 for the previous example.

The section until *peh* is complete runs unbroken except by intercalations by the *chazan* to the congregation's diurnations. After *peh* the *piyyut* is suspended, as with the Sephardi, for a direct quotation from the Levitical account: first "*Ve-chach*", then "*Ve-ha-Cohanim*". In that second section the actions in the Temple are mirrored in the synagogue: at "*korim*" the congregation kneels, at "*mishtachavim*" prostrate themselves, and remain in that position until the end of the paragraph when the angels' *Kedushah* is once again recited. Meshullam's *piyyut* resumes after the short closing paragraph "*Ve-aph*", but is suspended again after the *tsade* verses, for a second instalment of the Levitical allusions: "*Ve-chach*", "*Ve-ha-Cohanim*", "*Ve-aph*".

Meshullam resumes at *kaph*, but pauses once more in the middle of the *reysh* verses, to allow a different "*Ve-chach*" – the strange Cohanic counting which I've described previously. Four more *reysh* lines and again the "*Ve-chach*" that records the counting; the completion of the *reysh* lines and the first four *sheen* lines, before another variant on the '*ve-chach*' gives the Cohanic exquisition of the sins of Israel and for a third time the verse "*Ve-ha-Cohanim*" in which the kneeling and prostration again occur. "*Ve-aph*" again completes it. The remainder of the *sheen* lines lead to the final section of Meshullam's vast *piyyut*, with his acrostical signature worked into a series of scriptural allusions, and the opening line of *Ashrey* used as a peroration.

From this point on, the Sephardi and Ashkenazi versions become more similar, and often identical.

"*Ve-yom tov*" follows; then the "*Yehi ratson*" which incorporates the High Priest's prayer; a mere, straightforward alphabetical acrostic (have you, like I, become so used to them, and so bedazzled by the more complex elaborations, that you've come to think of the simple alphabetical acrostic as really quite straightforward? It isn't, I assure you – try one and see, even in English).

The *piyyut* "*Emet ma nehedar*" is a variation of the Sephardi "*U-ve-chen ha nehedar*" which prologued the "*Mareh Cohen*" prayer, as it does here. Of unknown authorship – again alphabetically acrostic, with that congregational refrain to each line: "*Mareh Cohen*".

"*Kol eleh*" and "*Ashrey ayin*" conclude the Temple service, as in the Sephardi ritual, and the *chazan*'s repetition resumes with "*Aval*", "*U-mey'rov*", "*Tachphu*", "*Tanof*", "*Al ta'as*", "*Keto'im*", "*Im ta'inu*", "*Ta'aval*", "*Tomar*", "*Orcha*", "*Ophel*", "*Titen*", and "*Ta'inu*", all of which repeat the Sephardi and have been described above. The short phrase "*Ma nedaber*" introduces "*Zechor*" and then the long tale of the Ten Martyrs.

✡

The Ten Martyrs

We enter, not for the first time, the realm of man-made myth. The tale of ten Rabbis, martyred by the Romans for their constancy to the Jewish faith and God – only, despite what is recorded in the anonymous *piyyut* (the *payyatan* signs his poem Yehudah *ha-Chazak* acrostically in the stanza "*Zechor be-rachamecha*", but this isn't a name, not even a nickname or a *nom de plume*; at most it's a sobriquet), the ten weren't all martyred at the same time; indeed, two of the eight lived at an entirely different epoch, long after the others had been killed - so this cannot be construed as history, even though it generally is. Two versions, then: first, the one we read on *Yom Kippur* and again on *Tishah b'Av*, the 9th of *Av* commemoration of the destruction of the Temple; then, what may really have happened.

First, the story as given in the *piyyut*. A Roman governor of Israel, possibly Lulianus, insisted on studying the *Torah* at the feet of the Rabbis, so as to be better informed of Jewish law; and then, having learned enough of it for his purposes, used it to destroy the Jews. He ordered that his palace be filled with shoes. Then he summoned the Sages, and asked them to clarify that the Jewish law prescribed the death penalty for the crime of kidnapping; which they did. The governor then noted that Joseph's brothers remained unpunished for the crime of kidnapping their brother more than sixteen hundred years before; and asked for clarification that in Jewish law the sins of the fathers were normally visited upon the sons (the shoes, incidentally, were a banal and obscure analogy which the Sages surely couldn't have been expected to read as a clue: some versions of the Joseph story – with the Prophet Amos as the source - have his brothers using the coins they received from the Ishmaelites to buy shoes).

The Sages requested three days, to appeal to God as the supreme authority on the matter and to gain His Judgement. Rabbi Yishmael as *Cohen ha-Gadol* was the man most suited to the task, and he duly purified himself and pronounced the secret name of God, then ascended the heavenly ladder and spoke personally with the Archangel Gabriel, who advised him that God required the conclusion of this unfortunate business, and that the Sages should therefore accept the verdict. Rabbi Yishmael and Shimon ben Gamli'el were taken first, Shimon asking that his head be cut off before Yishmael's, to save him having to witness the sacrifice of the chief sacrificer; and so it fell out, though it required the drawing of lots first. Watching Rabbi Yishmael go next, the Governor's daughter went into ecstasies of physical passion at his beauty and begged her father to spare him; when he refused, she insisted that the flesh of his face be flayed, so that she could stuff and preserve it as a bedside ornament – presumably as an *aide-de-branler*; a response which Rabbi Freud has never investigated, though his opinion on the matter would be worth the reading.

While Yishmael quivered under the lash, the angels in Heaven protested to the Almighty against his treatment, but were ordered into silence. These actions confirmed God's Laws, and thus they could not be contravened or countermanded. As with the *Kaddish* , we are called upon to justify the judgement.

Next, Rabbi Akiva, although there's a hint in the verse before Akiva's arrest of a small-scale massacre either of other Jewish leaders or even, possibly, of Roman torturers who refused. After Akiva – who went lacerating his own flesh with sharp-toothed combs – Rabbi Chananya ben Teradyon, who was burned, with saturated woollen sponges placed on his chest to slow the death-process as much as possible; his personal *Torah* Scroll was burned alongside him. Next, Rabbi Chutzpis the Interpreter, then Rabbi Elazar ben Shamu'a, Rabbi Chanina ben Chachinai, Rabbi Yesheivav the Scribe, Rabbi Yehudah ben Damah, and finally Rabbi Yehudah ben Bava, of whom the precise method of murdering isn't described, but only the fact.

Conflict of dates and known historic accounts reduce this to mere legend, an invention of the Middle Ages. Yet several of the ten did die as martyrs, each in their own time, and place, and manner. Who were they really?

The first was Rabban Shimon ben Gamliel ha-Nasi. The Gamliels were one of the great families of Israel in the Roman era, descended from Rabbi Hillel, the greatest of all Talmudic Rabbis, who came as leader of the Babylonian community to lead the Jews in the *yishuv*, the community in Israel. No less than six Gamliels figure amongst the alumni of Israel in the early Christian centuries, of whom the first of all was Hillel's grandson Gamliel *ha-Zakan* (the Elder or the Wise; in Hebrew the two conditions are for some reason deemed interchangeable). The second was his son, Shimon ben Gamliel of Yavneh, who succeeded Yochanan ben Zakkai as *Nasi* - leader of the *Sanhedrin* - around 80 CE, when the Temple had only recently been destroyed and ben Zakkai had persuaded Titus and Vespasian to allow a single *yeshiva* at Yavneh as the remnant of Judaism in the land. Shimon was much admired by Josephus – ironically, since Shimon had nothing but detestation for his admirer – who described him as "a man highly gifted with intelligence and judgement", and said of him that he could "by sheer genius retrieve an unfortunate situation in affairs of state" – a skill Josephus could recognise in others but not, alas, imitate himself. *Mishnah* also records his feats of valour, notably his prudence in the matter of the cost of birds purchased by women for ante-natal sacrifice, his capacity to juggle no less than eight flaming torches, and his athleticism in returning from the prostrate to the standing position in prayer with the use of just one finger on the ground. Shimon is himself quoted in *"Pirkei Avot"* ("The Ethics of the Fathers" 1:17): "All my life I have grown up among the wise, and I have found nothing of better service than silence; not learning but doing is the chief thing; and he who is profuse of words can cause sin." *Caveat scriptor*!

There were, of course, other members of the family who also took the name Shimon ben Gamliel, but it was he of *Yavneh* who bore the honorary title *Nasi*, Prince of Judah; most authorities agree that the one intended by this *piyyut* is the one I've described here, and this despite the fact that no one knows how he came to meet his death.

After Shimon, Rabbi Yishmael the High Priest. The astute will have noticed a conundrum in that name, for it was most unusual in that world torn between Pharisees and Sadducees to find a Rabbi appointed, or perhaps that should read anointed High Priest. Yishmael ben Elisha was the exception. A child at the time of the destruction of the Temple, he was taken as a captive to Rome but later ransomed by Rabbi Joshua, who became his teacher, alongside Nehunya ha-Kanah, at the *yeshiva* at Kfar Aziz, south of Hebron. As an adult Yishmael became a leading voice at Yavneh, the principal rabbinical seminary; he was present on the day Rabban Gamliel was deposed and Eleazar ben Azariah appointed *Nasi* in his place.

Yishmael's presence in the unhistoric tale of the Ten Martyrs isn't without particular significance, for in addition to his development of hermeneutics as the means of deducing God's commandments from the scriptures, he became embroiled in one especial controversy, precisely over the commandments for which suffering martyrdom was acceptable and those which prohibited it; Yishmael insisted that worshiping idols was acceptable if it were necessary to save a person's life, provided it wasn't done in public; a response which would become hugely significant amongst *marrano* and *converso* communities in Europe for the next two thousand years. As far as we know, Rabbi Yishmael died peacefully in his own bed, a martyr only to infirmity and old age.

Who else wasn't present on the date when the murder of the Ten Martyrs didn't actually take place?

Rabbi Akiva's death is perhaps the most renowned, though it too happened elsewhen, in the year 135 CE to be precise, more than half a century after Gamliel and Yishmael. Following the Bar Kochba revolt, the Romans were seeking all the leaders of Israel, and found Akiva reciting the morning *Shema*; throughout the long hours of his torturing, he never ceased reciting the *Shema* over and over. The Roman Commander Turnus Rufus was so astonished by this that he asked Akiva, "Have you no feeling of pain that you can laugh in the face of such intense suffering!" (every account of this that I've ever seen ends Rufus' statement with an exclamation rather than a question mark). Akiva is said to have replied, remarkably lucidly for a man in chains and beaten almost to the point of death: "All my life I have been concerned over a particular phrase of *Torah*. We are taught in the *Shema* to accept God's sovereignty and decrees 'with all our soul', which means obeying God even at the expense of our lives. This is an extraordinary thing to ask of any man, and I have often wondered if I would be given the privilege of performing it. Now that the chance has come, should I not grasp it with joy?" Saying which he uttered one last time the opening phrase of the *Shema*, drew out the *"Echad"* like an expression of derision for his persecutors, and died. Bravado? Of course bravado. Fiction? Of course fiction. But exemplary bravado, exemplary fiction, the sort from which archetypes are formed and future generations given courage to endure their personal torturings.

Rabbi Chananya ben Teradyon, the head of the academy at Siknin, acquired such a reputation for extraordinary acts of charity that Eliezer ben Yakov instructed his own followers that they shouldn't give money to any charity unless it was administered to the standards set by Chananya. Charity wasn't afforded to Chananya however, only by him. Like Akiva, he was rounded up in the wake of the Bar Kochba revolt; his wife also sentenced to death, and his daughter to slavery. The formal pretext was that he had violated a Roman edict against teaching the *Torah* in public – to which he could only, and proudly, plead guilty. The scroll he had used for the purpose was unrolled, and then wrapped around him like a shawl – though I can't help but wonder if they were mocking him or testing him, for they must have sensed that they were cladding him in spiritual armour, and that he might not burn. But burn he did, despite the saturated woollen sponges. Chananya too was guilty of bravado. As he burned, the letters written on the scroll became dislodged, fragments of half-charred parchment floating up into the air. "See," he called out to his daughter and disciples, "the human parchment is destroyed, but the sacred letters return to their creator" (sadly, I've made up these words: accounts of Chananya's death record only the ambience, not the specifics, of his bravado). However, we do know the words of the Roman executioner, who was deeply impressed by whatever it was Chananya said: "If I remove the wool from your heart, will I have a share in the World to Come?" I like this phrase, and not only for itself, but for the Jewish light is casts back on the Gospel stories of King Jesus. But that's by the by; Chananya confirmed the Roman's wish, the Roman swapped the wool for extra fuel, and then, somewhat in the manner of a worshipper of Mithras, threw himself into the same fire and was consumed. The two, it is said, entered Paradise locked in each other's arms.

Next, Rabbi Chutzpis the Interpreter. An Interpreter wasn't a translator from one language to another, though the need for such in Aramaic-speaking, Roman-governed Israel was great; rather, he was the man who explained to the bewildered congregation what the *Rosh Yeshiva*, the Senior Rabbi, had intended, in the esoterica of his *Talmudic* responsum or his *Shabbat* sermon. Chutzpis – this being a piece of Biblical apocrypha we should expect Biblical numerology – was a day short of his 130th birthday when he was killed; he did ask for the extra day, but it was denied.

Rabbi Elazar ben Shamu'a. Or Eleazar ben Shammu'a. Or plain Eleazar, without the patronymic, because everyone knows who is intended. Another of that small group of Cohen-Rabbis, he was one of the five principal students of Rabbi Akiva, and appears regularly as a source of authority in the *Mishnah*, usually endorsed by some anecdote or comment by Akiva. Eleazar doesn't belong on this list of martyrs, for he lived to an overripe old age and died in his bed; but perhaps he's included to honour the Rabbi who ordained him, Yehudah ben Bava, who was indeed martyred by the Romans. Eleazar may have been the founder of that potent movement in modern Judaism, which I will call "sentimental Zionism" and of which I am myself a member in good standing – a commitment to the Land and State of Israel that includes owning or renting a holiday home in Herzliya, joining an occasional Jewish Agency mission, and providing philanthropic support for clinics for wounded veterans of Israel's wars, but doesn't extend quite so far as to carry out the desire, prayed for daily and apparently now granted by the Almighty, of gathering in the exiles from the four corners of the Universe and re-establishing the Jewish community, not next but this year in Jerusalem. Eleazar's founding contribution? It's recounted (*Sifrey* Deuteronomy 80) that he and Yochanan ha-Sandler were sent to study amongst the Phoenicians, but got no further than Sidon, in southern Lebanon. Tears streaming from his eyes, Eleazar turned around and persuaded Yochanan to accompany him home. "Living in *Eretz Yisrael*," he declared, "is equivalent to all the *mitzvot* of the *Torah*." This isn't a statement that goes down well, in Borough Park, or in Golders Green, in St Kilda or on Bathurst Street.

Rabbi Chanina ben Chachinai. Not one of the famous five, but still one of Akiva's earliest students. Chanina's character would have appealed to Shlomo Agnon, I'm sure, though I've found no explicit reference in his writings – perhaps an obscure allusion: the uncomplaining wife of Reb Yudel Bok, in "The Bridal Canopy", the best book about *stadtl* Jewry ever written. Chanina's wife was so devoted to her husband, to the *Torah*, and to

132

her husband's devotion to the *Torah* (either that or it was the best ruse ever thought up by a woman cuckolding a man), that she encouraged him to stay at Akiva's *yeshiva* full thirteen years.

Rabbi Yesheivav the Scribe was a friend and rival, though not a pupil of Akiva, so renowned for his generosity that Akiva once restrained him from giving overmuch. Their chief disagreement, and I will state immediately that I side with Yesheivav on this, was over the issue of "*mamzerim* – children born out of wedlock". No, that needs re-phrasing, because "issue" has two meanings. The issue of the issue of "*mamzerim*". The offspring of all prohibited unions, according to Akiva, should be counted as "*mamzerim*". Yesheivav disagreed, regarding the legacy of sins to be a matter for God to decide, "even unto the third and fourth generation of them that hate Me", and not something for mere mortals to determine. During the Hadrianic persecutions following the Bar Kochba revolt, he hid at Sepphoris in the Galil with several other rabbis; but to no avail. The Romans found him, and executed him. He was ninety. His parting message to his disciples was "Support one another. Love peace and Justice. Perhaps there is hope."

Rabbi Yehudah ben Damah belonged to the group of scholars known as *Tanna'im*, as opposed to their colleagues and rivals the *Amora'im*. The word *Tanna* is of Aramaic origin, and though it's used to mean "to study" and "to teach", its etymology is clearly linked to the oral tradition, for that is the precise meaning of the Aramaic "*teni*". The *Tannaitic* period began with Hillel and Shammai around 20 CE, and ended with the final redaction of the *Mishnah* by Judah ha-Nasi around 200 CE. Within that epoch, the two significant dates are 70 CE, when the Temple fell and the seminary at Yavneh gave the *Tanna'im* a new pre-eminence; and 135, the year of the fall of Betar, following the Bar Kochba revolt, after which the writing down of the oral tradition, already understood as critical to the survival of Judaism as a religion, was extended into an urgent need for study and interpretation, lest what was now written down be misunderstood – a task that would lead to the creation of the *Gemara* and the supplanting of the *Tanna'im* by the *Amora'im*. Yehudah ben Damah belonged to the last generation of *Tanna'im* from the *Mishnah* period. We don't know how he died, except for his name being included, almost certainly apocryphally, in this list.

Rabbi Yehudah ben Bava was yet another of Akiva's colleagues. A pious man as well as a great scholar, he too defied the Roman law and taught *Torah* publicly (the modern mirror of this story is told in my novel "Going To The Wall": the Soviet Union institutionalised anti-Semitism in precisely the same way as the Romans). But the act for which the Romans finally took his life was his ordination of the last five of Akiva's students: Meir,

Yehudah, Shimon, Yose and Elazar. No sooner were they ordained than a Roman patrol tried to arrest them; as the *Talmud* records the tale (*Sanhedrin* 14a) ben Bava obstructed the patrol to ensure the students' get-away, but he himself was stabbed to death by Roman spears.

Ten separate deaths, some but not all of them through acts of martyrdom, two in one period, eight in another, all of them separate, many of them legendary or simply fictional; but united as though a single act of martyrdom in this *piyyut*. Twelve stanzas in all, each stanza is divided in two parts, and the first letter of each part provides an alphabetical acrostic; except for the last stanza which, as I've said already, spells out the acronym Yehudah ha-Chazak. The stanzas are separated by the refrain "*Chatanu tsureynu, selach lanu yotsreynu*", a mirror of the *Vidu'i* which allows the modern congregation both to treat the martyrdom as a burnt offering and thereby absolve its own sins vicariously, and also to acknowledge the key conceit that binds the Ten Martyrs, the notion that, however seemingly unjust, even barbaric, the fate of martyred Jews, it nonetheless "justifies the judgement", which is to say it's decreed through the mouth of the Archangel Gabriel as the ordinance of God. In this, some might argue, lies a mitigation of the Holocaust.

But it's also more than that. The very last words, recited by the *chazan* on behalf of the congregation, are:

"Look down from the heights at the spilled blood of the righteous, see it from Your chamber and remove the stains."

Which stains? The stains of blood? Or the stains of sin? It's left, deliberately I think, ambiguous.

Though nothing ambiguous in the implied criticism of the Almighty.

✡

Zechor Lanu

But it isn't enough to tell the story, however factual or fictional. It's someone else's story, not ours, and in Judaism no story is sufficiently recounted until it has been transubstantiated from the impersonal to the personal. So we recount history at the Passover, and state that "God brought *me* out of Egypt". So we remember the pogroms on their anniversaries, and fast, not just to remember those who died, but to feel a small amount of their suffering in our own bodies. So, now, after the telling of the tale of the Ten Martyrs, there is the making of the tale into something personal – for otherwise it's just history; for otherwise, why should we care?

And if we don't care, why should God care? And if God allowed them to die as martyrs, why should He treat us any differently, who aren't even a grain of salt as worthy? This is the ultimate conundrum – why should God care, since He has made death part of His process? We must all die – eventually. And if not now – when?

So we remind God that He has to care, because He has bound Himself in legal contract, and caring is one of the clauses. We remind God of the covenant, by quoting His own words back at him, and not once, not twice, but three times; the words in which He reaffirmed His covenant, in Leviticus 26:42, 45 and 44.

And yes, well done for noticing, we've read these lines before, during the *Selichot* of *Ma'ariv* in fact. No doubt it was the misordering of verses from Leviticus that drew your attention – but I'm pleased you were paying so much attention, this many hours into such an intense act of prayer and abstention. You are, however, wrong. Because we haven't read these lines before. We've read the identical words in the identical order from the identical source, but the context was very different, and the post-modernist Rabbis of the mediaeval period understood at least as well as we who invented post-Modernism do, that context is everything. Then we were discussing the Holiness of the Day, and thinking optimistically about the generations yet to come, and praising God in the matter of salvation for being compassionate, merciful and gracious. We were fawning, and coddling, like a happy child at its father's knees. We were speaking of the covenant in much the way a fiancée speaks of the ceremony she and her betrothed are planning. We recited the *"Zechor lanu"* hopefully, and optimistically, and smiling.

But now we're reciting it after hearing of the Ten Martyrs. The child at the father's knees is angry and disappointed. The woman waiting to receive her *get* is recalling why the marriage failed. Hope and optimism lie in the dust between us, destroyed. So we recite the *"Zechor lanu"* needfully and desperately, acknowledging our own sins, reminding God of His commitments to us, by quoting Him, again and then again. But daddy you said. But daddy you promised: Isaiah 43:25 and 44:22; Isaiah 1:18; Ezekiel 36:25. The last especially, Isaiah 56:7: "I will bring them to My holy mountain, and I will gladden them in My house of prayer." Yes, God – in Your house of prayer. We're standing here, even now. We're yearning to be gladdened.

✡

Shema Koleynu

Which prompts the question: does God listen? And if He does, a second

135

question, deeper than the first: does God hear our prayers? Every Jew, every religious person throughout the world, understands that talking to God is prayer, but that hearing God answer is schizophrenia. We don't really expect answers, not verbally (not even the "still, small voice" that Elijah heard in 1 Kings 19). We expect actions, in the world. And not necessarily from God. Whatever direction we face to pray, we know the true direction of prayer is inwards. And we certainly don't expect answers from within. We expect actions, in the world. Including the action of further prayer. Are you listening, God?

Nor is my question irreverent, for after *"Zechor lanu"* comes *"Shema koleynu* - hear our voice, Lord Our God...to our sayings give ear", an immense appeal to God that truly questions how far He has been paying attention, to our prayers today let alone to our martyrdoms in history. So deep is our concern that He might not be listening – the personalisation of the tale of the Ten Martyrs has left us traumatised – that we'll try every imaginable strategy to gain God's attention, opening the Ark to ensure there's no barrier between us, even trying the old stage trick of whispering one of His favourite lines, the way some actors playing Hamlet will whisper or even mime the "To be or not to be" speech, allowing the audience the space to speak the words themselves, and with it the deep and therefore empathetic pleasure of familiarity. "May the expressions of our mouths..." (the prayer-book explicitly instructs us to recite this "quietly", which is to say, in our own "still, small voice") "and the thoughts of our hearts, find favour before You.". It works too, for us at last if not for God. For out of the whispering comes forth self-assertion, and in the final verses of the prayer it's a very different voice that speaks to God, no longer pleading, but insisting, albeit plaintively. "Do not cast us away. Do not remove Your holy spirit from us. Do not forsake us."
Insisting, but plaintively.
"You will answer, my Lord, our God."
Definitely an instruction; almost a threat.
Until hope and optimism have overcome trauma, and been restored.

✡

But have we gone too far, said too much, spoken arrogantly – and in so doing committed yet another sin? With the Ark again closed, the two verses that begin *"Eloheynu"* are now recited, the first repeating almost the identical words that closed the previous prayer, but in a very different tone now, supplicatory again, no longer insistent. "Do not forsake us, nor cast us off, nor humiliate us, nor annul Your covenant with us..." (this fear is genuine, for at *Kol Nidre*, when all vows were annulled, is it not plausible that our covenant with God was annulled as well?)…"Expose our hearts to love You, and may we repent sincerely and wholeheartedly…Our God and God of our forefathers, forgive us, pardon us, atone for us."

Follows the beautiful melody *"Ki anu amecha"* before, yet again, we recite the *Vidu'i*, identical to the *Shacharit* version until the final verse, where *"ta'avur"* is here replaced by *"ka-katuv"*, quoting the Prophet Micah's assertion (7:18-20) that God "pardons iniquity and overlooks transgression. He has not retained His wrath eternally, for He desires kindness. He will again be merciful to us, He will suppress our iniquities, He will cast into the depth of the sea all our sins." Hope, and optimism, now fully restored.

✡

The Priestly Blessing

The *chazan*'s repetition is now resumed with *"Eloheynu"* and *"Retseh"*, after which there are two options for the community, depending on whether or not the *Cohanim* now ascend the *duchen* to confer the Priestly Blessing – a decision that itself depends upon the presence of a Cohen in the synagogue, for the Cohen is the descendant of the Temple Priesthood, and it's this ritual of the Temple Priesthood that's being re-enacted.

If there is at least one Cohen present, he will have left the prayer hall immediately upon the conclusion of the *Vidu'i* (some authorities suggest the *piyyut* that follow the *Vidu'i* were inserted explicitly to give the Cohanim and Leviyim time to exit and prepare for the ceremony of *duchening*), accompanied by any Levites present. The ceremony of the priestly blessing is performed every day; but today is *Yom Kippur*, and so the ceremony is different. Normally, once outside, the Cohen loosens the laces on his shoes, but doesn't yet remove them; on *Yom Kippur* he may well already be barefoot. Normally the Levites will assist the Cohen in the ritual washing of hands, with accompanying blessings, to ensure purity for the Priestly Blessing; but this is Yom Kippur, when washing is prohibited, and so his hands are merely rinsed, by pouring water from a jug. If he is indeed wearing any, the Cohen now slips off his shoes, for he may not ascend the *duchen* in a state of profanity – which leads me to wonder why he doesn't remove his socks as well, and have his feet washed, or at least rinsed, in the Moslem manner. The Levites cover their faces with their prayer shawls, for no one may look upon the face of the Priest while he recites the blessing, and re-enter the prayer hall. The Levites resume their places, standing with the congregation, who may have turned their backs (some communities do it this way; others regard this as the most derisory of acts and disallow it) or likewise covered their heads with their prayer shawls. The Cohanim follow immediately behind them, heads also buried in their prayer shawls, going directly to the *duchen*, the raised platform before the Ark – whence the nickname for the ritual, which should correctly be called *"Birkat ha-Cohanim - the Blessing of the Priests"*.

"Ve-te-arev lephaneycha" is recited, first by the congregation, then repeated by the *chazan*, a prayer for the return of God to Israel, and for the re-establishment of Temple worship, a prayer I cannot pray, as I don't believe that God ever left Israel, and I have no desire to see the re-establishment of Temple worship. The *chazan* then recites the *"Modim"*, while theoretically the congregation in an undertone counterpoints with the *"Modim d'Rabbanan"*, though I've never yet heard this recited anywhere, by anyone. Follows a lovely variant upon the *"Avinu malkeynu"* which is worth recording here in full, for it should be said in every church and mosque and shrine as well as every synagogue, at every opportunity:

"Our Father, Our King, remember Your compassion and suppress Your anger, bring an end to pestilence, bloodshed, famine, captivity, destruction, iniquity, plague, evil mishap, every illness, every obstacle, every strife, every sort of punishment, every evil decree and baseless hatred from upon us and from upon all members of Your covenant.'

And all those who aren't members of Your covenant as well. Amen.

So, once again, we ask God to inscribe us in the Book of Life, and the Cohanim recite their special *"Yehi ratson"* simultaneously to the *chazan* reciting *"Ve-chol ha-chayim"*; and then the most sacred moment of the entire day, the illusion – yes, even illusions may sometimes be sacred – that we have transcended time and returned to the Temple in Jerusalem, that the authentic High Priest is standing before us with his hands raised above his head, holding the fingers of both hands clenched in pairs, thumb stretched, second and third fingers held as if in a splint, fourth and fifth likewise, but stretched in a V away from the first pair, so that the five-fingered hand becomes the shape of the letter sheen (ש), the initial of the name that Abraham gave to God – *El Shaddai* - just as we do when descending into the waters of the *mikveh*, just as we do with the leather armbands of the *tefillin*. It's the same letter that's carved on most *mezuzot* and, because it renders one of the names of God, so it's forbidden to the congregation to look upon it – this the reason for back-turning or for covering the head with the prayer shawl. The ceremony is as theatrical as the inauguration of a President, with the *chazan* giving out the cues and prompts, the *Cohanim* – who are likely to be untrained lay people – responding.

The blessing for the Priestly Blessing is recited by the *chazan* in an undertone, with the voice raised only for the word *"Cohanim"* itself, alerting the congregation to the incipit to the ritual. The *Cohanim* in unison recite the blessing for the act of benediction, thanking God for making them *Cohanim*

– a necessary prelude to the ceremony that follows - after which the Priestly Blessing itself is given responsively, word by word, with a melody lullabied between the phrases and a long meditation recited by the congregation during the lullaby (though I've yet to hear anybody read the meditation).

Any person standing behind the Cohen will not be included in the blessing, which isn't a problem in most modern *shuls* where the Ark and *duchen* are fixed against the eastern wall and seats are all points westward; in *shuls* where this is not the case, the congregants should move.

The actual Priestly Blessing is broken down word by word, the *chazan* calling each and the *Cohanim* repeating it, with an extended chant between each of the three verses.

"*Yevarechecha adonay ve-yishmerecha* - may the Lord bless you and keep you.

"*Ya-er adonay panav eleycha vi-chunecha* - may He turn His face to shine on you and be gracious unto you.

"*Yisa adonay panav eleycha ve-yasem lecha shalom* - may he reveal Himself to you and bring you peace.

One last convention. After each phrase of the blessing, the congregation should reply "*Ken yehi ratson*", and not "*amen*". This is God's blessing upon us, not ours on Him. "*Ken yehi ratson*" acknowledges our faith in Him – "if it be Your will"; "*amen*" simply adds our agreement to whoever has uttered the prayer on our behalf.

After the blessing, the *chazan* recites a variant of the "*Yehi ratson*" which includes another of those strange pieces of mysticism: an alphabetical acrostic, based on the letters of the Priestly Blessing, which pretends to be one of the names of God, but which isn't even properly alphabetical; the verses referred to happen to provide twenty-two letters, which is a wonderful coincidence given that the Hebrew alphabet does too, but the letters here aren't the alphabet at all, and the language in which God created the world wasn't Hebrew anyway, which wasn't invented until millennia later.

The ritual is inordinately precise - the *chazan*, for example, is instructed not to begin the three-fold blessing until he's sure the congregation have finished their *amen* to the benediction blessing. Synagogues don't generally require complex choreography, but, as we've already seen, the Priestly Blessing is the exception. The first phase was merely one of timing the exit and entry accurately; the dénouement is much more complex. The *chazan* commences "*Sim shalom tovah*" immediately upon the congregation's completion of "*Yehi ratson*"; the *Cohanim* should turn back to the Ark precisely upon the commencement of "*Yehi ratson*", with their fingers still raised, and should only lower them when they are fully turned and the singing has begun. The *Cohanim* should recite *"Ribbono shel olam"* while *"Sim shalom tovah"* is being sung, the congregation simultaneously reciting *"Adir ba-marom"*, and the three should finish together, to enable them to recite in unison the closing phrase of the Book of Life, *"Be-sepher chayim"*, followed by *"Ve-ne'emar"*. The *Cohanim* should leave synagogue formally and re-enter it, rather than simply returning to their seats, departing at the last possible moment before *Kaddish* is recited, the final act in this *Musaph* service. Kafka records the appearance of a leopard in the synagogue with similarly fastidious detail.

And if no *Cohanim* are present in the *shul*, the entire ceremony is left out, save only the alternate phrases mentioned earlier, and the normal *Shabbat* morning recitation of the three-fold blessing by the *chazan*.

✡

The mood changes dramatically now – or perhaps dramatically is the wrong term, for the truly dramatic has just closed its stage-curtain. The Ark is opened for *"Ha-yom"*, for each line of which the congregation responds *"amen"*. The Ark is closed again for *"Ke-ha-yom ha-zeh"*, a further prayer for the restoration of the Temple and its sacrificial rituals; a further prayer for peace. *"Yehiyu le-ratson"* is repeated, and the full *Kaddish* recited - after which the *Cohanim* return, but for no great purpose except to shake hands and be wished well by their friends, because with that *Kaddish* the *Musaph*, the additional morning service, is technically at its end.

Many synagogues like to extend *Musaph*; however, on *Shabbat* and festivals, with the informal singing of *"Eyn keloheynu"*, or the formal recitation of the *"Aleynu"* to allow a second recitation of the *Kaddish* , on *Yom Kippur* these are both omitted. The reason given is worth recording. Each of the phrases in *"Eyn keloheynu"* is regarded as being equivalent to a blessing, and the song was introduced to ensure that the number of blessings recited on *Shabbat* and festivals wasn't less than those recited on a weekday, when the *Shemoneh Esreh* is said in full. But the *piyyutim* of *Yom Kippur* more than compensate for any shortfall. *"Eyn keloheynu"* also includes a reference to the incense service in the Temple; but on *Yom Kippur* the entire Temple Service is recounted, so it's unnecessary.

As to the omission of *"Aleynu"*. Though *Musaph* has ended, *Minchah* begins immediately, without a pause, so the two may be regarded as a single prayer service; as *Minchah* ends with the *"Aleynu"*, it would be prolix to say it now, at *Musaph*.

✡

140

Chapter Six: The Sacrifice Of Azazel

Minchah

If there is to be a break – an opportunity to rest from the rigours of prayer; no more than that; this isn't some university seminar on *Yom Kippur* where a pause for a cigarette, a cup of coffee and a digestive biscuit aids the social networking: this is *the thing itself* – then it will take place between the end of *Musaph* and the start of *Minchah*. Properly there shouldn't be a break at all, *Minchah* following straight on from *Musaph*; but if there *is* to be a break, there's nowhere earlier than this to take it, and to break between *Minchah* and *Ne'ilah* would be inexcusable. Most synagogues reckon to start *Shacharit* at around half-past nine, and to *daven* unbroken until around three o'clock, at which point they allow themselves up to a two-hour break; usually an opportunity to add an additional dimension to the ceremonies of prayer: a chance to question the Rabbi, to study text in open debate. It is even acceptable to rest, or sleep, though this is generally avoided, because doing so encourages guilt that one should not be doing so, and guilt is something we are trying strenuously to avoid on this of all days.

By five o'clock though we're back in *shul*, with roughly three hours left to make our last assault upon the compassion of the Almighty. Gathering in the troops, I always feel as Ernest Shackleton must have felt, forcing his men out on to the Antarctic ice for one last trawl. Or as Edmund Hilary must have felt, waking the men at dawn in the final base camp they would build on Everest. This is it, chaps. Play up and play the game time. There's the summit, just visible where the face of God disappears in cumulus and alto-stratus. United we stand. One last assault upon immaculate success.

It may be the last stretch, but it's also the hardest. Oxygen is thin as ice up here. Resources are strapped. The weight of our still unforgiven sins is heavier than rucksacks. The rocks are sharp on which we will now have to kneel for our *"Aleynu"*, instead of standing as we're used to doing. Is this not the point of the holy mountain at which Moses too had doubts, at which Jacob found himself needing a ladder, and the ladder held steady by the angels? No wonder *Minchah* begins by taking out the *Torah* Scrolls – at this juncture, we need God's help. Like the Israelites at Rephidim, we go into battle with our own souls, armed with God. (During my many years as prayer-leader, I always brought a bottle of smelling salts into *Minchah* and let those who wished to take advantage of it from now until the end; really it's just a placebo; but then, the exhaustion of the congregation is really all in the mind, and given that the multiplication of two negatives invariably makes a positive, what better method than placebo to cure the psychosomatic?)

The introductory prayers that accompanied the *Shacharit Torah* readings are omitted here. This isn't *Torah* ceremony, but *Torah* ritual – very different. In some communities a recitation of *"Korbanot"* and *"Ketoret"* forms a prologue, readings from Exodus 30:17-21, Numbers 28:1-8, Leviticus 1:11, Exodus 30:34-36; 7; 8, Leviticus 2:11, Psalm 46:8; 84:13; 20:10 and 32:7, and Malachi 3:4, all of which, but in a much briefer version than the one we read in *Shacharit*, give the Biblical instructions about the use of Offerings and Incense in the Temple, interspersed with *Talmudic* references that explain precisely how much Cyprus wine should be used, the process for grinding the spices, and an explanation of why fruit-honey isn't mixed. On *Yom Kippur*, remember, a day of abstinence from food. What kind of masochism is this, to stand in the synagogue discussing ingredients for recipes, salivating at the thought of cinnamon and aromatic bark?

But in the majority of communities, *Minchah* commences directly with the *Torah* reading. Two men open the curtain and the door, the *chazan* himself takes out a single scroll, while the congregation sings *"Va-yehi bi'n'so'a"* and the optional mediation is recited, *"Berich shemeh"*, a fragment of the Cabbalistic *"Zohar"*, which means "brightness", a reference to the gradations of emanations of God in the Universe; these emanations are the "physics" of the mystics, explaining both the full working system of the Universe, and also, because we don't stand at the highest rung of the ladder, the limits of our capacity to apprehend the whole. What we can do, however, is interpret what we do know, and ultimately this is what "The Book of Splendour" aims to do, by providing a mystical commentary or exegesis on the Five Books of Moses which employs four separate but simultaneous techniques that are in stark contrast to The Thirteen Laws of Hermeneutics of Rabbi Yishmael[20].

The first is *"Peshat"*, which is simply the obvious and literal meaning of the narrative. The second is *"Remez"*, which operates by deducing hints. The third is *"Derash"*, which is the interpretative or anagogical method. The fourth is *"Sod"*, the secret or mystical. Together, in Hebrew, the four acrostically spell the word *"Pardes"*, which, applying *"Peshat"*, means "an orchard"; applying *"Remez"* presumes it to be an apple orchard, probably because in Latin apple is *"malus"* which also means "evil", and it was an apple that was found in the Garden of the Hesperides in the Greek

---

[20] See "A Myrtle Among Reeds", chapter 7.

equivalent of Eden; applying *"Derash"* however, *"Pardes"* could be a citrus fruit, connected to the *etrog* of *Sukkot*, or it could be a pomegranate, connected to the Persephone myths of Crete; applying *"Sod"* informs us that the word "Paradise" in English is derived from the Hebrew *"Pardes"*, and in English Paradise is always a French farmhouse, close to the Loire Valley or deep in the Dordogne, and the associated fruit is obviously the grape. What even the most intense mystical interpretation cannot explain however, is whether the grape is red or white, and whether the wine is better with, or as so often nowadays, without a cork.

Where normally the *Torah* is taken out to the singing of three verses – *"Shema"*, *"Echad"* and *"Gadelu"* – on this occasion *"Gadelu"* alone is said, after which the Scroll is paraded round the *shul* for kissing, and *"Lecha adonay"* is sung. The Scroll is undressed, *"Av ha-Rachamim"* recited, and the Cohen called, not to the usual formula but with the verse *"Ve-tigaleh"*, after which the usual completing formula is used, *"Baruch she-natan…hayom"*.

The reading for *Minchah* of *Yom Kippur* is Leviticus chapter 18, in full, an inventory of forbidden sexual relationships which on the surface would appear to be irrelevant to the themes and purposes of *Yom Kippur*, except that, perhaps, of all our sins, many will have been sexual, and many of the rest, if Rabbi Freud's *midrash* on the subject is correct, are the consequences of our fears, hopes, ambitions and deficiencies in the same regard. And are we not naked before our mother, our father, our brother, our sister, in *shul* on *Yom Kippur*? To learn what is physically acceptable, whilst engaging in what is morally acceptable, we read Leviticus 18.

Exegesis of Biblical text is one of the best methods available to us to understand the ancient world. For one thing, nobody creates a legal prohibition against something that isn't taking place, so the injunction not to "uncover the nakedness" of your father or your mother suggests that incest was just as extant then as it remains today. More interesting is the verse that follows, "The nakedness of your father's wife shall you not uncover"; because it appears to be tautologous, a mere repetition of what was stated in the previous verse; except of course that "your mother" and "your father's wife" aren't necessarily the same person: a step-mother today as then, or several step-mothers in fact, because a man in Biblical times could take more than one wife. "Your sister" and "your father's daughter" in the next verse echo the theme; it's incest with a step-sister or a half-sister, as it is, according to the later verses, with an aunt or uncle, with a son-in-law or daughter-in-law. Sexual propriety extends beyond the family too: "you may not uncover the nakedness of both a woman and her daughter…or her son's daughter…this is plotted depravity". "Plotted depravity" is a phrase that leaves no room for argument; other translations prefer the gentler "lewdness", but Psalm 26:10 and 119:150, as well as Job 31:11, Ezekiel 16:27 and 22:9 and 11 all confirm the harsher is intended, and "heinous" the technical term favoured in legal circles for such a scale of inappropriate behaviour. Sexual prohibitions extend to include a woman and her sister, whether together or separately, a neighbour's wife, and a woman during menstruation. Only in the case of the neighbour's wife does the text specify carnal intercourse; in every other case the revelation of nakedness is all that's stated, but the inference is plain.

But it isn't only sexual tabu which is accounted here. Moloch worship is specifically mentioned and anathematised – perhaps because most of the incestuous sexual practices listed in this text were associated with Moloch worship.

On *Shabbat*, and on *Yom Kippur* morning, there are seven *aliyot*. In *Minchah* only three – Cohen, Levi, Israel, each with his blessings before and after, each receiving his "*Mi she berach*". After the reading *hagba'ah* and *gelilah* are performed as usual, but not "*Chetsi Kaddish* " as there's no *Maphtir* as such – in the sense that the final verses are not repeated. The *Maphtir* in fact was the portion read by the representative of Israel, the third *aliyah*, in this case the completion of the same chapter of Leviticus, with the strict prohibitions against both homosexuality and bestiality that suggest the world of the Bible and the world of cyberspace are closer than we might imagine, for what they prohibited back then is nowadays available for all to see, or simply fantasise.

Once complete, the *Maphtir* recites the *Haphtorah* blessings, and begins at once to read the *Haphtorah*, which in *Minchah* on *Yom Kippur* is the Book of Jonah.

✡

The Book of Jonah

This is not the place for a sermon on the text; my goal in this book is to trace the sources of the text, to describe how each piece of text fits into the broader scope and aim of prayer; and to point out, when they occur, any seeming conflicts and contradictions.

The story, then, in very brief. Jonah the son of Amitai (a mention in II Kings 14:25 allows us to place him historically in the reign of Jeroboam II, 786-746 BCE) is sent by God to Nineveh to call its people to repent their wickedness; God's intention is to destroy the city as He destroyed the Cities of the Plain, and this despite (I spoke of textual contradictions) His rainbow covenant with Noah, and His previous negotiations with Abraham to practice clemency in favour even of a minority of the good. Unwilling to be the mouthpiece for this calumny, Jonah flees on board a ship bound for Tarshish (Tartessus in southern Spain, at the mouth of the Guadalquivir river in Andalusia). A storm shakes the boat, and the superstitious sailors, wishing to propitiate the storm gods (a second contradiction, for Jonah's God and theirs are not the same, and yet their rites in favour of their gods succeed), cast lots to find out whose sins are being punished in this way. Jonah is heaved overboard, the storm abates, a great fish swallows Jonah whole, keeps him in its belly for three days, then spits him ashore (even initiates of the Zohar find it difficult to read this tale at the level of *peshat*).

Jonah is called a second time, and now responds by travelling to Nineveh, where he proclaims the coming end of the city, and calls for ceremonies of fasting and repentance to avert it. So successful is he, God grants the city clemency; a decision which only serves to infuriate Jonah, who either never knew or has forgotten the accounts of Noah and of Abraham, and who has suffered for his sins, and therefore believes, like any schoolchild, that justice should be doled out fairly and consistently, without regard to individual circumstances. Jonah sits outside the city gate, in the heat of the day, deep in sulk, waiting like a failed eugenicist for God to take his life – a request he's made because, again like any schoolchild, life simply isn't worth living if you don't get your own way every time and without contention (yes, I know I said wouldn't sermonise…but the story is so prone to sermons). In one of the great divine uses of analogy, God causes a castor oil plant to grow up beside Jonah, shading him from the sun; but then infests the plant with worms that eat it from the inside so it withers – an act of divine arbitrariness that couples this tale with that of Job. Lacking shade, and tormented by an east wind (the sirocco or chamsin), Jonah again asks God to let him die. God refuses, and offers a *derash* of his allegory, in which he explains (somewhat speciously it must be said) that Jonah didn't grow the plant, and therefore has no argument for caring about its fate; God on the other hand grew the city of Nineveh, and so He does care about its fate, and since the people have repented, so they should be granted full atonement, as Jonah was, when he emerged repentant from the belly of the whale. The telling of this story on *Yom Kippur* is obvious. The moral implications of the story, and especially the contradictory moral implications in view of Genesis 1:28, are worth a lengthy sermon.

There are other contradictions too. The king orders his people to wear sackcloth and to fast (3:7) when he already knows (3:5) that they're doing this. God provides Jonah with shade in the form of a castor oil plant, but in fact (4:5) "he made himself a shelter, sat in its shade and waited to see what would happen to the city", so the castor oil shade was utterly superfluous, except as allegory. The Thanksgiving Psalm in chapter 2 makes no sense either, since the language doesn't express thanks for the specifics of his release from the fish's belly, nor is it pertinent to the circumstances of Nineveh at the time of recitation. The book itself was probably written in the post-exilic period, which is to say after 530 BCE, but based on oral traditions passed down from the 8th century BCE; but this too is contradictory, because the story is set in the Israelite north and not the Judaic south. It's also hard to see Jonah as a Prophet, even as a minor Prophet, when only chapter 3:4 contains a phrase interpretable as prophesy, and the rest appears to be little more than a rattling good yarn told for questionable moral enlightenment. And why, one has to ask, was Jonah sent to prophesy to Gentiles, who weren't bound by the same Covenant of Sinai, who worshipped different gods, who owed no allegiance or suzerainty to a Hebrew Prophet – Nineveh at that time was in the territory of the Medean Persians, who practised Zoroastrianism? Probably, this was never a Jewish tale at all, but borrowed for its didactic value, in exactly the same way as the Chaldean Book of Job – Jonah means "dove" and the dove was the special symbol of Astarte, the moon and fertility goddess who ruled at Nineveh before the Persian conquest; we can imagine the priests of Astarte creating this tale, as a means of bringing back the ancient form of worship that had been suppressed by the invaders. Properly, in my view anyway, Jonah belongs in the *Ketuvim* or Literature section of the Bible, alongside Daniel and Esther, and not at all among the Prophets.

✡

Micah's 13 Measures

After completing the Book of Jonah, but before reciting the blessings, the *oleh* has one last, short reading, verses 18-20 from the Book of Micah, chapter 7, in which the Thirteen Measures, or Thirteen Attributes, are listed.

The full text reads, with my numbering in brackets to indicate the Thirteen Measures: "Who o God is like you (1), who pardons iniquity (2) and overlooks transgression (3) for the remnant of His heritage (4)? Who has not retained His wrath eternally (5), for He desires kindness (6). He will again be merciful to us (7); He will suppress our iniquities (8); and cast into the depths of the sea all their sins (9). Grant truth to Jacob (10), kindness to Abraham (11), as You swore to our forefathers (12), from ancient times (13).

Though the text is from the prophetic Book of Micah, a contemporary of Isaiah who was active in the kingdom of Judah in the late 8th century BCE, while the Assyrians were in process of conquering the Israelite north, tradition (*Rosh ha-Shana* 17b) holds that God taught these Thirteen Measures to Moses after the sin of the Golden Calf; though there's no evidence in the *Torah* to support this claim.

The title "The Thirteen Measures" doesn't come from Micah, and many prayer books prefer to call it "The Thirteen Attributes" which is hugely problematic, for there's already a text entitled "The Thirteen Attributes of Divine Mercy", namely the verse "*Adonay, adonay, el rachum ve-chanun*"[21]. And how do we deduce thirteen measures, or attributes, from this text? I've numbered them in their traditional deduction above. Some (2, 3, 5, 6, 7 and 8) are clearly descriptions of God's character; others (10, 11, 12, 13) of His role in past history; but a role is neither a measure nor an attribute. The first is simply a question, asked by us; or perhaps an exclamation. The fourth is a transmission of the same question into the future. As to the ninth, is it a reference to the ceremony of *Tashlich*, performed on *Rosh ha-Shana*, a personal *Azazel*-ritual that uses breadcrumbs in place of goats and chickens; or is it a literary allusion to the tale of Jonah? Either way, it too is neither a measure nor an attribute of God. Then why is it here?

The answer appears, again, to lie in mysticism, and specifically in the pages of the Zohar; *Parshas Naso* 131 to be precise. Here it's explained that there are two series of "Attributes of Mercy", the "*Letata*" or "Lower Ones", given by Moses in Exodus 34:5-7, and the source of "*Adonay, adonay, el rachum ve-chanun*"; and a second, higher series, which Zohar calls "Supreme Mercy", which were introduced by Micah. I find most mystical claims absurd, but this one isn't simply absurd; it's also profoundly offensive. If Micah intended his list to supersede that of Moses, then it was an act of hubris unworthy of a Prophet; we have to assume he didn't intend it, but is merely the victim of mystical expropriation. The claim that God taught these Thirteen Attributes to Moses after the sin of the Golden Calf may be intended by the Rabbis as an attempt to mitigate my allegation, but the simple fact is, the assertion that Micah's attributes are superior to those of Moses undermines the status of Moses, and of the *Torah* itself, and opens the door for prophesy to overrule *Torah*. It isn't a great distance from here to the assertion in the opening of the "*Pirkei Avot*" that the men of the Great Assembly have themselves replaced the Prophets, and by dint of the mystical claim about this passage, have taken unto themselves the authority not just to interpret Law, but to legislate. The addition of the Micah passage at this point is nothing less than a rabbinic *coup d'état*.

---

[21] See page 68.

✡

The *Haphtorah* blessings are now recited. The scroll has been redressed by now, and is taken to the *bimah* by the *chazan* for "*Yehalalu*", while two men reopen the Ark and Psalm 24 is sung, followed as always by "*U-ve-nuchah*" and the *chetsi-Kaddish* that always denotes a break between two stages of the act of prayer.

The returning of the scrolls allows an opportunity for a sermon, here as in *Shacharit* earlier. I offer my above comments on Micah as my sermon for the occasion.

✡

Amidah

Exactly the same silent *Amidah* as previously, including the *Vidu'i*. But the *chazan*'s repetition turns this into an entirely new *Amidah*, and once again it's the mediaeval poetry that makes the difference. The Ark is opened even before the three steps back are taken and the knees bent for the first "*Baruch*". The opening verse of the opening benediction, "*Avot*", is as normal, but then we make the announcement that, "*Mi-sod chachamim*," that based on the tradition of our wise and discerning teachers, and the teaching derived from the knowledge of the discerning, "I open my lips in prayer", a statement which transforms prayer into a facet of study, and thereby insists that *kavanah*, the intensity of concentration which prayer requires, incorporates the cerebral and intellectual alongside the emotional and spiritual. It isn't enough just to participate, to mouth the words, to recite the mantra of repeated liturgy, to be physically present. In the words of the *Shema*, "you shall love the Lord your God with all your heart, and soul, and might." With all the power of intellect as well, regardless of the cognitive dissonance.

Interesting though that a text compiled by Rabbis speaks of "*chachamim*" and not "*rabonim*" – wise men in the generic, rather than Rabbis in the specific – and recognises in addition "the teaching derived from the knowledge of the discerning", which thereby grants permission to the untrained, the amateur, the dilettante, to engage in their own deep thought, and draw their own conclusions; indeed, it actively encourages it. The opening line of "*Pirkei Avot*" claims authority for the rabbinacy, but never a monopoly on wisdom. "*Chachamim*" and "the discerning" embraces the universal , and even gives approval to an untrained amateur and dilettante like myself to undertake a book like this one.

The Ark is closed, and the congregations sits, because *piyyut* are the words and thoughts of inner man – the inner self transported outwards and thus made concrete – and do not merit the same honour of piety as words of God.

"*Eytan hikir emunatecha* - the mighty one recognised your truth", is a poem divided in three parts, each part invoking the merit of one of the three patriarchs. So, in this first part, acrostically *aleph* to *lamed*, Abraham is intended. The second part, completing the alphabetical acrostic, relates to Isaac, and the third part, which makes an acrostic on the name of the poet, Elijah ben-Rabbi Mordechai, relates to Jacob. Little is known of Elijah, save only that he was Italian, that he lived in the 10th or possibly the 11th century CE, and that he suffered the unfortunate fate of sharing the same name with the brother of the Shabtai Zvi, a 17th century Sephardic Rabbi and kabbalist who claimed to be the long-awaited Jewish Messiah, founded the Sabbatean movement, but then, at the age of forty, banished by his community as an apostate, let down his disciples by converting to Islam. But this Elijah also enjoyed the fortunate fate of having his *piyyut* commented on, and favourably at that, by no less a personage than Eliezer ben Nathan, the Ra'aven, who lived in Mayence in France from 1090 to 1170, was a contemporary of the *Rashbam* (Samuel ben Meir of Troyes, one of Rashi's grandsons) and Rabbeinu Tam[22], a member of that group known as the "*Rishonim*", and one of the earliest authors of *Tosafot*, the extension of Talmud into the commentaries of later Rabbis. Eliezer became the son-in-law of Eliakim ben Joseph of Mayence, one of Rashi's fellow students. Through his four daughters Eliezer became the ancestor of several learned families which exerted a major influence upon religious life in the subsequent centuries.

The three parts of Elijah's poem don't simply follow one after the other. After the Abrahamic evocation, congregation and *chazan* together offer up a short prayer in his name: "*Tzedaka teychashev lanu*", which includes an allusion to Psalms 103:10. The *Yom Kippur* addition "*Zachreynu*" is then interjected, and the regular last line of "*Avot*" – "*Melech ozer*", with the opening of the second of the Eighteen Benedictions, "*Gevurot*", the blessing for the resuscitation of the dead which is anticipated with the coming of the Messiah. Only then is the Isaac portion of the *piyyut* recited, "*Ma-ahav*", placed precisely here because we're told in the *Pirkei d'*Rabbi Eliezer (a section of *Midrash*) that Isaac's soul left his body when he realised his father on Mount Moriah had withdrawn his dagger from its scabbard and was prepared to strike; but that God returned his soul to his body in the same

---

[22] See page 53.

instant that the angel commanded him to restrain the proof of his loyalty. So Isaac uttered a blessing, thanking God for giving him back his life, and according to Rabbi Eliezer (and remember this is *Midrash*, where anything may be postulated, however implausible) it was precisely this *"Gevurot"* benediction that he recited, and which is to this day the second of the sections of the *Shemoneh Esreh*.

Once again the *piyyut* fails to find a *samech* (ס) acrostic when one is due, and interpolates a *seen* (ש) instead. After the *piyyut*, as with Abraham, a short prayer is recited by the *chazan* and the congregation, invoking Isaac's merit upon ourselves by symbiosis: *"Lephanav yekimeytnu* - may He raise us erect."

Follows *"Mi kamocha"* and the normal conclusion of *"Gevurot"*. The third section of the *piyyut*, *"Erelim"*, prologues the *Kedushah*, which is the praising of the angels, and of course it was these angels who ascended and descended on the ladder dreamed by Jacob when he slept the night at Bethel; and it was one such angel in the form of a man whom he wrestled to stalemate on the night preceding his return from exile at Penuel: the very wrestling-match in which he won that ultimate Jewish spur, the name of Israel. The mediaeval pietist recalls this, both through the angels' praise of Jacob, and through the giving of the divine sobriquet, "God of Jacob".

A short peripheral remark. Two of the greatest modern secular *payyatanim*, Leonard Cohen and Bob Dylan, have frequently plundered the Hebrew liturgy for lines, even for whole songs. Cohen's "Who By Fire" and "If It Be Your Will", and Dylan's "Forever Young" have already been referenced in this book. One line in Elijah ben-Rabbi Mordechai's *piyyut*, or actually one stich, one half-line, *"yah ya-ir eyney chashechim"*, the *yud* line in the acrostic of his name, gave Dylan one of the finest songs from his "Empire Burlesque" period: "In the merit of the Perfect One may He peer through the latticework, and may He give light to dark eyes."

After the *piyyut*, on this occasion, no personal prayer in invocation of Jacob, but a sequence of phrases recited by the *chazan* and repeated by the congregation, which restate the fundamental premises of *Yom Kippur*. *"Emunat* – faith." *"Yechaper* – atonement." *"Tephilateynu* – acceptance of prayer." *"Micha-el"* - the fusion of Earth with Heaven through the angels and through the act of prayer which binds this to the patriarchal incidents, so that all aspects of the physical and the metaphysical Universe are One.

At this point, in some congregations, the additional *piyyut "Ereley hod"* is recited, author unknown, before the introductory phrase in preparation for the *Kedushah*. Its place here is logical, as its refrain makes reference to the angel Micha-El, mentioned in the previous verse. Most anthologies of *piyyut* place "*Ereley hod*" alongside "*Ki rechuvo*", which is known to have been written by Yannai, who lived in the *yishuv* in Israel somewhere between the 3rd and 6th centuries CE. The placement suggests that Yannai may have been the author of both poems. Even if he isn't, the opportunity to write about him is irresistible, for he's one of the finest exemplars of the original Palestinian form of *piyyut*, one of its last too, and the teacher of Elazar ha-Kalir; but especially because scrolls of his work were amongst the truly important discoveries made when the Cairo *genizah* was opened and an entire historical library of Jewish manuscripts literally unearthed, in 1896; 250,000 fragments in total, including full page documents and a handful of books preserved in their entirety, penned by members of the Jewish community in Cairo over a period of 250 years, between 1000 and 1250 CE.

✡

Kedushah

No different from the regular *Kedushah* as far as "*Le-dor*" at the commencement of "*Kedushat ha-Shem*". As always "*Chamol*" is provided with two versions, some communities preferring "*Bi-kedushatcha* - for with Your holiness", others "*Ke-erchecha* - for like Your own measure" in the penultimate phrase. After this the regular "*Kedushat ha-Shem*" leads to an equally regular "*Kedushat ha-Yom* - the Holiness of the Day" ("*Atah bechartanu*" and "*Va-titen lanu*"), with additional phrases if *Yom Kippur* should fall on *Sabbath*; then the normal verses, "*Eloheynu*" and "*Zechor*".

The next *piyyut*, introduced by a phrase from the Book of Numbers (12:11), is "*Al na tashet* - please do not reckon…*" and the response "we have erred", is followed by "*El na rephah* - o God please cure…*", which is known in the Rabbinic literature as the "Song of Forgiveness for the Illnesses of Children" and recited not only on *Yom Kippur* but on all fast days – except that many congregations omit it altogether, on *Yom Kippur* and on other fast days. The poem is written in a complicated formal structure: a triplet, a varied refrain in which God is invited to answer us, but on each occasion to do so in recollection of a different historical occasion of His successful intervention; and then a repetition of the principal refrain, the "*chatanu* - we have erred" - which was the initial response to "*Al na tashet*". To make it still more complex, the poet runs an alphabetical acrostic through the three initial letters of each triplet, and in addition to the historical allusions contrives to include a substantial number of biblical references and quotations along the way. The historical line is always introduced with the word "*Aneynu*", reflecting the traditional prayer of that name used in daily services throughout the year as well as in special prayers elsewhere on *Yom Kippur*[23].

The verses *"Zechor lanu"*, *"Rachem aleynu"* and *"Mecheh pasha'eynu"* follow, preceding *"Shema koleynu"* in the regular manner. The Ark is opened for *"Shema koleynu"*, then closed again for the verses that begin *"Eloheynu"*. The responsive chant *"Ki anu amecha"* is followed by *"Anu azey panim"* and then, yet again, it's time for the congregational *Vidu'i*, the same format, standing, striking the left side of the chest with the right fist whilst reciting the alphabetically acrostical list of confessions from *"Ashamnu"* to *"Titanu"*, and then the further confessional verses *"Sarnu"* and *"Hirshanu"*. The *chazan* continues alone with *"Eloheynu"* and *"Hazdonot"* after which some congregations recite *"Atah meyvin"*, a double alphabetical acrostic believed to have been written by Eliyahu ha-Zaken, the brother-in-law of Chai Ga'on, or Chai ben Sherira, to give him his name rather than his sobriquet. Chai was the head of the *yeshiva* in Pumbedita – a *Ga'on* in those days was equivalent to a Rebbe in ours - though only after a fierce rivalry with Shmuel ben Hophni, who yielded only after Chai and Shmuel's daughter made a diplomatic marriage; Ben Hophni became, instead, the Ga'on, indeed the last Ga'on of all, at Sura.

"Shimcha mey-olam" is recited by the *chazan* and repeated by the congregation; *"Atah yodeyah"* is recited in an undertone by the congregation while the *chazan* recites it in full voice, and then all in an undertone recite the full *"Al chet"*, striking the chest, not at the start of every line as many do, but properly at the repetition in each line of *"She chatanu"*, clutching the fringes of the *tallit* in the gripped fist whilst doing so. So the act of flagellation is rendered sacred. *"Ve-al kulam"* is sung – but all this has been described and explained before.[24]

After *"Al-mitzvat aseh"*, *"Ve-David"*, one of many prayers and verses whose significance is largely overlooked, and only because Rabbis don't give sermons, nor scholars write treatises, on incidental passages of liturgy, preferring to focus on the larger texts of *Torah* and *Talmud*. This is a regrettable oversight. In *"Ve-David"*, for example, one of the most fundamental humanisms of Judaic faith and history is underscored, the recognition that error is implicit to humanity, even to the greatest exemplars of humanity, like David. All of us make errors – and in Judaic teaching, that is part of being what we are. It's acceptable. It's alright. All of us make errors, all of the time. Sometimes deliberately, sometimes in spite of our

---

[23] See page 78.
[24] See page 32.

best intentions. What matters isn't the error, but the saying sorry, and the making good. That's why the *selichot* prayers are available every day. That's why we have *Yom Kippur*.

And if we're still uncertain of the truth of this remark, the next verse, "*Al-tira*", affirms it. "Do not fear, o Jacob; repent o wayward children; repent o Israel; He neither slumbers nor sleeps…You are the Merciful, who accepts penitents; You promised us regarding repentance from earliest times – and because of repentance our eyes look hopefully to You."

"*U-mey-ahavtecha*" is the prologue to the *piyyut* "*Yom*". Rabbinical notes suggest that the original of this *piyyut* was considerably longer, and alphabetically acrostic; what remains today (I've been unable to locate the full version) is just four stanzas, and even these appear to be incomplete. The opening line gives the *aleph* of the acrostic, and appears to establish a structure by which each stanza would have had such a one-line opening, after which the next letter of the acrostic gives the verb relating to the action we are calling on God to perform this day. Thus "A day [on which]…today [such and such will happen]" through what must originally have been eleven stanzas, there being twenty-two letters in the Hebrew alphabet. All we have left is the opening *aleph-bet* pairing, the middle *mem-nun*, and the closing *kuph-reysh* and *sheen-tav*, though even this appears to me rather artificial.

"*Mi el kamocha*", yet another alphabetical acrostic which has lost the majority of its verses, is sung next, responsively, with the eponym as the refrain. Of the verses that haven't been lost, we have *aleph, bet, gimmel, dalet, hey, vav, kaph* and *lamed* in this version. Odd, because at *Musaph*, when we sang "*Mi el kamocha*", we had the same first six letters (though initialising different words and opening different phrases), but then *zayin, chet, tet, yud, sheen* and *tav* as well as two non-acrostical stiches, "*ve-noseh avon*", and "*ve-over al pasha*", none of which are repeated here. At *Shacharit* "*Mi el kamocha*" was different again, and again the words and phrases pursuant of the acrostic were different: *aleph, bet, gimmel, dalet, hey, vav, kuph, reysh, sheen, tav* – even more suggestive of missing verses than the other manifestations of the poem.

"*Ka-katuv*" and "*Eloheynu*" follow, the first congregational, the second recited by the *chazan* alone, and then the familiar concluding verses that include the ceremony of *duchening* at other times, but never during *Minchah*, even if there are *Cohanim* present in the synagogue to validate the rite. "*Retseh*", "*Ve-techezeyna*", the Thanksgiving "*Modim*" are as regular, and the same brief "*Avinu malkeynu*" that was recited at this point of the service in

Musaph is repeated here, a prayer for the destruction of all forms of destruction, and for the defeat of all forms of defeat, a splendid paradox that clearly requires a miracle to comprehend, as well as to perform.

"And inscribe all the children of Your covenant for a good life" includes bowing at prescribed moments, and then the *chazan*'s substitution for the Priestly Blessing does much the same, turning left and right as opposed to bowing up and down; and the congregation responding, not "*amen*", for this is a blessing not a prayer, but "*Ken yehi ratson* – if it be your will".

"*Sim shalom*" and a further request for our names to be inscribed in the Book of Life, and then, provided it isn't *Shabbat*, in which case this is omitted, a rendition, with the Ark open, of the long "*Avinu malkeynu*" – though still only in the partial form: the full is yet to come. All recite together until the phrase ending "*shiphrey chovoteynu*"; the next nine verses are recited *chazan* then congregation; all together recite the last set, from "*Hatsmach lanu*", but it's recited, not sung, as it will be in *Ne'ilah*.

So full *Kaddish* completes the prayers, recited twice to allow mourners their full opportunity to justify the judgement, with Psalm 27 interjected between the two - and *Minchah* is done.

Nor is there any pause between the ending of *Minchah* and the commencement of *Ne'ilah*. We are so high in the Himalayas now, ascending Everest, that oxygen is thin, and Everest indistinguishable from Sinai. No stopping to catch our breath – there is no breath to catch. This is where the Law of the Immaculate Failure comes into play: we can do nothing but set our sights on the summit, refuse to look down, and keep struggling limb by limb towards the summit. Those looking up at us from the minimal hilltops of suburbia think we're mad, but they've never ascended such spiritual heights, and therefore cannot know that madness and nirvana are first cousins, and in the Mosaic Code first cousin marriages are still permitted. Climb, climb, the gates of Heaven are just a gasp away; if you can't see them, it's simply the glare of sun on snow, and the grey-white cirro-cumulus of the clouds. Climb on!

✡

Chapter Seven: The Locking Of The Gates

Ne'ilah

In full *"Ne'ilat She'arim* - the locking of the gates". This is the climax of *Yom Kippur*, when the judgement inscribed in the Book of Life is formally sealed, and this is thus the last opportunity for sincere repentance. Which gates are being locked though? According to some rabbinical authorities it was the gates of the Temple itself (*"ne'ilat she'arei heychal"*), being closed at the end of the day; according to others, the gates of Heaven at nightfall (*"ne'ilat she'arei shamayim"*), when the last sacrifices have been tidied up. The second opinion is now favoured (though this doesn't automatically make it correct); and consequently we commence *Ne'ilah* before the sun has set and don't complete the prayers until night has fully fallen, a custom which I imagine must cause consternation in some parts of the equinoctial universe (in Israel, all through the year, darkness sets in at around 7pm, a function of being so close to the Tropic of Cancer; but when are they permitted to commence *Ne'ilah* in Finland?)

Historically, in Second Temple times, *Ne'ilah* didn't belong exclusively to *Yom Kippur*, but was the closing ritual on every fast day, and at the conclusion of the daily *"Mishmarot"* and *"Ma'amadot"*, the rotational duties required of each tribe under the terms of the national confederation. This lends weight to the argument that the act of locking refers to the gates of the Temple.

In Second Temple times it was also a much briefer ceremony. By the 3rd century CE we know that it contained an *Amidah* of seven benedictions, and a *Vidu'i* in which prayers specific to *Yom Kippur* had replaced others not thought appropriate (*"Atah noten yad"* for *"Atah yodeyah razei olam"* and *"Atah hivdalta"* for *"Al chet"*, for example). The *selichot* and *piyyut* weren't added until the early Middle Ages.

How long before sunset should we commence praying the *Ne'ilah* service? Yes, it matters. *Talmudic* sources tell us that one hour before sunset was the convention on all days of the year, because that was the time fixed for the closing of the Temple gates (which adds further weight to the argument). But on *Yom Kippur* the gates were left open until the last possible moment (which thereby diminishes the argument again), to allow even the least contrite to change their mind and make the choice to seek atonement; so the prayers should be delayed until the last possible moment, the point when sunset becomes twilight.

As with the normal *Ma'ariv* or evening service, as with the resumption after the Reading of the Law, the prayers begin with *Ashrey*, the alphabetical acrostic of Psalm 45 prefaced with a verse of Psalm 84 (5) and another from Psalm 144 (15), and concluded with a verse from Psalm 115 (18).

But this is no longer prayer. We have been conducting these rituals now for the best part of twenty-two hours, from sunset to almost sunset, without so much as a morsel of food or a drop of saliva passing between our lips. We've beaten our breasts and our consciences; we've racked our souls and our memories for further reasons to beat our breasts and our consciences and to rack our souls and memories; we've sung *piyyut* that we didn't understand, to melodies we couldn't follow; we've listened to interminable sermons full of platitudes and borrowed wisdom; we've been bored and restless for long periods, to the point of losing focus, talking to our neighbour, and accruing one more sin thereby that needed expiation. We've regained at last our lost composure, recognising that our understanding of the *piyyut* wasn't a necessity; that our ability to follow the complex melody didn't prevent us singing in our hearts; that lengthening the sermon was the Rabbi's entirely sensible way of differentiating holy space and holy time; that platitudes are merely wisdom we've already acquired, and no less wise for not being innovative, and no less true for being borrowed. We've transcended boredom, comprehending that boredom is a failure from within ourselves, and not a function of the ceremony; and in that moment of understanding we've moved a little further from our neighbour, found a space in which we can resume our *kavanah*, our concentration; and taking a long, deep breath, we've declared in our minds that this is almost over, the mountain-top is visible among the clouds, and one more effort only is required to get there.

Because this is no longer prayer. This is a last desperate appeal for mercy, clemency and forgiveness, framed in the language of prayer. This is the most intense three hours in the life of any Jew, for this is the Hour of Judgement, at the closing of the Day of Judgement, and it's *now, today*, and not in some imagined eschatological future. Now. Right now. And so, the Rabbis tell us, it's a time when tears are not out of place, as Pharaoh's daughter discovered (Exodus 2:6) when she found the child Moses "crying and she felt compassion for him". So, we're told, will God feel compassion for us – one of the great acts of self-delusion of any faith, but we're told we must believe it. And behold, six million cried in the death camps of Oswiecim, Chelmno, Sobibor, and nobody heard them, not this side of the closing gates, and not the other. Yet we're supposed to believe that He's listening to our pathetic mutterings at *Ne'ilah*. Those who cry are well advised to dry their tears, and make their own acts of repentance and forgiveness, now, in this life, on this side of the shuttered gates of Heaven. If God is listening, it's in *your* heart, not *His* ears. If your reputation as an "*ish tam ve-yashar* – a man perfect and upright" - is important to you (the epithet belongs to Job), it's not your reputation with God or your fellow Man that counts, but your reputation *with yourself.*

Nor do the Rabbis entirely disagree with me, though they may regard that last paragraph as tantamount to apostasy. They are not, however, such fools as to say so, for they are learned men, who know the sources for the rebuttal, who know that God has just as much to be convinced to accept our prayer, as we have to be convinced to add tears to our fervour. That's why the Ark is kept open through the whole repetition of the *Ne'ilah Amidah.* That's why the *Rosh Yeshivah* or the Rabbi or a respected senior member of the community leads this section of prayers, and not some ordinary member of the congregation. That's why we remain standing through the whole *Ne'ilah* service. That's why we chant the familiar prayers, but to melodies exclusive to *Ne'ilah.* That's why, in the *Selichot,* we combine every previous *selichah* into one complete digest. That's why we recite "*Avinu malkeynu*" in full, even if *Yom Kippur* falls on *Shabbat.* That's why, before we start, he who will serve as *chazan* for the service, will vocally exhort the whole community to tearful prayers and extra fervour. If God were truly so compassionate and all-forgiving, if the evidence of History were not so compelling against this piece of wishful thinking, none of this would be necessary.

U-va le-Tsi'on

Taken from Isaiah 59, verses 20 and 21, this is the Prophet's enunciation of the fifth and final covenant, the promised future covenant, the sending of the Messiah to redeem the world on the *Yom Kippur Yomey ha-Kippurim* if I may neologise a trifle ungrammatically:

"'A redeemer shall come unto Zion and to those of Jacob who repent from wilful sin.' So says the Lord. 'And as for Me, this is My covenant with them,' said the Lord. 'My spirit that is upon you and My words that I have placed in your mouth shall not be withdrawn from your mouth, nor from the mouth of your offspring, nor from the mouths of your offspring's offspring, from this moment and forever,'" says the Lord…'"

This is pivotal, and provides *Yom Kippur* with its ultimate validation: if we've achieved perfect repentance, perfect atonement, and therefore perfect forgiveness as a consequence of our day of fasting and mortification, have we not cleaned the entire slate of the Universe, and re-established the purity of Eden? And are those not precisely the circumstances, and the unique

157

circumstances, in which the coming of the Messiah is feasible? To complete *Yom Kippur* correctly is to pave the way of the Messiah. This is an enormous burden of responsibility, but also an enormous privilege.

Although we're not yet reciting the *Amidah*, nonetheless "*U-va le-Tsi'on*" contains elements of it, specifically the chant of the angels, "*Kadosh, kadosh, kadosh*". *Sotah* 49 (a), a key tractate of *Talmud*, declares that when the Temple was destroyed, so the beauty and pleasure of Creation also became denigrated, since when only two actions sustain the merit by which the world endures at all: the reciting of *Kaddish* at any time, but especially after *Torah* study, and the reciting of the *Kedushah* in "*U-va le-Tsi'on*". Why so? Rashi provides the answer a millennium later: because these are the two occasions when Man himself contributes to the sanctification of the Universe, and thereby restores the Temple metaphorically.

"*U-va le-Tsi'on*" is a combination of seemingly antithetical sources, the verbal praises of the angels in the firmament of Heaven, and the scriptural exegesis of one Yonatan ben Uziel, a pupil of Hillel in the first century BCE, who translated the Prophets into Aramaic, the daily language of his Israelite contemporaries, but who did not, despite the attribution over many centuries, also translate the Five Books of Moses into Aramaic; Uziel's translations were *midrashic*, and highly controversial, but his status as Hillel's greatest pupil saved, if I may use such a phrase in a Jewish book, and especially on *Yom Kippur*, his bacon.

Incorporating Uziel's Aramaic text with the Hebrew *Kedushah* makes for a Borgesian construction, or like Escher's lizards, which eat each other's tails: the prayer becomes itself an act of *Torah* study, while simultaneously reflecting the invocation to study *Torah* and the prayer recited after doing so. We should truthfully recite another *Kaddish* after "*U-va le-Tsi'on*". And of course, eventually, we do.

In addition to the Isaiaic and Psalmic references, "*Va'tisa'eyni ru'ach* - and a wind lifted me" - takes us into Ezekiel (3:12), and adds a fourth tier of literary complexity to this extraordinary poem. On *Yom Kippur*, as we've seen, the Book of Jonah is recited, as an exemplar of atonement and the call to responsibility; the Ezekiel quotation comes at precisely that moment when he too has been called to his duty, ordered by God to Babylon on behalf of the Jews in exile there. Where Jonah declined, and fled, only to be arrested by God and imprisoned in the belly of a whale, Ezekiel immediately accepted, and as the line tells us "a wind lifted" him, sent by God to ease and speed his transport – Nature itself providing the antithesis of its response to Jonah. And in the very sighing of the wind, what did

Ezekiel hear, but the voices of the angels reciting the second part of the *Kedushah*, which we recite now, as if in epiphany.

The prayer continues with another of the great catalogues of references, constructed like a cento of T.S. Eliot's by adding allusion upon allusion until something seemingly original has been achieved. *Targum Yonotan* again, Exodus 15:18, *Targum Onkelos*, 1 Chronicles 29:18, Psalms 78:38, 86:5 and 119:142, Micah 7:20, Psalms 68:20, 46:8, 84:13 and 20:10, an allusion that isn't quite a reference to Isaiah 65:23, Psalm 30:13, Jeremiah 17:7 (it's a matter of Jewish protocol, rather than *halachah*, that one cannot cite two of the major Prophets in any prayer or *piyyut* without also ensuring the inclusion of the third), and finally Isaiah 26:4, Psalm 9:11 and Isaiah 42:21.

I can't ignore the admonition stated baldly in *"U-va le-Tsi'on"*, because it applies to me, and to this book, in no uncertain terms. The second sentence of the penultimate paragraph invites: "May He open our hearts through His *Torah* and imbue us with love and awe of Him that we may do His will and serve Him wholeheartedly, so that we do not struggle in vain or create for no purpose." Study the *Torah* (and by inference all the prayers, all the scriptures, including the *machzor* for *Yom Kippur*) for the sake of God and not of Man. Do not study simply to show off how good you are at studying, or to make a literary reputation, or to earn money, or to acquire the admiration of your fellow-men and especially your fellow-women, or to put a published book on your resume and thereby help your job prospects. Study *Torah* for the sake of *Torah*. And also, one has to presume, to become one of those *"chachamim"*, "the discerning" so highly praised in the *Amidah* of both *Minchah* and *Shacharit*.[25]

"U-va le-Tsi'on" is followed by half-*Kaddish* , and then, in some communities, an extra *piyyut* is recited, a quadruple alphabetical acrostic whose closing lines spell out the poet's name as that of Yehudah ha-Levi ben Shmuel, one of the greatest *payyatanim* of the Golden Age, who was born in Toledo, in Spain, in 1080 and died en route to Israel, somewhere around 1145. Those occupied (I always choose my words advisedly) by the politics of modern Israel and contemporary Islam (so advisedly that I cannot bring myself to juxtapose "modern" and "Islam" in the same phrase and have therefore chosen to say "contemporary") would do well to read the poetry of Yehudah ha-Levi, and his fellow poets of North Africa and Spain in the early centuries of the second millennium BCE – ibn-Gvirol, Levi al-Tabban of Saragossa, Judah ben Abun, Judah ibn Ghayyat of Granada, the four ibn Ezra brothers, Meir ibn Kamnial, Solomon ben

---

[25] See page 148.

Mu'allam of Seville, Joseph ibn Migas, Baruch Albalia – why, even their names indicate how far the Jews were integrated into the Arab-Moslem world, and vice versa. It was a time when Jew and Moslem had no squabble, when Islam recognised and acknowledged the significance of Judaism as the source of Mohammed's teachings, when the two peoples knew that they were half-brothers, born of the same father, Abraham, and happily sat down to break bread together at his table.

Once more, then, the individual recitation of the *Amidah*, identical to the previous recitations except in very small but significant degree: in the *Modim*, where previously we had said "*U-chetuv le-chayim tovim kol beney vritecha*", "*ketuv*" is now replaced by "*chatom*": instead of asking God to write our names in the Book of Life, we ask Him instead to seal them there, because this is the *Ne'ilah* service, when the Book of Life, completed, goes through its galley proofs and is redacted. The same happens again a few lines later in "*Be-sepher chayim*".

Two other changes, which I've already mentioned; but now in detail. In place of "*Atah yodeyah*" we say "*Atah noten*", a final appeal for forgiveness based on the principle that so enamoured Heinrich Heine, that it's God who has called upon us to repent, and – the evidence is there in Jonah and the acquitting of the folk of Nineveh – wants us to obtain salvation. So here we are, God, saying sorry and asking pardon; and God will forgive, "because that's His job".

And of course, despite the inclusion of a full *Vidu'i*, there is no "*Al chet*", no breast-beating inventory of our sins and asking for extenuation: that time has gone. Instead we recite "*Atah hivdalta*" - a character witness by the chief prosecutor before the judge's summing up - and then complete the Eighteen Benedictions in the normal manner.

The *chazan*'s repetition begins in the normal manner too, with the blessing of the patriarchs, but is interrupted by the repetition of that key testament "*Misod chachamim*", the one that endorses the critical thinking of the individual, the enlightenment of the "discerning"; and then the first of several interjections of a *piyyut* invoking the patriarchs, ascribed to Rabbi Elazar ha-Kalir, the same man whose works graced the *Amidah* of *Musaph* earlier in the day. As with most of his poetry, the *piyyut* is an alphabetic acrostic, of which *aleph* to *gimmel* are recited here, and others follow as I shall describe. Mediaeval *machzorim* in fact included the whole of this particular *piyyut*, although modern *machzorim* (I've looked at Routledge, Birnbaum, Art Scroll, Singer, several others) appear to have decreed the exclusion of the second half, from *mem*, that is, to *tav*.

160

Elazar's contentions in these first four verses are tendentious to say the least, relying on *Midrash* rather than scripture and echoing the fantasies which sadly undermine that collection. Abraham had intimate knowledge of God and understood the necessity of a Creator from the age of three! God tested Abraham not once but on ten occasions! (*Tractate Avot* is Elazar's source on this occasion). There are times when it's our faith in faith, and not our faith in God, that's severely tested!

In response to Elazar the congregation and *chazan* reply "*Emunim…ha-yom*", a reflection of our having spent the entire day in prayer, but also the first of innumerable naggings that the time is rushing by, the hour of closure is almost on us, and we need to hasten lest we miss every available opportunity for yet one last act of penitence, one last contrition, one last plea for redemption. Speaking as one who led and organised these services year after year for more than a decade, timing by now is everything; about an hour and three quarters is sufficient for *Ne'ilah*, but two hours should be left, in order not to have to hurry "*Avinu malkeynu*".

"*Zachreynu*" and "*Melech ozer*", followed by "*Atah gibor*", then the second of Elazar's interjections, *hey* to *chet*. In the first Abraham's virtues were extolled; now it's Isaac's turn. Elazar cites Genesis 21:12, where Isaac is declared "the Patriarch's only offspring", not a rejection of Ishmael's paternity, only of his right to inherit; and though this isn't the time or place, the reference is one of several in the scriptures which appear to corroborate a view of ultimogeniture in the Biblical epoch – inheritance by the last-born, not the first, as we might expect today. The second reference to Genesis is more pertinent to the occasion: in 26:18 we're told that Isaac left the city of Avi-Melech and took up residence as a shepherd in the desert: a choice of rural idyll over urban decadence, at least in Elazar's interpretation, because he declares that Isaac did so in order "to avoid the snares of evil". But Elazar would have known the tractate of *Midrash* called "*Beryeshis Rabbah*", and there Avi-Melech is castigated for being outwardly an exemplar of moral uprightness, but in actual practice (*BR* 64:2) a man of inveterate wickedness. It's precisely these two vices – the hypocrisy as well as the wickedness *per se* – from which Elazar presumes Isaac to have fled; and the admonition upon us on *Yom Kippur* is self-explanatory. Elazar then makes his third reference, this time to Genesis 26:12. where Isaac's fortunes were enriched a hundredfold precisely because he'd taken the right spiritual and moral stance in relation to Avi-Melech. Again, self-explanatory.

But most important of all, any reference to Isaac must inexorably evoke the *Akeda*; and after all, we studied it in detail earlier this morning, and surely there must have been good reason. Like the dog in Steinbeck's "Of Mice And Men", shot half-way through the novel so that we're prepared for the shooting of Lenny later on, so now the image of the *Akeda* comes home to roost. In the congregational response to Elazar we ask God for salvation and redemption, but also for resuscitation. Why resuscitation? Because we're hungry and thirsty at the end of the long fast? No, that wouldn't require resuscitation, because exhausted and bedraggled we may be, but not close to death. Chapter 31 of the *Pirkei d'*Rabbi Eliezer provide us the explanation: when Abraham placed the knife on Isaac's neck, he didn't physically die either, but he passed through a kind of spiritual death, which our modern psychologists would call a "trauma", not in its source-meaning of "dream" but in its medical understanding as "life-changing damage". When evening approached, Rabbi Eliezer tells us, Isaac went out into the fields to pray (we know this from elsewhere in the scriptures; Eliezer makes the assumption that, since this was Isaac's adult practice, he would have done so on the day of the *Akeda* too – it's the kind of retrospective logic in which the *Talmudists* indulge consistently, and which, I suppose, we must allow them); and his prayers were rewarded by the sending of "life-giving dew", with which he was able to be revived. At roughly 5.45 on a late autumn evening, twenty-two hours into our fast and prayers, some manna of Earl Grey, some life-giving dew of Assam or Darjeeling, even a herbal ginseng, a blackcurrant infusion, a liquid extraction from the coffee bean, most certainly wouldn't go amiss. But alas, we can't yet do anything but refuse it.

"*Mi kamocha*" as usual, then *tet* to *lamed* of Elazar's *piyyut*; Jacob now, the third of the patriarchs. "The radiant image" of the first phrase recalls *Targum Yonatan* rather than the original version of Genesis 28:12 – as I said before, Yonatan probably wasn't the translator, though the work is attributed to him; as I said before, the translations were *Midrashic*, which means interpretative and expansive, rather than literal word-for-word resumptions of one language in another; in the *Targum* the image of Jacob is physically engraved upon the Throne of Glory, a somewhat surprising hypocrisy from a God who will not allow His people graven images.

The second of Elazar's references is the one that troubles me beyond the merely tongue-in-cheek. "When he who was perfect saw that awesome place, he awoke, he gazed, and he trembled with fear." The evidence of the Book of Genesis doesn't corroborate this claim for Jacob's perfectness; but leave that apart. In all these references and our congregational responses, the intention is to bring the experiences of the patriarchs to bear upon us today, to complete that chain of history which is the prologue to the "Ethics of the Fathers", by making the past personal and thereby the present meaningful. What Abraham knew can become our knowledge; how Isaac revived can inspire our revival. But why, with Jacob, introduce the ladder of Bethel and the vision of the angels ascending and descending on the ladder? We're in *Ne'ilah*, when we're licensed to speak the *Kedushah* in our own names, because we have equality of status with the angels. Are we intended to imagine that this synagogue is Bethel, that this congregation is the host of angels? What is Bethel, etymologically I mean? *Beit-El*, the House of God – a stele or dolmen or stone pillar generally, rather than the fully erected house, as we know from the fact that the Phoenicians and Greeks used the word *baetylos* to describe the same construction. And we, like Jacob, as we say these lines, are we intended to wake up, startled awake by what we're reciting, waking to the recognition of the true holiness of this holy place, our habitual and comfortable daily synagogue where we have our seat, our place to store our *tallit*, waking to the terrible recognition that this must be more than habit, more than comfort, more than ritual and routine, that this is a sacred act of inner duty?

For me, this is the moment when the significance of *Ne'ilah* hits home, and I begin my personal last scaling of the summit – perhaps by ladder now, and perhaps that's the answer to my concern in the previous paragraph. Jacob's Ladder is introduced, precisely because we're on a par with the angels at this moment, precisely because now, and only now, we too are permitted to begin climbing. But we've been climbing for twenty-two hours already. We're in the clouds now. Look closely as you climb, and you should soon be able to discern the ornamentation on the gates of Heaven, you should soon be able to answer those significant questions that have always troubled you (do we all go in by the same door, men and women, Jews, Christians and Moslems? Is there a special entry for atheists, so that God can have the last laugh? Do they need security guards? Will I get a stamp on my passport? I wonder who made it here, and who get sent to the other place?) No wonder the congregational response this time is placed in bold type in almost every version; no wonder the response cites Psalms, and not *Midrash*. "*Yimloch* - the Lord shall reign forever, your God, O Zion – from generation to generation." "*Halleluyah* - You, o holy one, are enthroned upon Israel's praises; please o God." And then, once more, the nag that time is passing: "*Shema na*".

What did the remainder of Elazar's *piyyut* consist of? Sadly I've been unable to locate a copy of it anywhere – all references to it suggest the *piyyut* was lost in all but its *machzoric* cento. I imagine that it went on to cite the virtues of those Jewish leaders who came after the three patriarchs – Moses, inevitably, David, Solomon, others. No doubt Reform scholars and Rabbis would like to think it moved from the patriarchs to the matriarchs, but that's implausible; about time though it is that modern Judaism has opened its doors to women, it's nonetheless a lie and a calumny to suggest the patriarchal wives had that role in previous times. They absolutely did not. Biblical Judaism was hopelessly patriarchal. Sarah was a good wife but a lousy breeder until Hagar proved a better one; and other than getting her servants to prepare a meal for the angels at Hebron, no other role than this was ever ascribed to her, except the strange events in Egypt, which don't exactly describe Abraham as uxorious. Rebecca is first a wife and mother, but in the few paragraphs allotted to her she's shown as an unscrupulous manipulator whose engendering of sibling rivalry and rejection of her first-born would arouse the attention of the welfare services were it to be the case today. Rachel belongs amongst the nymphette literature with Lolita and Juliet; Leah is left as uncharacterised as a cameo in a Jeffery Archer novel; and as to Bilhah and Zilphah, they are breeding machines, and then abandoned to the harem. No, women can put on *cipah* and *tallit* and stride to the *bimah* to *leyn* from the *Torah* as much as they like, and modern Judaism is delighted to bid them welcome; but it's a falsehood to evoke Lilith and Chochma in the cause of matriarchy, or to write novels about these Biblical women that pretend or fantasise a society like today's, because women had neither role nor status in the epoch of the Bible, and history may be altered in the writing, but not in the reality. Women who wear wedding rings today should understand that their matriarchal heroines wore them too, not on their finger, but through their nose; a symbol of property no different from the purchasing of cattle.

Having expiated that little piece of patriarchal guilt on behalf of my fellow Jews, and having recited the *Kodesh* and the *Kaddish*, the *Kedushah now* completes the Jewish holy trinity, with its introductory "*U-ve-chen*" and then the interjection of an anonymous *piyyut*, alphabetically acrostic but in an unusual structure: "*Sharey armon - meherah tiphtach le-vo'arey dat amon*".

The poem is split in lines of two columns. Each phrase begins "*Sharey*", the second word of that phrase giving the first acrostic. Each sister-phrase begins "*Meherah tiphtach le*", and its next word gives the second acrostic. The sense of the piece relates specifically to *Ne'ilah*, the locking of the gates, the "*sharey*" in question being the gates of the Temple in Jerusalem, so that we are restored – if I may be permitted the usage of the term – to Roman Jerusalem before the destruction by the Titanic hordes. One conundrum though: here we are awaiting the locking of the gates, which implies they must be open, and yet the *piyyut* calls for their opening. Greater minds than mine have discussed and disputed the matter without reaching a consensus; Rav (Obadiah ben Abraham of Bertinoro, a 15th-century Italian Rabbi much admired for his populist commentary on the *Mishnah*), for example, holds that the *payyatan* is asking God to open the Heavenly Gates, which seems to me absurd since the literal words are plain for all to see; Rabbi Yochanan (there are innumerable Rabbi Yochanans in Jewish history; it is unclear which of them is being referenced here) insists that it is indeed the Temple gates, but offers no explanation on my point. I venture to suggest that the anonymous *payyatan* wrote a poem calling for God to open the Temple gates, i.e. to hear and receive prayer, and the compilers of the *machzor* thought, "oh look, there's a *piyyut* with no obvious home, where shall we put it?", and since it referred to the Temple gates they put it in *Ne'ilah* and didn't think till afterwards that maybe they were wrong. Or perhaps I'm wrong, but I like my explanation, because I like there being an arbitrary, human element to all this ritual, I like the idea that Rabbis sometimes get things wrong albeit for the right reasons, I like the element of chance, of hazard, and I like especially the fact that there need to be some things to which even the most rigorous scholars have eventually to say, I'm sorry, I just don't know.

So *Kedushah*, and it's precisely the regular three part *Kedushah* that we've grown used to, so no need for further explanation: the angels' *Kedushah*; "*Kedushat ha-Shem*", constituted of "*Le-dor*", "*Chamol*", "*Be-eyn*", "*Od yizkor*", the four paragraphs each beginning "*U-ve-chen*", then "*Ve-timloch*" and "*Kadosh*"; and "*Kedushat ha-Yom*", containing "*Atah vechartanu*", "*Va-titen*", and finally "*Eloheynu*": once again, the customary pattern.

Selichot next, prefaced with the call – I think Rav was jumping ahead to this in his attempted explanation of the previous *piyyut* – to open the Heavenly Gates precisely now when the Temple Gates are closing; and a third time-nag, stated by the *chazan* and echoed by the congregation, so that there must be some concern that God will call us whiners and be irritated by us, as all wives are irritated by all husbands when all husbands get irritated by the perpetual lateness of all wives. But no matter, for even if God is irritated, placebo is at hand: an immediate apology, itself a touch whining and overstated: "We implore you – please o God, forbear, forgive, pardon, be compassionate, be merciful, atone, suppress error and iniquity". As though the Almighty is likely to be impressed by our possession of a thesaurus!

I've demonstrated previously that, in Jewish circles, flattery is the highest form of strategic planning for forgiveness. We begin, not by confessing our sins, but by detailing the virtues of He whom we would ask to forgive us; in this instance, by reciting the Thirteen Attributes of Divine Mercy, just as we did in evening prayers on *Kol Nidre*. As I've given my exegesis there, I shan't repeat myself here, but simply note that a measure of arm-twisting is also involved, a reminder to God that there exists a covenant, that it takes two to covenant, and that His part of the bargain must by definition include forgiving. And yes, of course He knows. But it's deemed meritorious to remind Him every now and again. And then again. To remind someone else of their part of a bargain serves also to remind ourselves of ours.

And if reciting the Thirteen Attributes isn't enough, we sing once more that most beautiful of melodies, and not once but three times: "*Adonay, adonay, el rachum ve chanun*" before making the formal request for forgiveness in "*Ve-salachta*". And then the final passages of *Selichot* begin in earnest, and remember, this is the last chance, the key moment, pun intended, before the locking of the gates, and so the *kavanah*, the intensity of these moments, must needs be prodigious. In a sense, from now to the moment when the gates shut fast, the words we say are unimportant, but only the intensity of our saying them, the dignity with which we stand, the sincerity with which we pray, the obduracy of our hearts in persevering through the thirst and hunger and exhaustion.

"*Ke-rachem* - as a father has mercy on his children, have mercy on us". "*Selach na* - forgive the iniquity of your people". "*Va-yomer adonay* - and God replied (the source is Numbers 14:20) — "'*Salachti ki-devarecha* - I have forgiven according to your words.'"

That last phrase always surprises me. Such a brief statement, recited so quickly that we almost fail to notice it. It tells us everything we long to know, and yet we walk right through it, as though it were a single flower in a desert, and we so fixed on distant sand, we trample it and don't even realise it was there. "I have forgiven according to your words." What, already, before we got our last prayers in, before the gates shut? This isn't how it's supposed to happen, Lord. You're meant to wait, to draw your verdict afterwards, when we've done: theatre critics don't file their copy half way through Act 5, when Edmund still has the perfidy to send to have Lear and Cordelia hung, when Regan and Goneril are still alive. Not yet, God. It's too early. We need still more confession.

Either that, or we're dealing in wilfulness and obstinacy of a kind that implies serious masochism.

Because we go on making supplications, calling on God as though He hadn't just proven He was listening, and responding. "*Hateh elohay aznecha* - incline your ear, o God*".

But the words are clear. At exactly that moment, without hesitation or equivocation. God has heard our words. God has forgiven us. Apparently it's that simple.

The *piyyut* "*U-mi ya'amod*" is one of the most remarkable in the entire liturgy, but alas we do not use the full text (some *Machzorim* publish it, but no congregations use it in full). What we're given are just six lines, broken into columns again, or stiches to give them their correct appellation. They are in fact the last six lines of twenty, and they count down alphabetically from *vav* to *aleph*, each stich taking the same letter, so that the original must have been a forty-stich double reverse alphabetical acrostic, which sounds like some obscure Olympian gymnastics of the mind, and is, as you'll discover if you try to write one: how much less mediaeval *piyyut* there might have been, had the world already discovered Free Cell and Sudoku! With, as we shall see very shortly, an additional fragment, "*Shilum*", itself acrostical, rendering the author's name, Shlomo *ha-Katan*, Solomon the Small, and leaving a conundrum that I shall deal with in a moment.

In the meanwhile the first rendition of "*El melech yoshev*", repeated interminably as a refrain to the *Selichot*, and always followed by yet one more elucidation of that extraordinarily powerful refrain "*Adonay, adonay, el rachum ve chanun*"; and by this stage of the proceedings we are chanting with much the same relief and fervour that you'll hear "You'll never walk alone" on Spion Kop when it's two-one to the home team and injury time approaching: it has become our anthem, and though nothing is ever certain, and though our nerves are badly frayed, we are confident that we're definitely winning.

"*Shilum*" follows, in a marvellous literary image transmogrifying the linguistic sacrifices of our prayers into the actual bullocks of the Temple Altar; and simultaneously providing us with the author's acrostical signature, Shlomo ha-Katan, and that conundrum that I mentioned earlier. For there's nothing to inform us anywhere who was this Shlomo. A trawl of mediaeval literature reveals absolutely nothing; the index of the Encyclopaedia Judaica doesn't even mention him; and that final brick in the multi-lingual Tower of Babel, the absolute authority on all knowledge in the human Universe, Tractate Google (*pace D'vei* Kipedia), carries no reference to him either. Is it then an error in the text? But no, it cannot be, for the acrostic is carefully laid out at the opening of each stich. Shlomo *ha-Katan* it clearly is.

But perhaps it's possible to deduce who this Shlomo might have been, and to do so using precisely the methodology of hermeneutics given us by Rabbi Yishmael as the means of deducing law from Biblical account. We know that Shmuel *ha-Katan* was a *tanna* of the second century CE, of the era of Gamliel II; he was famous for writing a strict anathema against the early Christians, who in those days were almost entirely Jews for whom Christianity was a Reform movement rather than a new religion in its own right. That text, "*Birkat ha-Minim*", commissioned by Gamliel, also inveighed against sectarians of other kinds, including Sadducees, Boethusians (followers of Boethus who rejected the concepts of afterlife and resurrection) and Essenes; and especially against informers. It was from this latter part of his text that the paragraph of the daily *Amidah* "Against

Heretics – *Ve-la-malshinim*" – was taken, technically the nineteenth of the Eighteen Benedictions of the Standing Prayer. *Ha-Katan* obviously wasn't Shmuel's family name, but a sobriquet that he acquired, and not because of his physical stature, but because of the height of the esteem in which he was held: the Prophet Samuel was obviously Samuel the Great, and perhaps it would be more accurate to translate "*ha-Katan*" in this context as "the Lesser".

But that was Shmuel *ha-Katan*, and this is Shlomo *ha-Katan*. Applying the first of the Thirteen Laws of Rabbi Yishmael[26], "*Mi-kal va-chomer*", and the second law, "*Mi-gezerah shava*", we can presume that *ha-Katan* was also intended as a sobriquet for Shlomo, and that it intended to compare him with King Solomon, who wasn't a Rabbi despite his proverbial wisdom, but who was a *payyatan* of the highest order, as evidenced by his composition of the "Song of Songs". Applying the third law, "*Mi-binyan av mi-katuv echad, u-mi-binyan av mi-shney chetuvim*", we can draw conclusions from the text that place it no earlier than the mediaeval period: the use of the acrostic began much earlier, but no one before the 10th century ever employed the sort of complex pun contained in the connection between the eponymous "*Shilum*" and the name of the *payyatan* on the one hand; and between the verse itself and the act of "*Shilum ha-Torah*" or completion of the reading of *Torah* which is implicit both in the positioning of this verse within the "completing" rite of *Ne'ilah* and in the deliberate use of scriptural references from all three sections of the *Tanach* as well as the *Talmud* (I trust my sentence has conveyed the scale of the complexity by example). Applying the twelfth law, "*Davar ha-lamed me-inyano, ve-davar ha-lamed mi-sopho*"; we can place the writing of the piece in Moorish Spain or North Africa rather than in Catholic Europe, both from the choice of vocabulary ("*shachat*" rather than "*She'ol*" for the Pit), from the fact that the text appears in both Sephardi and Ashkenazi *machzorim*, and especially from the Talmudic reference, which is to *Tractate Rosh Hashana*, a fragment of the Babylonian that was only later incorporated into the Palestinian *Talmud*. Of course, this is all just speculation, but what's wrong with speculating? And doing so, who might we consider worthy enough, from amongst the poets of that era, to name him "a second Solomon"? Solomon ibn-Gvirol is the one who comes to my mind, and a comparision of this *piyyut* with his famous poem on his sickness suggests a stylistic similarity close enough for him to be my choice. Let the serious scholars prove this dilettante right or wrong!

Returning to the liturgy, "*El melech*" again, "*Adonay*" again, and then "*Merubim*", the next *piyyut*, written by the 12th century French Rabbi Yoseph

---

[26] See the companion volume to this book, "A Myrtle Among Reeds", for a full explanation of the Thirteen Laws of Hermeneutics

ben Yitzchak Bechor Shor, from Orléans to be precise, and with sincere apologies to those who were "unconvinced" by my "entirely bogus" argument previously in favour of Shlomo ibn-Gvirol as the author of the *"Shilum"*, let me now propose another option for the authorship of that work, and suggest that the positioning of *"Shilum"* immediately before *"Merubim"* may not be coincidental, especially given the opening line of the *"Shilum"*, "May our lips' payment of bull-offerings be reckoned as sincere". The reference to bull-offerings is the essential here, for Rabbi Yoseph took his somewhat unusual *"kinnu'i"* or family nickname, *"Bechor Shor"*, from Deuteronomy 33:17: "His glory is like the firstling of his bullock (*bechor shur*)." The family claimed to be one of the most ancient in Israel, direct descendants of Aaron and the priests who conducted the very sacrifices to which the *"Shilum"* refers, and which, if we read the *piyyut* as belonging to a member of that dynasty – they bore the name for several centuries after Yoseph ben Yitschak and produced many distinguished *tosafists* and *payyatanim* - would suggest that the transmogrification of the bullocks wasn't just from sacrifice to prayer, but also from prayer to poetry; a wonderful conceit that I for one hope is grounded in authenticity. It cannot, of course, have been Yoseph who wrote *"Shilum"*, because the acrostic spells the name Shlomo. But the *"kinnu'i"* *"Bechor Shor"* evolved into the family name Shor, and became pre-eminent in France during the 15th and 16th centuries as various of its rabbinical members married into other rabbinical families. They were also noted amongst Ashkenazi families as being of those who had early on intermarried with Sephardim; and yes, amongst the later members of the family, there were a number of Solomons.

Whoever wrote it, we can note that *"Merubim"* is once again acrostical, and that again the majority of it is missing. The acrostic is a simple linear form, the first line that we have beginning with the mem of *"Merubim"* and continuing through the lines to *tav*, the final letter of the alphabet. What has happened to *aleph*-to-*lamed* is not clear. After these verses *"El melech"* and *"Adonay"* are once again repeated, then four short stiches of *piyyut* which give us the author's signature, Yoseph, in the traditional manner, before *"El melech"* and *"Adonay"* still one more time.

"Zechor", the next *piyyut*, is in the autograph of *Me'or ha-Golah*, "The Light of Exile", the poetic pseudonym afforded to Rabbi Gershon ben Yehudah, one of the first great *Talmudists* of Rhineland Germany and the man to whom is credited the spiritual ambience of Germany Jewry in the Middle Ages. Born in Mainz around 960, he later became head of the *yeshiva* there, and made his name with two famous *"takkanot"*: rulings based on actual cases which reform or reconstitute an earlier interpretation of the law. Of the two, it's the *"cherem"* – the prohibition – against bigamy that had the

169

greatest impact, because it brought to an end the long-standing debate within Judaism resulting from Jacob's possession of two wives and two concubines.

"*Zechor*" in its original form was considerably longer than the abridged version recited here in *Ne'ilah*; indeed, all that we have here appears to be the epilogue containing the author's signature, and not the actual *piyyut* at all. Its opening statement – "remember the covenant of Abraham" – isn't simply another reference back to the patriarchs, but more particularly an allusion to Leviticus 26, in which God promises to remember His covenant with the patriarchs in times of national difficulty. Coming as it does from a legalist like Gershon it isn't a surprising reference: the use of precedent, of case law; the reminder to God that He too can be held in breach of contract when the Book of Life is sealed. It's a daring and dignifying stance, whose origins also lie with Abraham – the argument over numbers at Sodom and Gomorrah. But it's fundamental to the Jewish religion, and one of the principal ways in which Judaism is different from any other of the world's religions. God is king and ruler, but Man is no mere valet or butler or stable-boy; designated as such in the closing moments of Creation, Man stands before the throne of God as Vizier-of-Earth, and the Prime Minister always has the right to challenge, criticise, advise and even admonish the figurehead President.

A sequence of short prayers is recited next, responsively, *chazan* first, then the congregation: "*Enkat*", "*Yisra'el nosha*", "*Yachbiyeynu*" and "*Yashmiyeynu*", then "*Adonay adonay*" again, but this time without a preliminary "*El melech*". In every case these short prayers are the remains of earlier *piyyut* which the redactors of the *machzor* chose to expurgate. "*Enkat*" was written by Rabbi Silano, in Italy, in the 9th century CE. "*Yisra'el nosha*" came from the pen of another Italian, Shephatiah of Oria, again in the 9th century CE. "*Yachbiyenu*" belongs three centuries later, in Dampierre in France, where it was written by Yitzchak ben Shmuel (the *Ri*, as he's commonly known), one of Rashi's grandsons. "*Yashmieynu*" is attributed to Shlomo ben Shmuel, a 13th century *payyatan* and Rabbi from Wuerzburg, whose other claim to fame is that his is the name on the oldest surviving illuminated Jewish manuscript – coincidentally here, it's Rashi's commentary on the Bible that forms the written part of that manuscript, whose illustrations could easily have been made by a non-Jew, given the Latinate style. Only the featureless human faces denote that a mediaeval Jew must have created these.

"*Ezkerah*", the next *piyyut*, contains the autograph Amitai ben Shephatiah of Oria. Amitai's grandfather, who bore the same name sixty years earlier, was also a liturgical poet; the father, Shephatiah, wrote the *piyyut* of which "*Yisra'el nosha*", which we have just read, four verses before "*Ezkerah*", is the only surviving fragment. Once again we have only the *payyatan*'s signature but not the body of the poem, which must lead us to ask: why did the editors reduce the text? No answer is given in any of the scholarly works I've studied; but chrono-logic tells me what the answer must have been: prayer has now become severely time-restricted. We're praying to the clock. Deadlines exist, beyond which we may not seek extension. If we recite this *piyyut* in full, another will have to be shortened later. Priorities must be established. This, it seems to me, isn't the appropriate ambience for prayer. But this is how it is, now, as we approach sunset, and the end of *Ne'ilah*. We are no longer praying against sin, but against time.

This time *"El Melech"* is restored, and as always it leads into another recitation of the painfully uplifting *"Adonay adonay"*, after which the beautiful and famous *"Rachem na"* – surprisingly famous, given that the text is barely more than a single line. Very little Hebrew liturgy is known outside the synagogue-attending world. Those who have seen Schindler's List will know the highly Litvak rendering of the *Kaddish* from the scene towards the end where, salvation and redemption now approaching with the advance of the Russians, Schindler's pot-makers present him with a ring, and then light candles and recite the Mourner's *Kaddish*, believing him to be their saviour when in reality he's made them his. The Polish-American composer Mark Warshawsky made, in the early years of the 20th century, a version of the closing phrase of the *Kaddish* – *"Oseh shalom bimromav"* – which has become widely known. But purchase a CD of *chazanut*, to hear the great cantors of the world performing their religious Jewish opera, and the *"Rachem na"* will be the one you most remember, a powerfully plaintiff, inward keening of intense *kavanah* which, despite its brevity, is long enough to last for ever.
"Rachem na - please have mercy."

Like *"Sha'arey"*, the verse which follows, *"Rachem na"* really belongs to *Hoshana Rabah*, the closing ceremony of the festival of *Sukkot*, when the palm leaves are beaten on the ground and the prayers for rain are chanted. Like so much of this liturgy, both verses are ascribed to Elazar ha-Kalir, of whom I've already written earlier in this book.

"El melech" and *"Adonay"* yet again, and then the keynote of these *Selichot*: the triple sorrow (sorrow, which is connected with grief in English, is from the same root-word that gives us "sorry"): forgiveness, pardon, atonement: *"Eloheynu ve-elohey avoteynu, selach lanu, mechal lanu, kaper lanu"*. Followed by the beautiful *"Ki anu amecha"* for which every community has its own melody, yet all of them – all the many I've heard anyway – sharing the same atmosphere of folk-song, almost of children's lullaby. Much needed at this stage. Much needed.

"Anu azey phanim" follows, and then – no, we haven't reached the end of the *Selichot* after all, but their beginning, despite the pronouncement in *"Ke-rachem"* that "I have forgiven according to your words". Everything until now transpires to have been preliminary, preparatory. The *Vidu'i*, the full confession, the final throwing over the cliff of the *Azazel* of our personal sins, remains to be recited. Even now.

"Eloheynu – may our prayer come before You; do not ignore our supplication…for we are not so brazen or so obstinate as to say…we are righteous and have not sinned…rather, we and our forefathers have sinned." We, *and our forefathers*. Not just the living individual, but the past that's always imminent in the present, the actions of those who came before us, and which have created the present that we inhabit. The sins of the fathers, even unto the third and fourth generation. Redemption, not just from sin, but from history. As though we look into the mirror to identify ourselves, but history has distorted the mirror, and we are unable to see ourselves simply as ourselves, we can only see our reflection in a form that contains and imprisons those distortions. To make the image clear, to render the image purely "me" without distortion, I must redeem myself from sin, and redeem myself from history too. How? By redeeming history. It's perhaps the most important lesson of the entire process of *Selichah*. That what we inherit from our parents isn't just the condominium in Florida and the leftovers of the bank account after death duties have been paid. It's also the world in whose creation they participated. The sins they left behind, which it becomes our responsibility to expiate. Truth and Reconciliation, to use the phrase the South Africans adopted, after the fall of apartheid. *Vergangenheitsbewältigung* in the German – the struggle to come to terms with the past.

There's no *"Al chet"* in this *Vidu'i* however, no need for the long enumeration of all the world's and worldly sins. Enough to say at this late stage that we have contributed to their commission, that we as individuals take our share of personal responsibility, that we admit that nobody is innocent, not least ourselves, in however small a degree. But we do beat our breasts, to make the act of contrition physical, reciting the now familiar *"Ashamnu"*, *"Sarnu"*, *"Atah noten"* and *"Atah hivdalta"*, and then the formal, customary ending of the *chazan*'s repetition: *"Eloheynu"* first, with additional phrases should *Yom Kippur* fall on *Shabbat*, and then the *"Avodah"* once more: *"Retseh"* and *"Ve techezeyna"*, followed by the *"Modim"* in its regular format, the *chazan* reciting the regular *"Modim"* aloud while the congregation in an undertone recites the *"Modim* of the Rabbis" – though I've yet to hear a single congregation actually do this.

172

The version of *"Avinu malkeynu"* recited here isn't *that "Avinu malkeynu"* but it's a nice piece of choreography to place it here; those who have begun to nod off into reveries of chicken soup will hear the words, wrongly assume we've reached the great climactic moment, and return to prayer. It isn't *that "Avinu malkeynu"*, but it stirs the blood in readiness, for arduous though that recitation will be, it's also the most joyful and potent moment of the entire twenty-five hours…but I'm rushing ahead. For now we simply ask God to remember…and most especially, so specially it's printed in bold capitals, to **seal all the children of Your covenant for a good life**. All the children. That's a wonderful phrase. When Warshawsky wrote the version of *"Oseh Shalom"* that I mentioned earlier, he made a slight but significant variation to the closing phrase: "He who makes peace in the heavens, may He make peace upon us, and upon all Israel." Warshawsky changed *"Ve-al kol Yisrael* - upon all Israel", to *"Ve-al kol ha-olam* - upon all the world". Here we have "all the children of Your covenant". But which covenant? There are five in total, of which the last four are the Covenant of Circumcision (*Brit Milah*), the Covenant of the Law (*Torah*), the Covenant of *Shabbat*, and the Prophetic Covenant, the promise of a future Messiah. But the first covenant of all was made with Noah, in the setting of the arc of the rainbow into the sky as a promise that God would never punish the world again by sending universal destruction; and the seven Noachic Laws, derived from that covenant, are deemed by Jews to apply to all the world, regardless of race, creed, religion, secual orientation or colour. Who then are "all the children of Your covenant"? Like Warshawsky's variation, they are all the children of the world, and this prayer, made by Jews on the Jewish fast of *Yom Kippur*, is in fact a universal prayer for universal peace.

And if there's any lingering doubt in the reader's mind that this is so, the phrase that follows proves it. "Everything alive will gratefully acknowledge You." "Everything alive". The herbs of the field and the fish of the sea are as much a part of Man's Viziership as are his fellow-men. The ice-caps too, if you'll pardon for me mentioning them, the polluted rivers, the rat-infested cities, the slums of the impoverished and the slave-factories where children work twelve-hour days to sew on our designer labels. If you'll forgive the dreadful pun (on *Yom Kippur*, and especially at *Ne'ilah*, everything is forgivable, provided the apology is sincere – and mine here is, I swear) global warming may just be the tip of the iceberg.

Then *"Yevarechecha"*. What else should come after a prayer for universal peace and brotherhood than God's acknowledgement of His part in the covenant, and the ensuing bestowal of the benediction? The Priestly Blessing, given by the High Priest from the *duchen* in the Temple, as it's given on his lap by the father to his son, and the grandfather to his grandson.

After *"Yevarechecha"* we always say or sing *"Sim shalom tovah"*, but joyfully, please, joyfully. After all, we've been asking God for forgiveness and we've waited for a sign. *"Yevarechecha"* was that sign. More than just a sign – an affirmation. Our prayers have been accepted. Redemption has been granted. The Book of Life for at least the coming year contains our names. Sing joyfully. Joyfully. And then add what's no longer a prayer but our own affirmation of the affirmation:

"In the Book of Life, Blessing, and Peace, and Good Livelihood, Good Decrees, Salvations and Consolations, may we be remembered and sealed before You..." Sealed. That's the keyword. Sealed. The book is closed. No more contrition. No more asking, begging, pleading. It's done. It is written... "before You – we and Your entire people the family of Israel for a good life and for peace."
In bold capital letters, because this, this, this is **IT**.

And now, now we can release all our pent-up hunger and exhaustion and emotion in the longest mantra ever written.

Avinu malkeynu chatanu lephaneycha...ve-hoshiyeynu
Avinu malkeynu eyn lanu melech eleh ata
Avinu malkeynu aseh imanu lema'an shemecha
Avinu malkeynu chadesh Aleynu shana tova
Avinu malkeynu batel mey-Aleynu kol gezerot kashot

Twenty-one verses, all commencing with the same phrase, *"Avinu malkeynu"*, in the same slow melody, and with that opening phrase chanted not once in each line, but as many as four times – only three if the remaining lines of the verse are too many for a fourth to fit. Twenty-one verses, before there's the option of an interruption, to chant – few communities do this, but it's available – a Cabbalistic prayer for sustenance, once again using that familiar opening *"Yehi ratson lephanecha"*.

And then resume, two more verses chanted responsively, *"Avinu malkeynu chatmeynu be-sepher zechuyot"* and *"Avinu malkeynu chatmeynu be-sepher selichot u-mechilah"*, and then a recognition, that there are simply too many verses, we're breathless this close to the summit, we simply can't sustain the mantra, not so many repetitions on the same opening word, the same melody, it's overpowering us, we're fingernail-widths from the final summit, and we may not make it. Forget the melody, forget the repetitions, forget the communal participation. Simply – recite. Each for himself or herself, simply recite, each line, *"Avinu malkeynu...Avinu malkeynu...Avinu*

174

malkeynu…", a further twenty verses, and then, once again resume the communal, once again repeat the phrase, once again chant the melody, for one last time, for the forty-third time in total, "*Avinu malkeynu*", and now, the last, the forty-forth (unless you have the Salonika edition, which has fifty-three verses, or the Yemenite, which only has twenty-seven, or the Sephardi, which has twenty-nine, or Amram Ga'on's, which had twenty-five, or a copy of the original, which only had twenty-two), sung to its own melody, more languid and more exquisite even than "*Adonay, adonay el rachum ve-chanun*": "*Aseh imanu, tzedakah va-chesed, ve-hoshiyey-ey-ey-nu*".

But what an extraordinary moment. Why have we sung this final, concluding crescendo, but ended on the dominant and not the tonic? Is the song unfinished? It feels unfinished. For non-musicians reading this, imagine singing Happy Birthday to someone, and getting to that final line, "Happy Bir…" but stopping there. What was the composer thinking? That prayers for forgiveness are as infinite as the repetition of sin, and therefore he couldn't bring himself to return to the tonic chord, but held the dominant. And not just a dominant, but a dominant seventh, which even more strongly implies the tonic. And not just a dominant seventh, but a dominant seventh in the relative minor. Why, o why, do Reform synagogues allow themselves the indulgence of repeating that last verse over and over again, and of returning to the tonic every time? Because they like the tune, and everyone can join in? Please, this is an act of worship, not a Simon and Garfunkel concert. They've surely missed the most important point of the entire twenty-five hour ritual.

But it's over, even though it isn't yet over. We can't just terminate on a minor chord, on a sub-dominant, on a lingering last note. We must remember why we're here. Recite the first line of the "*Shema*", the declaration of our faith, and say it loud and proud and clear. We must bless and thank God for sustaining us through this time, for allowing us ephemerally to stand beside and at the level of the angels. And so, in their words: "Blessed be His holy name and His glorious kingdom for ever and ever." Not once, but three times, once for the past, once for the present, once for the future. And then the human acknowledgement as we return to the mundane level of our own lives. "*Adonay hu ha-Elohim. Adonay* is God." Not once, not three but seven times, His holy number, the number of *Shabbat*, of the walls of Jericho, of the Jubilee.

So the *chazan* recites the *Kaddish* one last time, because every period of prayer and study always ends with the *Kaddish*. And…how neat and tidy and dramatic it would be to write that, as whatever version of "*Oseh Shalom*" draws its last breath, the *shofar* is sounded for the last time…but it doesn't happen quite that way. In an almost unprecedented breach of the laws of

Kaddish, Kaddish itself is rendered up to a hiatus, its solemn flow interrupted. It would be too easy to do it the neat and dramatic way, and have the community rushing out before the last solemnities were done. But that is avoided in the breach. It isn't at the very end, but here, after the verse beginning *"Yitbarach"*, that the *shofar* is sounded, that the congregation stands formally to make their vow "Next year in Jerusalem" (in the case of more than half the Jews in the world, their first vow of the new year, and already a vow they have no intention whatsoever of fulfilling); and only then is the *"Kaddish"* completed. And remember, the Ark was opened right at the start of the *Amidah* of *Ne'ilah*, and is still open now. You cannot leave the synagogue while the Ark is open. Only when *"Oseh Shalom"* has been finished are the doors and curtains of the Ark drawn closed, only then may we do what we've waited twenty-five hours to do: to go and stuff our faces and our throats with food and drink, to return from the sacred to the profane realm, to start enumerating all the many sins we shall come back to repent next year. For all that we've lived a while as angels, we're only human, after all.

✡

EPILOGUE

And no, I haven't forgotten *Ma'ariv*. No error, merely a recognition of reality. Properly speaking, no one should leave after *Ne'ilah*, because there are still the evening prayers for the commencement of the following day. The *chazan* for *Ma'ariv* is enjoined by the sages not to prolong the prayers unnecessarily, because people are weak from fasting. And no doubt, in the synagogues of the profoundly religious, *Ma'ariv* is recited and there's still a *minyan*. But I'm a realist. Most Jews will start to wrap their *tallitot* away as soon as the *shofran* lifts the ram's horn to his lips. The *shofar* is the dinner gong in most people's ears. And anyway, as Rabbi Yitzchak of Vorki[27] famously wondered, why *daven Ma'ariv*, a service which is essentially the *Shemoneh Esreh* with bookends, why say prayers for forgiveness, when we've just spent the entire day in synagogue atoning for previous sins, and God has just given us a clean sheet to take away with us? Vorki answered his own question with a parable: A peasant insulted the king. Being a benevolent ruler, the king didn't want to punish a man who was clearly too ignorant even to realise he had insulted the king. Instead, he ordered the man to be given an education, and when it was done the man appeared again before the king. Memory washed over him and he recalled the previous occasion, understood how rude he'd been, and fell to the ground in horror and repentance. This, said Vorki, is how we should be at the end of *Yom Kippur*, and we need the *Selichot* of *Ma'ariv* to make that repentance formal. It's a nice idea but I prefer my own view. Having already made one vow that we don't intend to keep...let's go eat.

---

[27] The last chacham to be quoted in this book, and most appropriately, for the Vorker Rebbe was a disciple of my own ancestor, Rabbi Menachem-Mendl of Kocke, and Kalish, which was his domain, includes the village of Praszka, from which my family came – thus does one make history and prayer personal, and complete the process of redemption.

ACKNOWLEDGMENT

In addition to an index of references, which I have provided, a scholarly work is supposed to provide a bibliography of sources as well; this I have not done, and only because the number of works I have consulted are simply too many list, including both traditional works of Jewish scholarship in book form, and the many hundreds of pages on the Internet that turned up in my searches. My thanks are due to all of them.

ABOUT THE AUTHOR

David Prashker was born in London in 1955 and has lived in France, Israel, Canada and the United States, where he is currently based.

He is the author of thirty books, including contemporary and historical novels, short stories, poetry, songs, plays and scholarly works. You can follow his blog at apps.theargamanpress.com/Blog/ or find him at his website Davidprashker.com.

For more information about his books, go to:

theargamanpress.com.

www.ingramcontent.com/pod-product-compliance
Lightning Source LLC
LaVergne TN
LVHW051054080426
835508LV00019B/1868